The Case for Scottish In

Scottish nationalism is a powerful movement in contemporary politics, yet the goal of Scottish independence emerged surprisingly recently into public debate. The origins of Scottish nationalism lie not in the medieval battles for Scottish statehood, the Acts of Union, the Scottish Enlightenment or any other traditional historical milestone. Instead, an influential separatist Scottish nationalism began to take shape only in the 1970s and achieved its present ideological maturity in the course of the 1980s and 1990s. The nationalism that emerged from this testing period of Scottish history was unusual in that it demanded independence not to defend a threatened ancestral culture but as the most effective way to promote the agenda of the left.

This accessible and engaging account of the political thought of Scottish nationalism explores how the arguments for Scottish independence were crafted over some fifty years by intellectuals, politicians and activists, and why these ideas had such a seismic impact on Scottish and British politics in the 2014 independence referendum.

BEN JACKSON is Associate Professor of Modern History at the University of Oxford and co-editor of *Political Quarterly*. He is the author of *Equality and the British Left* (2007) and co-editor (with Robert Saunders) of *Making Thatcher's Britain* (2012).

The Case for Scottish Independence

A History of Nationalist Political Thought in Modern Scotland

Ben Jackson

University of Oxford

CAMBRIDGE
UNIVERSITY PRESS

CAMBRIDGE
UNIVERSITY PRESS

University Printing House, Cambridge CB2 8BS, United Kingdom

One Liberty Plaza, 20th Floor, New York, NY 10006, USA

477 Williamstown Road, Port Melbourne, VIC 3207, Australia

314–321, 3rd Floor, Plot 3, Splendor Forum, Jasola District Centre, New Delhi – 110025, India

79 Anson Road, #06–04/06, Singapore 079906

Cambridge University Press is part of the University of Cambridge.

It furthers the University's mission by disseminating knowledge in the pursuit of education, learning, and research at the highest international levels of excellence.

www.cambridge.org
Information on this title: www.cambridge.org/9781108835350
DOI: 10.1017/9781108883733

© Ben Jackson 2020

First published 2020

Printed in the United Kingdom by TJ International Ltd, Padstow Cornwall

A catalogue record for this publication is available from the British Library.

Library of Congress Cataloging-in-Publication Data
Names: Jackson, Ben, 1975– author.
Title: The case for Scottish independence : a history of nationalist political thought in modern Scotland / Ben Jackson, University of Oxford.
Other titles: Nationalist political thought in Scotland, c.1960-2014
Description: Cambridge, United Kingdom ; New York : Cambridge University Press, 2020. | Includes bibliographical references and index.
Identifiers: LCCN 2020009199 (print) | LCCN 2020009200 (ebook) | ISBN 9781108835350 (hardback) | ISBN 9781108793186 (paperback) | ISBN 9781108883733 (epub)
Subjects: LCSH: Scotland–Politics and government–20th century. | Nationalism–Scotland. | Self-determination, National–Scotland–History–20th century. | Scotland–History–Autonomy and independence movements. | Home rule–Scotland.
Classification: LCC DA765 .J33 2020 (print) | LCC DA765 (ebook) | DDC 941.1086–dc23
LC record available at https://lccn.loc.gov/2020009199
LC ebook record available at https://lccn.loc.gov/2020009200

ISBN 978-1-108-83535-0 Hardback
ISBN 978-1-108-79318-6 Paperback

For Edward and Jacqueline

Contents

Acknowledgements

This book is about a subject that I have been thinking about for a long time, since my earliest interest in politics, which I would date from around 1990. But I was prompted to write the book by the more recent debates about Scottish independence that culminated in the dramatic 2014 referendum. Around the time of the referendum, I wrote two articles that are distant ancestors of the following pages: 'The Political Thought of Scottish Nationalism', *Political Quarterly*, 85 (2014), pp. 50–6 and 'The Left and Scottish Nationalism', *Renewal*, 22 (2014), pp. 15–23. Although this book grew out of those pieces, and the odd paragraph or sentence draws on material previously published in them, my interpretation – and, I like to think, my understanding – of the independence movement has evolved since then. But I remain committed to the view that a critical analytical task is to take a political movement's ideals seriously and to investigate – as rigorously as possible – how those ideals came to inspire that movement's supporters, activists and leaders. That is what I have tried to do with the objective of Scottish independence in this book.

Throughout my work on this project I have been fortunate to enjoy the support of many individuals and institutions. The Faculty of History at Oxford University and University College, Oxford provided supportive and lively intellectual homes in which to write this book. For outstanding research assistance, I am indebted to Nicholas Garland, Cara Pacitti and James Stafford – without them it would have taken me a lot longer to get this project off the ground. Earlier versions of some of the ideas in the book were first presented to the Political Thought Seminar at Oxford University; the Modern British History Seminar at Cambridge University; and the Scottish History Seminar at St Andrews University, as well as in more informal talks at Oxford, at Queen Mary University of London, and at the 2015 'Changin Scotland' event at the Ceilidh Place in Ullapool. I am grateful to the audiences on all those occasions for their insightful comments and questions. Many friends, colleagues and students have discussed this book (and related topics) with me over the years and have helped me with useful suggestions that have influenced my thinking (though they may not have been aware of it). For this, thanks are due to Lise Butler, Alex Campsie, Aled Davies, Madeleine Davis, Christina de Bellaigue, Nicholas Garland, Matthew Grimley, Scott Hames, Gerry Hassan, Catherine Holmes, Michael Kenny, Colin Kidd, Gillian Lamb, Deborah Mabbett, Gregg McClymont, Murdo Macdonald, Ross McKibbin, Cara Pacitti, Jon Parkin, Malcolm Petrie, Lewis Pope, Jacob Rowbottom, Robert Saunders, Max Shock, Peter Sloman, Sophie Smith, James Stafford, Florence Sutcliffe-Braithwaite, Jim Tomlinson, David Torrance, Stuart White and Oliver Zimmer.

I must also thank the three anonymous referees for Cambridge University Press who greatly improved the manuscript with their searching and perceptive comments. More generally, I owe a huge debt to Cambridge University Press for their commitment to this project – Liz Friend-Smith has been a supportive and wise editor and working with Atifa Jiwa and the rest of the expert editorial team has been a great pleasure.

My research on this book benefited from the helpful and efficient assistance of the staff at the Bodleian Library, Oxford; the National Library of Scotland; and Nuffield College Library, Oxford. I am grateful to Clara Young and Shelagh Wright for permission to quote from unpublished material and to Heidi Egginton at the National Library of Scotland and to Sarah Bromage at the Scottish Political Archive for getting in contact with the copyright holders for me.

For a book about Scottish history by someone who lives in Oxford, I wrote a surprisingly large amount of this text in Warsaw. This was only possible because of the generous hospitality (and childcare) of Irena Stemplowska, Ryszard Stemplowski, Maria Stemplowska-Rymarz and Paweł Rymarz. The discipline of trying to explain the intricacies of Scottish nationalism to interlocutors without any stake in the subject was another important benefit of these trips to Poland. Meanwhile, back in Scotland, the support of my family was crucial. My parents, Edward and Jacqueline Jackson, lived through the period that the book covers and their insights, encouragement and once again childcare kept the project going. My brother, Daniel Jackson, and Alison O'Donnell have been busy with their own family, but their thoughts about the book's subject and related issues were invaluable.

Other, more important things happened in my life during the writing of this book. I can't say that my daughters Helenka and Hania exactly helped with writing it. But they filled my days with many other diverting activities that were far more valuable uses of my time than working on the book. Zofia Stemplowska has learned a lot more than she ever wanted to know about Scottish nationalism over the last few years. In spite of having plenty of better things to do, her advice and comments on the text were crucial to the book making it to the finish line, while it was only thanks to her encouragement and support that I was able to start writing it in the first place.

Abbreviations

EC	European Community
EEC	European Economic Community
EU	European Union
ILP	Independent Labour Party
IMG	International Marxist Group
NPS	National Party of Scotland
SDP	Social Democratic Party (1981–8)
SLP	Scottish Labour Party (1976–81)
SNL	Scots National League
SNP	Scottish National Party
STUC	Scottish Trades Union Congress
UCS	Upper Clyde Shipbuilders

Abbreviations

Introduction
Dreaming Scotland

if our debates, agreements and disagreements did not influence
how North Britain is governed, then democracy here does not exist.
Alasdair Gray, 2014[1]

On 18 September 2014 Scotland held a referendum on whether to
become an independent country, the third referendum on Scotland's
constitutional status to be staged in the space of some thirty-five years.
The advocates of 'yes' lost, polling 45 per cent, but the most remarkable
feature of the referendum was the large increase in popular support for
independence during the campaign and then for the Scottish National
Party (SNP) at the subsequent British general election in 2015 (at which
the SNP polled 50 per cent of the Scottish vote). In these years Scottish
nationalism emerged as a genuine mass movement for the first time in
Scottish history. Nationalism not only dominated Scottish electoral
politics at Holyrood and Westminster but was also now capable of
mobilising a large number of activists, inspiring a swathe of associated
civil society groups, generating avid online communities based around
sympathetic websites, and even providing a sufficiently engaged reader-
ship to make viable a new daily print newspaper, *The National*, which
reports events from a pro-independence perspective that contrasts with
the otherwise largely pro-Union Scottish print media.[2] In telling the story
of Scottish nationalism's journey to this historical high watermark, it is

---

[1] Alasdair Gray, *Independence: An Argument for Home Rule* (Edinburgh, Canongate, 2014),
p. 10.
[2] Excellent analysis of the 2014 referendum and its impact can be found in Iain McLean, Jim
Gallagher and Guy Lodge, *Scotland's Choices: The Referendum and What Happens Afterwards*
(Edinburgh, Edinburgh University Press, 2013); Neil Davidson, 'A Scottish Watershed',
New Left Review, no. 89, 2014, pp. 5–26; Jonathan Hearn, 'Nationalism and Normality:
A Comment on the Scottish Independence Referendum', *Dialectical Anthropology*, 38
(2014), pp. 505–12; Iain Macwhirter, *Disunited Kingdom: How Westminster Won a
Referendum But Lost Scotland* (Glasgow, Cargo, 2014); Peter Geoghegan, *The People's
Referendum* (Edinburgh, Luath Press, 2015); Lindsay Paterson, 'Utopian Pragmatism:
Scotland's Choice', *Scottish Affairs*, 24 (2015), pp. 22–46; Aileen McHarg et al. (eds.),
The Scottish Independence Referendum: Constitutional and Political Implications (Oxford,

striking how recently the cause of independence emerged as a focus of Scottish public debate. The origins of Scottish nationalism lie not in the medieval battles for Scottish statehood, the Scottish Reformation, the Acts of Union, the Scottish Enlightenment or any of the other familiar historical milestones that regularly crop up in debates about Scottish identity. Rather, an influential separatist Scottish nationalism began to take shape only in the 1960s and 1970s, and achieved its present ideological maturity in the course of the 1980s and 1990s.

The nationalism that emerged from this testing period of Scottish history was unusual, in that it did not primarily demand independence for Scotland in order to defend a threatened ancestral culture. Instead, Scottish nationalists emphasised that independence was the most effective way to promote the political agenda of the left in a neoliberal era. Insofar as an ancestral culture was believed to be threatened by the British state, it was the culture of social democratic corporatism, which Scottish nationalists regarded as well suited to Scotland's long-standing egalitarian and democratic traditions. In the face of the neoliberal restructuring of the British economy that emanated from London, Scottish nationalists interpreted growing opposition to the Conservative Party in Scotland as expressive of a deep political divergence that could only be resolved by the creation of a new Scottish state.

This book examines the political thought of this Scottish nationalism. What are the key influences and arguments that produced this now ubiquitous case for Scottish independence in such a short period of time? How have the major ideas deployed in this nationalist discourse been combined to create a politically powerful ideology? How has the case for Scottish independence changed over time? My answers to these questions will provide the first systematic account of the development of the ideology of modern Scottish nationalism. They will also help us to understand why the arguments of Scottish nationalists grew more persuasive to Scots (and even to some living in the rest of the UK) over the course of the late twentieth and early twenty-first centuries. While the answer in part relates to shifting political and economic circumstances, this book shows that a

Oxford University Press, 2016); Neil Blane and David Hutchison with Gerry Hassan (eds.), *Scotland's Referendum and the Media* (Edinburgh, Edinburgh University Press, 2016); Charles Pattie and Ron Johnston, 'Sticking to the Union? Nationalism, Inequality and Political Disaffection and the Geography of Scotland's 2014 Independence Referendum', *Regional and Federal Studies*, 27 (2017), pp. 83–96; Michael Keating (ed.), *Debating Scotland: Issues of Independence and Union in the 2014 Referendum* (Oxford, Oxford University Press, 2017); Edward Fieldhouse and Christopher Prosser, 'The Limits of Partisan Loyalty: How the Independence Referendum Cost Labour', *Electoral Studies*, 52 (2018), pp. 11–25.

full response to this question can only be given by scrutinising how this changing context – in essence Scotland's recent history – was interpreted, conceptualised and rhetorically redescribed by a range of intellectuals, politicians and activists. Some of these figures were officially affiliated to the SNP while others were not, but their overall impact was to construct a reading of Scottish identity as politically distinctive from that of England and oriented towards self-determination.

The years between the 1960s and 2014 saw the formation of a vision of Scottishness that was broadly 'civic' or voluntarist in its mobilisation of democratic political values and institutions that were said to set Scotland apart from England and in its conception of Scottish citizenship as a status that encompassed anyone resident in Scotland regardless of ethnicity or country of national origin. Inevitably, though, this construction of Scottish identity also defined the boundaries of the nation, and justified the cause of national independence, by drawing on historicist myths or even inherited or 'organic' cultural resources. Although modern Scottish nationalism has usually presented itself as an unimpeachably 'civic' doctrine that reflects liberal democratic values rather than ancestral tradition, no nationalism can in practice restrict itself to a purely political national identity, since it is necessary to substantiate and legitimate that identity in each case by reference to a particular (and unchosen) history and culture.[3] As many commentators have pointed out, Scottish nationalism conforms to this pattern by blending civic ideals about a democratic and egalitarian nation with mythic narratives about Scotland's history; claims about cultural distinctiveness; and even the occasional evocation of the particularity of the Scottish landscape.[4]

The Rise and Fall and Rise of Scottish Nationalism

Although there are some significant gaps, the broad outlines of the history of Scottish nationalism have been well told by historians and

---

[3] Here I follow Oliver Zimmer, 'Boundary Mechanisms and Symbolic Resources: Towards a Process-Oriented Approach to National Identity', *Nations and Nationalism*, 9 (2003), pp. 173–93, from which I take the voluntarist–organic distinction. For persuasive criticism of the traditional contrast drawn between 'civic' and 'ethnic' nationalisms, see Jonathan Hearn, *Rethinking Nationalism* (Basingstoke, Palgrave, 2006), pp. 88–91; Bernard Yack, *Nationalism and the Moral Psychology of Community* (Chicago, University of Chicago Press, 2012), pp. 23–43.

[4] Jonathan Hearn, *Claiming Scotland: National Identity and Liberal Culture* (Edinburgh, Polygon, 2000); David McCrone, *Understanding Scotland: The Sociology of a Nation* (2nd ed., London, Routledge, 2001), pp. 177–8; Murray Stewart Leith and Daniel Soule, *Political Discourse and National Identity in Scotland* (Edinburgh, Edinburgh University Press, 2011); Andrew Mycock, 'SNP, Identity and Citizenship: Reimagining State and Nation', *National Identities*, 14 (2012), pp. 53–69.

political scientists. Initiatives to safeguard Scottish identity within the Anglo-Scottish Union, including forms of devolution or home rule, have been traced back over many centuries and rightly seen as inherent in the nature of the Union itself, which created a multinational state in which a significant amount of Scottish autonomy was either preserved or subsequently negotiable.[5] The focus of this book, however, is a more radical form of Scottish nationalism than these efforts to render Scottishness compatible with a persisting political union with England, namely the objective of leaving the 1707 Union of Parliaments and founding a new Scottish state ('independence'). As Michael Keating has reminded us, nationalism need not be state-seeking in this sense. The history of Scottish nationalism could therefore be told more broadly as a story about the rise of demands for an elected Scottish assembly of some kind from the late nineteenth century onwards.[6] While that is an important approach to the history of the Scottish national movement, I have a more specific objective in mind here, which is to understand the precise rationale political actors have offered for supporting state-seeking nationalism and to chart the emergence of independence as an influential social ideal in late twentieth-century Scotland. The aim of Scottish independence was only systematically articulated for the first time in the interwar period, with the SNP founded as the primary political vehicle for this goal in 1934.[7] Yet the SNP achieved little popular success during the 1930s, 1940s and 1950s. The first serious nationalist electoral breakthrough occurred in the 1960s, with Winifred ('Winnie') Ewing's (b. 1929) victory for the SNP in the 1967 Hamilton by-election and the subsequent rise in the vote share of the SNP during the 1970s, culminating in the SNP claiming eleven seats at the October 1974 general election.

Why did the SNP establish itself as a serious electoral competitor in the 1960s and 1970s? This period saw the intersection of several powerful historical trends that benefited Scottish nationalism: economic crises that rocked both Labour and Conservative governments in quick succession and opened political space for third parties; the initial stages of the long process of deindustrialisation that would ultimately reshape Scotland's

---

[5] Lindsay Paterson, *The Autonomy of Modern Scotland* (Edinburgh, Edinburgh University Press, 1994); Graeme Morton, *Unionist-Nationalism: Governing Urban Scotland 1830–60* (East Linton, Tuckwell Press, 1999); James Mitchell, *The Scottish Question* (Oxford, Oxford University Press, 2014).

[6] Michael Keating, *The Independence of Scotland* (Oxford, Oxford University Press, 2009), pp. 42–3.

[7] Michael Fry, *Patronage and Principle: A Political History of Modern Scotland* (Aberdeen, Aberdeen University Press, 1987), pp. 201–15; Colin Kidd, *Union and Unionisms: Political Thought in Scotland, 1500–2000* (Cambridge, Cambridge University Press, 2008).

economy; the marked decline of social deference to Britain's elites, which began to erode traditional political loyalties and alignments; and, more indirectly, the final dissolution of the British Empire, which raised large questions about the ideological character and credibility of Britishness. In this context Scottish nationalism could be presented as a modernising force that was in tune with the widely felt desire for greater local control over the remote state and economic bureaucracies that towered over everyday life. Long-standing and distinctive Scottish cultural resources were mobilised by nationalists to make the case that changing Scotland's constitutional status could address Scotland's economic problems and what was widely believed to be a growing sense of popular alienation from the British state. The discovery of North Sea oil in Scottish waters in 1969 significantly enhanced the economic credibility of this proposition and gave the SNP a powerful platform to campaign on in the mid 1970s.[8]

But the 1970s popular breakthrough of the SNP was not consolidated. Labour's panicked attempt to introduce devolution in Scotland (and Wales) as a means of diffusing the nationalist challenge was defeated in the 1979 referendum.[9] Instead, the 1980s and 1990s saw the development of a broader nationalist politics that transcended the SNP and initially coalesced around the demands for a devolved Scottish parliament articulated by the cross-party Scottish Constitutional Convention (which the SNP declined to participate in). This more ecumenical nationalism was mobilised in response to the Conservative government elected in 1979 and the emergence of Thatcherism as the Conservative solution to the economic and social tensions of the 1970s. The SNP still made the case for independence, but it was only after the creation of the Scottish Parliament in 1999 (following the second referendum on

---

[8] Jack Brand, *The National Movement in Scotland* (London, Routledge, 1978); Keith Webb, *The Growth of Nationalism in Scotland* (Harmondsworth, Penguin, 1978), pp. 66–138; Christopher Harvie, *Scotland and Nationalism: Scottish Society and Politics 1707 to the Present* (London, Routledge, 2004 [1977]), pp. 162–88; Ewen Cameron, *Impaled upon a Thistle: Scotland since 1880* (Edinburgh, Edinburgh University Press, 2010), pp. 201–319; Paula Somerville, *Through the Maelstrom: A History of the Scottish National Party 1945–67* (Stirling, Scots Independent, 2013); Peter Lynch, *SNP: The History of the Scottish National Party* (Cardiff, Welsh Academic Press, 2013), pp. 69–169; Jimmi Østergaard Neilsen and Stuart Ward, '"Cramped and Restricted at Home?" Scottish Separatism at Empire's End', *Transactions of the Royal Historical Society*, 25 (2015), pp. 159–85; Tom Devine, *Independence or Union: Scotland's Past and Scotland's Future* (London, Penguin, 2016), pp. 125–52; James Mitchell, *Strategies for Self-Government* (Edinburgh, Polygon, 1996), pp. 172–221; Mitchell, *Scottish Question*, pp. 87–186; James Mitchell, *Hamilton 1967: The By-Election That Transformed Scotland* (Edinburgh, Luath, 2017).

[9] While a majority of the voters at the 1979 referendum supported devolution for Scotland, they were not a large enough proportion to meet the threshold of 40 per cent of the electorate voting in favour for the measure to pass.

Scotland's constitutional status in 1997) that the party began to make significant electoral progress. Enthusiastically embracing their new status as a potential governing party, the SNP was able to position itself to the left of Labour as it shifted to the centre to govern at Westminster from 1997. From its platform as the Scottish government after 2007, the SNP was able to take advantage of the 2010 election of a new Conservative-led government committed to economic austerity to present independence as a chance to escape from a right-wing British state.[10]

But while the historical arc of Scottish nationalism is fairly clear, the role of ideas in this narrative has remained imprecise. The arguments marshalled by nationalists have evolved since their earliest iterations but the trajectory of the ideology of Scottish nationalism has not been thoroughly investigated. As Ewan Gibbs and Rory Scothorne have powerfully argued, existing accounts of Scottish nationalism have ascribed too little weight to the political ideas used by politicians, intellectuals and activists.[11] Gibbs and Scothorne have made this point in relation to the broader trend towards greater Scottish political autonomy in the late twentieth century, encompassing both the politics of devolution and independence, but the point is particularly important for understanding the recent rise in support for a Scottish state. Scottish independence is as yet only a theoretical project. It rests on a counterfactual – a new Scottish state – the nature of which must be imagined by its proponents in the course of political debate. We can therefore deepen our understanding of why this has become such a persuasive political objective by attending to the visions of an independent Scotland set out by prominent nationalist intellectuals. Such theorists were critical to the emergence of modern Scottish nationalism because their writings shaped the political arguments and concrete proposals for a new Scottish state that nationalists successively issued to the electorate. More generally, it is striking how fundamentally the work of a relatively small number of independence-supporting intellectuals has recast the terms of Scottish political debate since the 1960s. As Gerry Hassan has observed: 'Scottish nationalism has

---

[10] Cameron, *Impaled upon a Thistle*, pp. 320–71; Devine, *Independence or Union*, pt. II; Mitchell, *Strategies*, pp. 127–33, 221–49; Mitchell, *Scottish Question*, pp. 187–274; James Mitchell and Rob Johns, *Takeover: Explaining the Extraordinary Rise of the SNP* (London, Biteback, 2016).

[11] Ewan Gibbs and Rory Scothorne, '"Origins of the Present Crisis?": The Emergence of "Left-Wing" Scottish Nationalism, 1956–79', in Evan Smith and Matthew Worley (eds.), *Waiting for the Revolution: The British Far Left From 1956* (Manchester, Manchester University Press, 2017), pp. 163–8. Two exceptions to this general pattern are Webb, *Growth of Nationalism*, pp. 139–65; Peter Lynch, 'From Social Democracy Back to No Ideology – The Scottish National Party and Ideological Change in a Multi-Level Electoral Setting', *Regional and Federal Studies*, 19 (2009), pp. 619–37.

supplied over the last thirty to forty years several of the leading thinkers on Scottish politics: Tom Nairn, the late Neil MacCormick, Neal Ascherson and several more.' As this book will show, what Hassan has called 'this nationalist renaissance in ideas' has radiated far beyond the ranks of partisan supporters of the SNP.[12]

The Intellectual History of Scottish Independence

Social scientists have demonstrated that Scotland's economy, social structure and underlying values are not in fact significantly different from England's, which suggests that an explanation of the political divergence between the two nations should be sought elsewhere, in the realms of politics and culture.[13] As David McCrone has helpfully put this point, the rise of a more pronounced Scottish 'frame of reference' was evident in the way both public policy and media debate were structured in Scotland from around the 1970s onwards (for example, McCrone sees the advent of dedicated Scottish television news bulletins as an important step in this direction). This growing public sense of Scottish cultural distinctiveness (McCrone continues) functioned as a 'prism for translating social change into political meaning and action' – in effect as a cognitive frame – that then directed political outcomes in Scotland down a markedly different course than in England.[14] How this revised Scottish 'frame of reference' was culturally constructed is a complicated subject that remains open for debate. But one dimension of this process was certainly an ideological one: it entailed the development of a revised conceptualisation of Scottish political identity, a daunting task that drew on a range of cultural resources curated by leading journalists, academics, activists, politicians and other intellectually inclined public figures.

One fertile qualitative method to study the work of these groups is to approach it ethnographically, using interviews and face-to-face observation as well as published sources to investigate how new conceptions of Scottish identity were internalised and mobilised by these elites in the late twentieth and early twenty-first centuries. Both Jonathan Hearn and Gerry Hassan have undertaken important studies in this vein, which document how certain pervasive historical narratives about Scottish egalitarianism and democracy became staple themes in elite discourse

---

[12] Gerry Hassan, 'The Forward March of Scottish Nationalism', *Renewal*, 19 (2011), p. 55.

[13] Keating, *Independence*, p. 48; Cairns Craig, *The Wealth of the Nation: Scotland, Culture and Independence* (Edinburgh, Edinburgh University Press, 2018), pp. 21–2.

[14] David McCrone, 'Cultural Capital in an Understated Nation: The Case of Scotland', *British Journal of Sociology*, 56 (2005), pp. 65–80, quote at p. 79.

in Scotland and widespread in the rhetorical appeals made respectively by the campaigns for devolution and independence.[15] Hassan has also sought to demythologise this rhetoric in a penetrating critical investigation of the way in which these historical narratives have coalesced into the conventional wisdom of contemporary Scottish political debate.[16]

This book examines similar themes to those broached by Hearn and Hassan but does so using the tools and methods of intellectual history. The focus in the following pages is on the longer-run development over time of key concepts and arguments articulated by Scottish nationalists, as revealed by a close reading of a wide range of relevant texts, both published and unpublished. In other words, the focus of this book is less on the dissemination and social circulation of ideas among political actors explored by Hearn and Hassan and more on their initial conceptualisation and theorisation. The distinctive feature of this intellectual historical approach is the space it affords to the detailed scrutiny of the meaning of complex texts. This book for the most part consists of an in-depth investigation of three aspects of these texts: their intellectual sources and historical contexts; the logical and rhetorical structure of their central claims; and their reception and appropriation by other theorists and by political actors.

One dimension of the intellectual history of this period has already been well documented – the cultural history of Scottish literature, drama and art.[17] The creative arts have certainly been highly influential in shaping Scottish identity since the 1960s. Many more Scots will have read the novels of, say, William McIlvanney (1936–2015) or Alasdair Gray (1934–2019) than will have encountered, or even heard of, the majority of the texts that form the source material for this book. The cultural sphere is therefore a crucial domain in which changing ideas about Scottish identity and experience can be pinpointed (and some reference will be made later to the political contributions made by leading Scottish cultural figures). As Scott Hames has shown, the precise causal significance of culture in the rise of Scottish nationalism is itself a contested issue. On the one hand, literary scholars have frequently argued that Scottish writers,

---

[15] Hearn, *Claiming Scotland*; Gerry Hassan, *Independence of the Scottish Mind: Elite Narratives, Public Spaces and the Making of a Modern Nation* (Basingstoke, Palgrave, 2014).

[16] Gerry Hassan, *Caledonia Dreaming: The Quest for a Different Scotland* (Edinburgh, Luath Press, 2014).

[17] See, inter alia, Robert Crawford, *Devolving English Literature* (Edinburgh, Edinburgh University Press, 2000); Robert Crawford, *Scotland's Books* (London, Penguin, 2009); Cairns Craig, *The Modern Scottish Novel* (Edinburgh, Edinburgh University Press, 1999); Cairns Craig, *Intending Scotland* (Edinburgh, Edinburgh University Press, 2009); Craig, *Wealth of the Nation*; Michael Gardiner, *The Cultural Roots of British Devolution* (Edinburgh, Edinburgh University Press, 2004).

artists and entertainers fostered a sense of cultural distinctiveness after the 1960s that was itself responsible for reviving Scottish national identity and popularising demands for greater Scottish political autonomy. On the other hand, those very same debates about Scottish self-government after the 1960s were gripped by anxiety that Scottish 'culture' was itself perceptibly weakening and losing its distinctiveness due to the intrusion of the unreconstructed union-state. Hames has concluded that 'culture' therefore occupies an ambivalent status – cited as both a cause and an effect of Scottish home rule – in much analysis of this period.[18]

We will return to the elusive role of culture in Scottish nationalist ideology – and the complexities of what the term 'culture' can connote – later in this book, but the main point to stress at this stage is that the kind of intellectual history pursued here is one that is largely (although not completely) distinct from the arts and popular entertainment that feature in many cultural histories of this period. Instead, it is mainly located in what Hames has called 'the grind' of 'machine politics' – the more technocratic world of constructing political speeches, manifestos and policy documents, genres of writing that ultimately cannot solely rely on the suggestive language of the novelist and the poet.[19] However important the arts have been to the growth of Scottish nationalism, a more analytical register is *also* required to satisfy the demands of political debate and it is here that the less aesthetically pleasing practice of writing non-fiction books, pamphlets, articles and speeches provides some necessary additional intellectual fuel for democratic argument. In these venues we can trace the development of the ideology of Scottish nationalism – understood as a conceptual framework for guiding political action – rather than the cultural representation of Scottish experience.[20]

In recent decades, the role of political theory in framing political decision-making and policy debate has been successfully integrated into the historiography of modern Britain but principally in relation to metropolitan or English sources and discourses.[21] This book joins a recent

---

[18] Scott Hames, *The Literary Politics of Scottish Devolution* (Edinburgh, Edinburgh University Press, 2019).

[19] Hames, *Literary Politics of Scottish Devolution*, pp. 78–116.

[20] For this approach to the study of ideology, see Michael Freeden, *Ideologies and Political Theory* (Oxford, Oxford University Press, 1996).

[21] Gareth Stedman Jones, 'Rethinking Chartism' in his *Languages of Class* (Cambridge, Cambridge University Press, 1984), pp. 90–178; Michael Freeden, 'Stranger at the Feast: Ideology and Public Policy in Twentieth-Century Britain', *Twentieth Century British History*, 1 (1990), pp. 9–34; Jose Harris, 'Political Thought and the Welfare State 1870–1940: An Intellectual Framework for British Social Policy', *Past and Present*, 135 (1992), pp. 116–41; Philip Williamson, *Stanley Baldwin* (Cambridge, Cambridge University Press, 1999), pp. 12–18; Dean Blackburn, 'Still the Stranger at the Feast?

wave of scholarship that has sought to widen the scope of this literature to encompass the distinctive and vibrant traditions of political controversy found in Scotland.[22] It therefore takes as its focus the Scottish public sphere: the gamut of books, journals, magazines, newspapers and conferences where Scottish political debate raged, policy objectives were conceptualised, and new political messages were forged. As Rory Scothorne and Scott Hames have observed, the decades after the 1960s were particularly fertile years in the Scottish public sphere because of the profusion of small magazines – titles such as *Scottish International*; *Cencrastus*; and *Radical Scotland* – that hosted intense debates about politics and culture which resonated far beyond their initially rather selective readerships.[23] These magazines comprise one important body of source material for this book, alongside a variety of other published and unpublished texts.

Although we will trace in these sources the ideas of political actors who were quite radical insofar as they sought to challenge the existence of the British state, the demographic composition of these theorists of Scottish nationalism nonetheless reflected the daunting social constraints on which groups in late twentieth century Scotland could access the time and space necessary to produce intellectual work: most were university graduates (though some entered university from working class families) and the vast majority were men. Scottish nationalism as a political movement has featured many notable female politicians, from Winnie Ewing to the victor

Ideology and the Study of Twentieth Century British Politics', *Journal of Political Ideologies*, 22 (2017), pp. 116–30.

[22] Kidd, *Union and Unionisms*; Malcolm Petrie, 'Anti-socialism, Liberalism and Individualism: Rethinking the Realignment of Scottish Politics, 1945–70', *Transactions of the Royal Historical Society*, 28 (2018), pp. 197–217; Gibbs and Scothorne, '"Origins of the Present Crisis?": The Emergence of "Left-Wing" Scottish Nationalism'; Rory Scothorne, 'Nationalism and the Radical Left in Scotland, 1968–92' (PhD thesis, Edinburgh University, in progress). For similar thoughts about the need for more research on Irish political thought, see Richard Bourke, 'Reflections on the Political Thought of the Irish Revolution', *Transactions of the Royal Historical Society*, 27 (2017), pp. 175–91.

[23] Rory Scothorne, 'The "Radical Current": Nationalism and the Radical Left in Scotland, 1967–1979', *H-Nationalism*, 25 May 2018, at https://networks.h-net.org/node/3911/discussions/1862513/left-and-nationalism-monthly-series-%E2%80%9C-%E2%80%98radical-current%E2%80%99 (accessed 2 October 2019); Hames, *Literary Politics of Scottish Devolution*, pp. 58–65; 132–4. See also Linda Gunn and Richard Cleary, 'Wasps in a Jam Jar: Scottish Literary Magazines and Political Culture 1979–99', in Aimee McNair and Jacqueline Ryder (eds.), *Further from the Frontiers* (Aberdeen, Centre for Irish and Scottish Studies, 2009), pp. 41–52; Richard Price, 'Some Questions About Literary Infrastructure in the 1960s', in Eleanor Bell and Linda Gunn (eds.), *The Scottish Sixties: Reading, Rebellion, Revolution?* (Amsterdam, Rodopi, 2013), pp. 93–114; John Herdman, *Another Country: An Era in Scottish Politics and Letters* (Edinburgh, Thirsty Books, 2013), pp. 82–3.

of the 1973 Govan by-election, Margo MacDonald (1943–2014), to Nicola Sturgeon (b. 1970), the second SNP First Minister of Scotland. More generally, the SNP has a decent (though far from ideal) record of female representation in party life and among its candidates for public office.[24] But in our period the Scottish public sphere was still predominantly a masculine one, particularly the small group of intellectuals who had the leisure to debate the national question. This of course reflected underlying inequalities in access to education and employment opportunities and in the distribution of care work. One consequence of this is that the voices that can be heard in the sources are mostly male ones.

In writing an intellectual history of Scottish nationalism, I am following in the footsteps of two brilliant works of Scottish history that have sought to uncover the ideological foundations of modern Scottish politics. Christopher Harvie's *Scotland and Nationalism* is a more panoramic work than this one, covering Scottish history since 1707, and it encompasses the Scottish arts as well as the analytical texts discussed in this book. Harvie used the confluence of intellectual, social and political history to contrast the emergence of demands for greater Scottish political autonomy after 1945 with the earlier era of Scottish history under the Union in which Scottish identity was preserved (Harvie argued) in civil society rather than the state. Harvie was influenced by the 1970s Scottish vogue for the Italian Marxist theorist, Antonio Gramsci, which we will return to later in this book. Appropriating what he took to be a Gramscian interest in the role of 'organic intellectuals' (that is, intellectuals associated with the cause of a particular class or social group rather than constituting a separate class of their own), Harvie's account of Scottish history centred on the emergence of a more explicitly nationalist intelligentsia in Scotland in the second half of the twentieth century, although even in later editions the book focused more on the period up to the 1970s (the first edition was published in 1977) than on subsequent ideological developments in nationalist circles. Indeed, as a pioneering work *Scotland and Nationalism* inevitably devoted more space to a detailed narrative of the history of Scottish nationalism than to an anatomy of its political thought of the kind pursued in this book.[25]

---

[24] Catriona Burness, 'Drunk Women Don't Look at Thistles: Women and the SNP 1934–94', *Scotlands*, 2 (1994), pp. 131–54; Fiona MacKay and Meryl Kenny, 'Women's Political Representation and the SNP: Gendered Paradoxes and Puzzles', in Gerry Hassan (ed.), *The Modern SNP* (Edinburgh, Edinburgh University Press, 2009), pp. 42–54.

[25] Harvie, *Scotland and Nationalism*; on Gramsci, see pp. 7–8, 85, 157–61; see also Christopher Harvie, 'Nationalism, Journalism and Cultural Politics', in Tom Gallagher (ed.), *Nationalism in the Nineties* (Edinburgh, Polygon, 1991), p. 33.

A second work that has fundamentally shaped the terms of my account is Colin Kidd's *Union and Unionisms*. Kidd powerfully argued that a variety of unionisms dominated Scottish political thought until the 1970s, constituting a rich array of languages that supported Scottish distinctiveness within the larger structures of the British state (although rereading the book after 2014 it is striking that Kidd did not discuss the social democratic unionism of the Labour Party, the nationalist contestation with which is a key theme of the following pages). Methodologically, Kidd demonstrated the potential of the study of political thought to enliven Scottish historiography, as he sought, through a careful analysis of central doctrinal debates in Scottish public life over five centuries, to destabilise the distinction drawn between nationalism and unionism in much writing on Scottish history. Kidd argued that in his period it was in fact hard to detect a categorical distinction between the two, as unionists were fervent advocates for Scottish distinctiveness and nationalists, when they first appeared in the mid-twentieth century, sought a place for an autonomous Scotland within larger British or imperial structures.[26] Although the arguments of Harvie and Kidd are different, both identify a late twentieth-century rupture in Scottish political thought, with the emergence for the first time of a serious and committed separatist nationalist ideology. Compared with these wide-ranging works, the task of this book is the more chronologically delimited one of identifying the character of this nationalist turn in Scottish political thought and clarifying the political, economic and historical claims that underpinned it. For that reason, my account of Scottish nationalism largely begins where Harvie and Kidd stopped, namely the 1960s and 1970s, and complements their analyses by examining the case for independence as it was constructed in the five decades before the referendum of 2014.

However, their work also underlines the complexity of the meanings of 'nationalism' in a Scottish context and thus the necessity of a clear definition of terms at the outset. In general terms, 'nationalism' refers to a movement that seeks to advance the identity and capacity for self-rule of a community that understands itself as a 'nation'. The precise definition of a 'nation' is a complicated issue, but roughly speaking it refers to a historically extended community linked to a specific territory that shares some form of common culture and a collective belief in the nation's existence.[27] With respect to the case of Scotland, Kidd has

---

[26] Kidd, *Union and Unionisms*, especially pp. 300–4.

[27] Anthony Smith, *Nationalism* (2nd ed., Cambridge, Polity, 2010), pp. 5–9; David Miller, *On Nationality* (Oxford, Oxford University Press, 1995), pp. 21–7.

observed that although the standard terminology of Scottish political debate contrasts nationalism with unionism, their relationship is in fact more complicated than a straightforward distinction between the two implies. Scottish unionisms have been historically animated by a concern to defend Scottish national identity through a Union that protects Scottish distinctiveness, whereas Scottish nationalists have imagined an independent Scotland as entering new forms of relationship with supranational organisations, whether the EU, NATO or some form of looser association with England, Wales and Northern Ireland. While the terminology used in everyday political speech can be vague and misleading, this book will concentrate on a subset of nationalist arguments that *do* represent a schism from the broad church of Scottish unionism, namely those that advocate the dissolution of Scotland's Union with England, Wales and Northern Ireland and the creation of a new 'independent' Scottish state. This form of nationalism is different from the demands for greater Scottish autonomy within the Union because it identifies separation from the British state as the most authentic and effective form of Scottish self-government. As this book will demonstrate, one distinctive feature of Scottish nationalist ideology after the 1960s is the much greater specificity and coherence imparted to this goal by leading writers and politicians. In the rest of this book I will at times use the shorthand 'nationalists' to refer to these advocates of Scottish independence but this is for reasons of linguistic convenience – it is difficult to generate a suitable alternative label to refer to these political actors – and it should always be read with the implicit caveat that this represents only one influential current of a much broader Scottish national consciousness that does not adhere to a univocal stance on the relationship between Scottishness and the Union.

The Structure of the Book

The book will track the evolution of the case for independence through five thematic, although loosely chronological, chapters, each of which (with the exception of Chapter 1) explores the historical development of a central ideological theme in nationalist arguments for a new Scottish state. The first chapter sets the stage for subsequent analysis by sketching in the evolution of nationalist ideology before *c.* 1960, with a view to identifying the continuities and discontinuities with the arguments for independence that were deployed after that date and which will be documented more fully in the rest of the book. While there were certainly important differences in the ideas about class, democracy and the state espoused by supporters of Scottish independence between the middle and the end of the twentieth century, this chapter shows that there were also some affinities with respect to favouring a more decentralised and participatory Scottish polity (which early nationalists saw as having a deep connection with Scottish constitutional history).

The second chapter examines the cultural case for independence, understood in a broad sense as the view that the Union threatens the autonomy of Scotland's distinctive institutions, particularly its egalitarian and communitarian character as expressed through its democratic intellectual and educational traditions. Although widely discussed by Scottish nationalists, the cultural argument was considered to be a false start by many influential figures in the movement and the chapter concludes by reviewing why many leading advocates of independence looked to alternative intellectual sources, or translated the cultural case into a political one, to advance their cause.

The third chapter turns to the nationalist critique of the British state and demonstrates how indebted independence supporters have been to the New Left's characterisation of Britain as an antediluvian relic that historically evaded an adequate process of modernisation. In particular, the chapter illustrates the importance of 'imperialism' to nationalist thinking, insofar as nationalists saw the fundamental weakness of British national identity as its close connection with empire and the economic 'decline' of the British state as related to its loss of colonial possessions. However, the chapter also documents the fading away of the Marxist and economistic elements of this critique of Britain over the course of the 1980s and 1990s, to be replaced by a robust, but avowedly political, democratic republicanism, which identified the British state's chief shortcoming as a failure to become a proper bourgeois democracy.

The fourth chapter analyses nationalist attempts to yoke together Scottish independence and the egalitarian politics of the left. From an initial embrace of the radical participatory politics of the 1960s to a later enthusiasm for the heritage of the British labour movement, nationalists have presented independence as the route to a socialist Scotland. But as this chapter also demonstrates, the early twenty-first century saw some key nationalists turning away from this agenda and embracing instead a revisionist social democracy that accepted some significant capitalist constraints on the politics of independence.

The fifth chapter focuses on the concept of sovereignty and the twofold role it has played in nationalist thought. First, the chapter shows that an increasingly important argument for independence has been that a long-standing Scottish tradition of popular sovereignty is fundamentally in tension with the English notion of parliamentary sovereignty. Indeed, a rudimentary but highly effective argument for Scottish independence from the 1980s onwards was simply that in the absence of a Scottish state Scotland is often governed from Westminster by a party that the Scottish people did not vote for. On this account, Scottish independence is supported by the principles of democracy. But, second, the chapter also demonstrates that from the 1980s onwards Scottish nationalists frequently argued that the era of absolute state sovereignty had ended. Instead, an independent Scotland would be one among a whole raft of 'post-sovereign' European states, sharing membership of the European Union and pooling sovereignty where appropriate to advance their interests. The conclusion draws together these strands of argument, reviews the changing balance between them in nationalist political thought, and weighs up the strengths and weaknesses of the case for independence revealed by the 2014 referendum.

1   The Ideology of Early Scottish Nationalism

> The great achievement of the SNP from 1942 to 1964 was simply to have survived. But its survival has been based entirely on a very limited conception of nationalism.   Hanham, 1969[1]

Scottish nationalism understood as support for an independent Scottish state is notable by its absence from most of Scotland's history after 1707. Although the initial organised advocacy for greater Scottish democratic autonomy within the United Kingdom emerged in the late nineteenth and early twentieth centuries, and was incubated within radical Liberalism and the early Scottish labour movement, the goal of Scottish independence only received its first clear and sustained modern articulation after the First World War, with the foundation of the Scots National League (SNL) in 1920. The SNL was succeeded shortly afterwards by the formation of the National Party of Scotland (NPS) in 1928 and the subsequent historic foundation of the SNP in 1934. The SNP merged together the NPS with the less radical Scottish Party, which had itself only started in 1932. From the interwar years until the 1950s, the cause of Scottish nationalism was an unpopular one, chiefly prosecuted by small organisations which were often plagued by high levels of internal disagreement about party strategy and objectives (although a significant amount of this disagreement related to the strategic question of whether a gradualist, devolutionary road to independence was more appropriate for Scotland than one that sought independence in the first instance).[2] As Douglas Young (1913–73), one of the leading nationalists of the

---

[1] H. J. Hanham, *Scottish Nationalism* (London, Faber, 1969), p. 179.

[2] Hanham, *Scottish Nationalism*; Jack Brand, *The National Movement in Scotland* (London, Routledge, 1978), pp. 169–264; Michael Keating and Richard Bleiman, *Labour and Scottish Nationalism* (London, Macmillan, 1979), pp. 21–149; Richard Finlay, *Independent and Free: Scottish Politics and the Origins of the Scottish National Party 1918–1945* (Edinburgh, John Donald, 1994); James Mitchell, *Strategies for Self-Government* (Edinburgh, Polygon, 1996), pp. 172–204; Paula Somerville, *Through the Maelstrom: A History of the Scottish National Party 1945–67* (Stirling, Scots Independent, 2013); Peter Lynch, *The SNP: The History of the Scottish National Party* (Cardiff, Welsh Academic Press, 2013), pp. 29–68.

period (and an accomplished classicist and poet), once remarked: 'He who would serve Scotland must have the patience of Prometheus and the epidermis of a rhinoceros.'[3] This chapter will discuss the Sisyphean labours of these early Scottish nationalists as they tried to construct a persuasive case for independence before the 1960s. The aim of the chapter is not to offer an exhaustive account of the nationalism of this period but simply to set the scene for the rest of the book by clarifying the ideological resources that were already available for advocates of independence in the mid-twentieth century. Having done so, we will then be in a better position to understand how their successors after the 1960s departed from (but also elaborated on) this first wave of nationalist political argument.

The ideology of the early national movement was a fissiparous one, with diverse, and at times contending, strands of nationalist thought coexisting in an uneasy partnership with one another. These tensions were exacerbated by the significant number of literary and cultural figures who attached themselves to the cause of Scottish nationalism in this period, adding the heady but not always politically advisable language of the poet and the novelist to the more mundane policy deliberations of a minority party. The poet Hugh MacDiarmid (1892–1978) was the leading figure in this 'Scottish renaissance' and his extraordinary political journey from cultural nationalism to something he called 'fascism' to communism, although an outlier, did reflect something of the protean quality of nationalist thought in this period.[4] MacDiarmid was the sort of charismatic literary figure that the more pragmatic founders of the SNP sought to marginalise from strategic or tactical influence in the party.[5] Although John MacCormick (1904–61), perhaps the most dynamic and influential of the early Scottish nationalists, described MacDiarmid as 'politically one of the greatest handicaps with which any nationalist movement could have been burdened',[6] as an *intellectual*

---

[3] Douglas Young to Andrew Dewar Gibb, 18 October 1943, Andrew Dewar Gibb Papers, National Library of Scotland, Acc. 9188/4. On Young's career, see Gordon Pentland, 'Douglas Young', in Gerry Hassan and James Mitchell (eds.), *Scottish National Party Leaders* (London, Biteback, 2016), pp. 145–64.

[4] Stephen Maxwell, 'The Nationalism of Hugh MacDiarmid' and Neal Ascherson, 'MacDiarmid and Politics', both in Paul Scott and A. C. Davis (eds.), *The Age of MacDiarmid* (Edinburgh, Mainstream, 1980), pp. 202–23, 224–37; Bob Purdie, *Hugh MacDiarmid: Black, Green, Red and Tartan* (Cardiff, Welsh Academic Press, 2012). Hugh MacDiarmid was a pen name – he also published some non-fiction under his real name of Christopher Grieve.

[5] Iain McLean, 'The Rise and Fall of the Scottish National Party', *Political Studies*, 18 (1970), pp. 357–9; Finlay, *Independent and Free*, pp. 83–5, 93–6.

[6] John MacCormick, *The Flag in the Wind* (London, Gollancz, 1955), p. 35.

influence MacDiarmid's writings – and the work of other leading figures
in the interwar Scottish renaissance such as Neil Gunn (1891–1973) and
Lewis Grassic Gibbon (1901–35) – have been inspirational for succeeding generations of Scottish nationalists.[7]

Nonetheless, the main body of activists who threw themselves into this
seemingly hopeless cause were of a different sociological type to the more
mercurial artists and writers. Scottish nationalism in this period was
primarily a movement drawn from (a small minority of) Scotland's
Presbyterian professional and small business classes and the early ideas
of Scottish nationalism often reflected the preoccupations of this social
stratum (MacCormick, for example, was a lawyer).[8] MacDiarmid himself once remarked that this generation of nationalists were 'a gang of
dullards with no cultural interests and certainly no personal intellectual
or artistic gifts'.[9] Like many of MacDiarmid's polemical pronounce-
ments, this is inaccurate. While Scottish nationalism in its early years
was dominated by middle-class professionals, it is nonetheless possible to
delineate a distinctive underlying philosophy – and even a streak of
romanticism – that animated nationalist political argument and from
which (or so I will argue) later Scottish nationalist thinking represented
a break.

As with subsequent iterations of the creed, Scottish nationalism in this
period took as its fundamental goal the creation of a new democratic and
independent Scottish state – 'the restoration of Scottish national sovereignty by the establishment of a democratic Scottish government' – with
the proviso that this state could then decide to share certain economic,
social or military institutions with the rest of the United Kingdom or the
British Empire if this proved to be in the Scottish national interest.[10] This
objective was conceptualised as a return to Scotland's status prior to the

---

[7] Scott Lyall, *Hugh MacDiarmid's Poetry and Politics of Place: Imagining a Scottish Republic*
(Edinburgh, Edinburgh University Press, 2006); Scott Lyall, 'Hugh MacDiarmid and
the Scottish Renaissance', in Gerard Carruthers and Liam McIlvanney (eds.), *The
Cambridge Companion to Scottish Literature* (Cambridge, Cambridge University Press,
2012), pp. 173–87; Margarey Palmer McCulloch, *Scottish Modernism and Its Contexts
1918–59: Literature, National Identity and Cultural Exchange* (Edinburgh, Edinburgh
University Press, 2009). Although note that not all of the writers and poets of the
interwar Scottish renaissance personally supported independence.

[8] Richard W. Mansbach, 'The SNP: A Revised Political Profile', *Comparative Politics*, 5
(1973), pp. 188, 196, 210; Stephen Maxwell, 'Social Justice and the SNP', in Gerry
Hassan (ed.), *The Modern SNP: From Protest to Power* (Edinburgh, Edinburgh University
Press, 2009), p. 120.

[9] Hugh MacDiarmid, *Cunninghame Graham: A Centenary Study* (Glasgow, Caledonian
Press, 1952), p. 10.

[10] SNP, *Statement of Aim and Policy of the Scottish National Party* (Stirling, Scots
Independent, January 1947), p. 1.

Union, 'the restoration of Scotland to her former position of political independence', although the immediate context of this goal was in fact a more modern one, namely the post-1918 view that 'international peace' was best promoted in a world in which 'the right of every nation to self-government' was recognised.[11]

Small Is Beautiful

Why did the nationalist pioneers regard independence as a desirable objective? One strand of argument in this period was cultural, and sought independence as a means to defend Scotland's indigenous Celtic culture and languages from Anglicisation.[12] But a romantic culturalism was never at the core of the case for independence made by Scottish nationalists, not least because it was difficult in the Scottish case to manufacture a potent narrative about national oppression from those materials alone. Instead, nationalists focused on the growing divergence between the socioeconomic interests of Scotland and England, something that could only be registered democratically by creating a new Scottish polity in which those interests could be represented in a politically effective way (rather than making an appearance as a minority view at Westminster).

The economic and political dramas of the interwar years enabled this argument to acquire greater plausibility. In the 1920s and 1930s a newly democratic Britain, with a party system in flux, was forced to grapple with an economic slump that had a highly unequal impact across the nations and regions of Britain. Areas dominated by traditional export-oriented heavy industry, such as the central belt of Scotland, were perceptibly economically weaker after the First World War than before. This in turn facilitated a more potent nationalist critique of the impact of the Union on Scotland's industrial development.[13] The founding generation of the NPS and SNP argued that, because of Scotland's marginal status within the Union, its unemployment rate was higher than in England, its level of economic growth lower, and insufficient public spending was forthcoming from the Treasury for Scotland's needs. Furthermore, nationalists expressed anxiety about the loss of indigenous

---

[11] Angus Clark, 'Scotland a Nation', *Scots Independent*, No. 1, November 1926, pp. 1, 2.

[12] Hugh MacDiarmid, *Albyn* [1927], in Hugh MacDiarmid, *Albyn: Shorter Books and Monographs*, ed. Alan Riach (Manchester, Carcanet, 1996), pp. 1–39; Hon. Ruaraidh Erskine of Marr, *Changing Scotland* (Montrose, Review Press, 1931).

[13] Ewen Cameron, *Impaled upon a Thistle: Scotland since 1880* (Edinburgh, Edinburgh University Press, 2010), pp. 48–53; Richard Finlay, 'National Identity in Crisis: Politicians, Intellectuals and the "End of Scotland"', *History*, 79 (1994), pp. 242–59.

control over Scottish businesses as the ownership of important companies passed into foreign (predominantly English) hands. They also believed that, in the absence of Scottish statehood, it would not be possible to prevent the population decline that nationalists thought would follow from the high levels of emigration from Scotland in the 1920s and 1930s.[14]

Although this analysis had some similarities with the later case for independence we will investigate in this book, the way in which nationalists of the mid-twentieth century conceptualised Scottish interests differed significantly from their successors. One of the distinctive features of Scottish nationalism before the 1960s was that it located the demand for independence within a wider critique of large-scale economic and political organisations, whether capitalist or socialist, and emphasised the importance of revitalising Scotland's rural communities as a means of diffusing more widely large concentrations of power, wealth and population. As John MacCormick put it in 1933, this was a distinctive 'radical' view which favoured 'neither capitalism as we now know it, nor socialism as expressed by the Labour Party'. MacCormick argued that the members of the NPS

believe in the private enterprise of individuals but are suspicious of monopolies, trusts or combines or anything which, in short, though still privately owned, has reached dimensions too great for individual responsibility in ownership. They believe in small holdings, in small towns, in small independent business, in everything that is the reverse of either large scale capitalism or socialism.[15]

Archie Lamont (1907–85), an eminent geologist and long-standing nationalist activist, spoke for many in the movement when he argued that 'the small unit of government – call it commune, or soviet, or simply parish council – and the independent farmer, fisherman, or craftsman – not the wage slaves – are the principal agents for harmonising freedom and private enterprise in national democracy'.[16] A self-governing Scotland was therefore presented as a logical extension of this philosophy, given the manifest advantages of decentralised government and active citizenship. Lamont thought, for example, that in nations with populations of over roughly ten million people the government 'seemed to lose touch with those it represented and to become dehumanised', whereas smaller nations were less bureaucratic and the people closer to their rulers.[17]

---

[14] Lewis Spence, *The National Party of Scotland* (Glasgow, National Party of Scotland, 1928) [reprinted from *Edinburgh Review*, 1928]; Charles Stewart Black, *The Case for Scotland* (Edinburgh, National Party of Scotland, 1930).

[15] John MacCormick to Duncan H. MacNeill, 8 February 1933, quoted in Finlay, *Independent and Free*, pp. 110–11.

[16] Archie Lamont, *Small Nations* (Glasgow, William MacLellan, 1944), p. 78.

[17] Archie Lamont, *Scotland and the War* (Glasgow, Scottish Secretariat, 1943), pp. 1, 22.

This outlook had a long lineage, stretching back to a rich vein of eighteenth-century radical republican political thought that emphasised the desirability of a polity composed of free citizens who possessed roughly equal amounts of property. More immediately, in British political debate the distributism of Hilaire Belloc (1870–1953) and G. K. Chesterton (1874–1936) had sparked an enduring subaltern strand of political argument about dispersing property ownership as widely as possible as a coherent alternative to the concentration of property in either private or state hands. The virtues of decentralising the economy *and* the polity formed an important part of the Liberal Party's public profile as it struggled to carve out political space for itself in the British party system of the 1930s and 1940s, and the ideology of Scottish nationalism in the same period followed a broadly similar path.[18] However, the proponents of independence added to this general argument a historically specific narrative about Scotland as a small, relatively non-hierarchical nation traditionally inclined to self-determination – as revealed, for example, by the medieval wars of independence – that had been swept away from its authentic character by the economic opportunities – and at times coercion – of Union and Empire. But as the economic returns of industrialisation and imperialism began to fade, and as it became increasingly apparent that the twentieth century was to be an era of centralised political and economic control from London, nationalists believed that Scots would in due course prioritise their primary national identity as the basis for a freer and more communal separate Scottish state.[19]

The most prominent nationalist exponent of these ideas was Robert McIntyre (1913–98), SNP leader from 1947 to 1956 and briefly the party's first MP in 1945 (by profession he was a doctor – a consultant – with a particular interest in public health issues).[20] Ideologically,

---

[18] Ben Jackson, 'Property-Owning Democracy: A Short History', in Martin O'Neill and Thad Williamson (eds.), *Property-Owning Democracy: Rawls and Beyond* (Oxford, Wiley-Blackwell, 2012), pp. 33–52; Stuart White, '"Revolutionary Liberalism?" The Philosophy and Politics of Ownership in the Post-War Liberal Party', *British Politics*, 4 (2009), pp. 164–87; Peter Sloman, *The Liberal Party and the Economy* (Oxford, Oxford University Press, 2015), pp. 116–25, 190–5, 234; Malcolm Petrie, 'Anti-socialism, Liberalism and Individualism: Rethinking the Realignment of Scottish Politics, 1945–1970', *Transactions of the Royal Historical Society*, 28 (2018), pp. 197–217.

[19] Oliver Brown, *Scotland: The Satellite!* (Glasgow, Scottish Secretariat, 1958), pp. 68–9; Oliver Brown, *The Anglo-Scottish Union of 1707: Then and Now* (Stirling, Scots Independent, n.d. [*c*.1959]).

[20] Richard Finlay, 'Robert McIntyre', in Hassan and Mitchell (eds.), *Scottish National Party Leaders* (London, Biteback, 2016), pp. 177–99; 'Robert McIntyre (1913–98)', *Oxford Dictionary of National Biography* (Oxford, Oxford University Press, online ed., 28 May 2015), at https://doi.org/10.1093/ref:odnb/59442 (accessed 2 October 2019); Dick Douglas, *At the Helm: The Life and Times of Dr Robert D McIntyre* (Portessie, Buckie, NPFI Publications, 1996).

McIntyre has been perceptively described by H. J. Hanham as 'a neo-Lockean populist who believes in a property-owning democracy'. McIntyre wanted 'to see property so widely distributed that even urban man has something to fall back on – whether it is a workshop in the backyard or a croft in the Highlands'.[21] He combined these distributive ideas with a staunch commitment to the democratic rights of small nations. McIntyre was critical of the rise of Soviet communism, and totalitarian ideologies more generally, since these were creeds that were complicit in the suppression of many ancient European nations: 'nations with histories like our own – small countries, usually, which have had to defend themselves against powerful and imperial neighbours'.[22]

McIntyre drew on a diverse set of sources to make this case, including a language of individual rights derived from Christian personalism. Personalism was an influential twentieth-century philosophical and theological current that sought to defend both the dignity of the person and the necessarily social character of that personhood against the growth of materialism and totalitarianism. It played a key role in the ideological formation of continental Christian democracy in the mid-twentieth century.[23] McIntyre's use of personalist ideas in the same period meant that his political thought – and the SNP's – bore some resemblance to the Christian democracy that shaped for example West Germany and Italy after the Second World War. McIntyre desired a Scotland 'where freedom and that respect for persons which comes from our Christian heritage is not sacrificed on the altar of materialism, and where that very Christian respect for persons ensures to all an adequate material standard'.[24] Personalism was also present in the SNP's more systematic statement of its aims and policies agreed at the party's 1946 conference, which contained the telling line: 'Scottish nationalism is based primarily on spiritual values, on the recognition of the needs of the individual and the right to express himself fully and freely within the framework of a community knit together by the ties of an enduring tradition.'[25] Personalists characteristically emphasised that individuals could only realise their full individuality as members of a wider community and through

---

[21] Hanham, *Scottish Nationalism*, p. 174.

[22] Robert McIntyre, 'The Challenge of Today', *Scots Independent*, No. 299, July 1951, p. 1.

[23] Carlo Invernizzi Accetti, *What Is Christian Democracy?* (Cambridge, Cambridge University Press, 2019), pp. 53–79; Samuel Moyn, *Christian Human Rights* (Philadelphia, University of Pennsylvania Press, 2015). As Moyn observes, personalism was for example influential in the drafting of the new Irish Constitution of 1937: pp. 39–49.

[24] Robert McIntyre, 'National Party Annual Conference: Chairman's Opening Remarks', *Scots Independent*, No. 262, June 1948, p. 1.

[25] SNP, *Statement of Aim and Policy*, p. 3. Intriguingly, this line appears at the start of the section headed 'Local Government'.

social relationships. McIntyre tweaked this communitarianism to add that participation in the life of a nation represented an essential element of such a rich social context. 'Nationalism', he argued, was in fact 'the self-consciousness of a nation, the affirmation of its personality'. The individual, the family and the nation were, he said, 'the new political trinity' that demanded popular support.[26]

McIntyre believed that both Labour and the Conservatives offered similar projects of centralisation and overwhelming bureaucratic power, one predominantly public sector, the other in the private sector (reflecting, perhaps, his reading of Peter Drucker's *The End of Economic Man* [1939]). After 1945 McIntyre was highly critical of the regime of economic planning and nationalisation that Labour presided over since it represented 'the joint concentration of economic and political power'.[27] Nationalisation had made no difference to the distribution of power, McIntyre argued, since the nationalised industries were simply 'new business empires' controlled by the state. McIntyre thought that the era of classical economic conflict between workers and owners was in the past, displaced by a new 'struggle for power' that raged across both private and public institutions to secure greater individual freedom and democratic control over a 'managerialist' model of social organisation run by an elite class of bureaucrats. Scottish self-government, and stronger local democracy, he claimed, would enable Scots to enjoy greater personal liberty and a deeper democracy by reducing the scale of government and economic organisations.[28] In his successful campaign at the Motherwell by-election in 1945, McIntyre argued: 'Scotland has no need of a highly centralised state interfering in the private lives of the people'; instead, 'a self-governing Scotland would depend on the natural organisation of the family and the local community for its stability'. He emphasised the importance of empowering local government in order to 'let the community of Scotland be reborn'.[29] Reflecting

[26] Robert McIntyre, 'Bannockburn Day: Opening Remarks by Chairman', 21 June 1952, speech notes, Robert McIntyre Papers, National Library of Scotland, Acc. 10090/70.

[27] Robert McIntyre, 'Nationalists Annual Conference: Chairman's Opening Remarks', *Scots Independent*, No. 275, July 1949, p. 1; McIntyre, 'National Party Annual Conference'. The influence of Drucker is suggested by Hanham, *Scottish Nationalism*, p. 175. On Drucker's economic philosophy, see Daniel Immerwahr, 'Polanyi in the United States: Peter Drucker, Karl Polanyi and the Mid-Century Critique of Economic Society', *Journal of the History of Ideas*, 70 (2009), pp. 445–66.

[28] Robert McIntyre, 'Freedom, Power and Democracy', *Scots Independent*, No. 286, June 1950, p. 1; Gwynfor Evans, Roy Lewis, J. E. Jones et al., *Our Three Nations: Wales, Scotland, England* (Cardiff, Plaid Cymru/SNP/Common Wealth Party, 1956), pp. 7–17.

[29] Robert McIntyre, Motherwell by-election pamphlet, 1945, Robert McIntyre Papers, National Library of Scotland, quoted in Finlay, 'Robert McIntyre', pp. 188–9. See also the stress on empowering Scottish local government in SNP, *Statement of Aim and Policy*, p. 3.

McIntyre's ideas, the SNP characterised itself as aiming at 'the diffusion of economic power' to protect both freedom and democracy, with the key economic implication that it was crucial 'to eliminate or to subject to strict supervision all private monopolies and to restrict state monopolies to the minimum'.[30]

The heterodox social credit ideas of Major Clifford Douglas (1879–1952) were also a significant influence on the national movement's economic philosophy.[31] McIntyre, for example, warned that 'the community of Scotland cannot enter into its rightful inheritance while the wealth of the country is in the hands of alien government, international finance and private monopolies', a form of argument that showed the imprint of social credit on nationalist economic thought.[32] Douglas's ideas were tied into a set of economic theories that were discredited in the eyes of professional economists but which nonetheless tapped into widespread concerns about the malfunctioning of capitalism between the wars and mobilised deeply felt hostility towards what Douglas referred to as 'cosmopolitan finance' (as this language suggests, Douglas's social credit ideas also made use of anti-Semitic tropes, which MacDiarmid – a keen advocate of social credit – was also guilty of using).[33] Douglas sought to counteract what he regarded as capitalism's tendency to suppress consumer purchasing power with a universal income or 'social dividend' for all citizens, subsidised prices, political and economic decentralisation, and public control of the financial system.[34] Douglas was an important reference point for Hugh MacDiarmid, who supported a 'neo-Gaelic economics' that situated Scottish cultural revival in the context of a new economic model that was hostile to usury and prioritised autarchic economic development.[35] Other nationalist thinkers and leaders were less extravagant than MacDiarmid

---

[30] SNP, *Statement of Aim and Policy*, p. 5.

[31] Hanham, *Scottish Nationalism*, pp. 174–5; Brand, *National Movement in Scotland*, pp. 204–8.

[32] Robert D. McIntyre, *Some Principles for Scottish Reconstruction* (Glasgow, SNP, 1944), p. 3.

[33] Hugh MacDiarmid, *At the Sign of the Thistle* (London, Stanley Nott, 1934), p. 63; Purdie, *Hugh MacDiarmid*, pp. 38–42.

[34] C. B. MacPherson, *Democracy in Alberta: Social Credit and the Party System* (Toronto, University of Toronto Press, 2013 [1953]), pp. 93–141; Francis Hutchinson and Brian Burkitt, *The Political Economy of Social Credit and Guild Socialism* (London, Routledge, 1997).

[35] MacDiarmid, *Albyn*, pp. 34–8; C. M. Grieve, 'Wider Aspects of Scottish Nationalism', *Scots Independent*, No. 13, November 1927, pp. 3–4; C. M. Grieve, 'Neo-Gaelic Economics', *Scots Independent*, No. 14, December 1927, pp. 21–2; C. M. Grieve, 'Neo-Gaelic Economics II', *Scots Independent*, No. 16, February 1928, pp. 53–4; Purdie, *Hugh MacDiarmid*, pp. 25–48.

in their economic philosophy and some were sceptical about adopting 'Douglasism' wholesale.[36]

However, although MacCormick chastised MacDiarmid for his 'woolly thinking, which could encompass within one mind the doctrines both of Major Douglas and of Karl Marx', Scottish nationalism nonetheless absorbed into its worldview staple social credit themes such as the desirability of national control over finance and the need to develop a home market for goods rather than focusing on exports.[37] The latter point proved to be a useful point of attack for nationalists on the 1945 Labour government. The Attlee government's focus on production for exports was consistently singled out by the SNP as demonstrating the misplaced priorities of a British state that was not economically self-sufficient in the way that Scotland – with its lower population – could be.[38] The SNP was committed to banning 'the export of raw materials for processing abroad' (unless 'exceptional circumstances' applied) and to legislating to ensure that businesses based in Scotland were owned and controlled by Scots.[39] Nationalists therefore mainly construed the benefits of Scottish independence in economic rather than cultural terms, but the economic analysis they subscribed to was one that sought to go beyond the ideological distinction between socialism and capitalism in the name of what they believed to be a distinctively Scottish model of economic relationships.

Before the 1960s, the Scotland of nationalist imagination was predominantly agrarian rather than industrial. Independence was often desired precisely because it would at last allow the deep-seated problems of rural Scotland to be addressed. Tom Gibson (1893–1975), one of the leading early figures in the nationalist movement (and who eventually served as SNP president in the 1950s), saw Scotland and England as fundamentally different in part because of their divergent geological and hence agricultural structures. In particular, he argued, 'the physical nature of Scotland lends itself to farming in small-holdings', unlike in England, but he added that the encouragement of such smallholdings should be seen as one element of a much-needed wider revitalisation of Scottish

---

[36] See for example Ronald Muirhead to Tom Gibson, 25 March 1933, Tom Gibson Papers, National Library of Scotland, Acc. 6057/1/4.

[37] MacCormick, *Flag in the Wind*, p. 35.

[38] 'Scotland's Answer to the Crisis: Manifesto by the National Party', *Scots Independent*, No. 255, November 1947, pp. 1–2; John Galloway, 'Employment in Scotland', *Scots Independent*, No. 260, April 1948, p. 1; McIntyre, 'National Party Annual Conference', pp. 1–2; 'Policy Resolutions by National Party Conference', *Scots Independent*, No. 280, December 1949, p. 6.

[39] SNP, *Statement of Aim and Policy*, p. 11.

agriculture, encompassing afforestation, cottage industries, land reclamation and fishing. This could only be undertaken, Gibson argued, by a new Scottish state with the powers to invest in Scottish land and to focus the Scottish people's energies on a project of national redevelopment rather than merely encouraging Scots to emigrate to colonies around the world (as the British state did).[40] More precisely, as Robert McIntyre put it, an independent Scottish state would seek land reform involving 'the limitation of private ownership of land and the encouraging of owner cultivators responsible to the community for their good husbandry'.[41] SNP policy in the 1940s regarded further industrialisation of rural areas as undesirable. For rural Scotland, the party argued, 'crofting is socially and ethically desirable', since it created a healthy local community, and could be made economically viable by combining it with 'part-time employment in local industry such as weaving, forestry, fishing or other local productive activities'.[42]

The problem of significant levels of emigration from Scotland, and related anxieties about inward migration from Ireland and England, weighed heavily on the minds of many Scottish nationalists in this period.[43] An uneasy mix of voluntarist and organic themes percolated through this aspect of the case for independence, as the 'excessive proportion' of residents in Scotland who had not been born in Scotland was identified as an important argument for Scotland to gain sovereign control over immigration: 'If our national culture and distinctive characteristics are to be maintained, *if the Scottish race is to survive*, Scotland must regain the power to regulate the entry of all aliens.'[44] Yet the hostility to Irish immigration, and Catholicism, that animated such sentiments was contested by other leading figures in the national movement. MacDiarmid, for example, welcomed Irish immigration as a bracing new cultural influence that would counteract the hostility to the arts bred into

---

[40] Tom Gibson, 'The Land: The Problem Stated', *Scots Independent*, No. 2, December 1926, p. 3. Gibson was a businessman who worked in the steel industry for much of his career: see Richard Finlay, 'Thomas Hill Gibson (1893–1975)', *Oxford Dictionary of National Biography* (online ed., 4 October 2012), at https://doi.org/10.1093/ref:odnb/71329 (accessed 2 October 2019).

[41] McIntyre, *Some Principles for Scottish Reconstruction*, p. 8; see also SNP, *Statement of Aim and Policy*, p. 6.

[42] 'Policy Resolutions by National Party Conference', p. 6.

[43] Finlay, 'National Identity in Crisis', pp. 251–2.

[44] 'The Irish Menace', *Scots Independent*, No. 2, December 1926, p. 2; emphasis in the original. For similar examples, see also George Thomson, *Caledonia or the Fate of the Scots* (London, Kegan Paul, 1927), pp. 10–17; Spence, 'National Party of Scotland', pp. 5–7; Andrew Dewar Gibb, *Scotland in Eclipse* (London, H. Toulmin, 1930), pp. 53–62.

Scottish society by the dominance of a dour Calvinism.[45] MacCormick, meanwhile, later argued that Irish immigrants had been insufficiently integrated into Scottish national life precisely because the Scots 'were themselves sadly deficient in national feeling'. When Scotland has 'a sufficiently healthy national life of her own', MacCormick said, 'she will find no difficulty in absorbing strangers in her midst and turning them into good Scottish citizens'.[46]

Democratic Sovereignty and Its Limits

The aspiration to recover Scotland's powers as a sovereign nation raised a significant question about how a small state such as Scotland could exercise control over its own affairs without cutting itself off from international trade, collective security and, most importantly in the mid-twentieth century, participation in the British Empire. Most Scottish nationalists recognised this as an important issue for the cause of Scottish independence and thought that Scottish sovereignty would need to be attenuated in certain respects in order to enjoy secure borders and a flourishing economy. But this was not accepted by everyone involved in the early years of the Scottish national movement. Significant fissures emerged over how far the ultimate goal of nationalism was to secure Scotland a self-governing status *within* the British Empire, perhaps analogous to the position of the existing dominions such as Australia or Canada, or even for Scotland to assume the special role of an equal 'mother nation' of the Empire alongside the rest of the United Kingdom. Other voices within nationalism adopted a more pungently anti-imperial stance, seeing Scottish independence as a cause that was about liberating Scotland from participation in colonialism (or indeed liberating Scotland from officially becoming a British colony, which is one way of interpreting the goal of converting Scotland into a dominion like Australia and New Zealand). From this latter perspective, some nationalists argued that the virtues of small-scale national self-government represented the future of humanity – since a somewhat deglobalised world system with many small nations would avoid the aggressive imperialism and expansionism that had cursed world politics in the first half of the twentieth century. As Richard Finlay has shown, there were many twists and turns over which of these competing visions of Scottish nationalism had the upper hand within the movement, but broadly speaking the Scottish Party had been strongly imperialist in orientation, favouring a Scottish

[45] MacDiarmid, *Albyn*, pp. 3–4, 28–30.   [46] MacCormick, *Flag in the Wind*, pp. 52–3.

parliament within the context of larger British and imperial structures. The merger of the Scottish Party with the NPS therefore diluted the clarity of the latter's commitment to independence so that the SNP's early years offered a policy profile that was less separatist and anti-imperial than either the SNL or NPS. Instead, the broad initial objective of the SNP was a self-governing Scotland that nonetheless shared with England the governance of Empire, arrangements for defence and foreign policy, and a customs union.[47]

However, this moderation of the SNP's policy stance proved to be only temporary. By the end of the 1940s a more sovereigntist view was once again ascendant in the SNP, as the exponents of less radical positions gradually left active service in the party or, in the case of John MacCormick, turned to non-party organisations as the vehicle for making progress on the Scottish question.[48] The SNP therefore faced the 1950s and the decomposition of the British Empire committed to a more separatist stance on Scottish statehood than in the 1930s, although the party did stress that its central argument was precisely that Scotland should possess the sovereign power to determine for itself which supranational treaties and international relationships to enter into. It was therefore conceivable that some sort of confederation or even federation might be possible within the British Isles 'but it must be a federation freely accepted and operated by equal nations'.[49] After the Second World War, the SNP emphasised the importance of international cooperation, with an independent Scotland aiming to enjoy 'a particularly intimate relationship with the other countries of the British Isles', as well as 'the closest direct political and economic relations with the self-governing dominions' and the wider world through the United Nations.[50] By the late 1940s, Robert McIntyre and Douglas Young had begun to see the nascent moves towards European integration as a further arena of international relations in which an independent Scotland could flourish as a full and enthusiastic participant.[51]

---

[47] Richard Finlay, '"For or Against?" Scottish Nationalists and the British Empire 1919–39', *Scottish Historical Review*, 71 (1992), pp. 184–206; Finlay, *Independent and Free*, pp. 112–19, 130–3, 152–8.

[48] Malcolm Petrie, 'John MacCormick', in Hassan and Mitchell (eds.), *Scottish National Party Leaders* (London, Biteback, 2016), pp. 55–61.

[49] 'Scotland – Free or Fettered?', *Scots Independent*, No. 305, January 1952, pp. 8–9.

[50] SNP, *Statement of Aim and Policy*, p. 4.

[51] Robert McIntyre, 'European Union', *Scots Independent*, No. 260, April 1948, pp. 1–2; Robert McIntyre, 'England Turns Back: The National Idea', *Scots Independent*, No. 287, July 1950, p. 3; Douglas Young, *The International Importance of Scottish Nationalism* (Glasgow, Scottish Secretariat, 1947), pp. 16–17.

All of this was a better fit with the party's political economy than the earlier 'imperialist' turn in Scottish nationalism. As we have seen, Scottish nationalists located the commercial future in small-scale industry and the repopulation of rural areas, trends that would express certain historic qualities of Scottish identity. As the nationalist lawyer Duncan MacNeill (1893–1981) wrote in 1943:

> Scotland will be seen as a country organised to allow the fullest scope to the individualism of the citizen; a country of which the political dynamic is peace; a country which, beneath its romantic trappings and superficial patriotism, was in fact simply a settlement of men inspired by the desire for liberty, otherwise peace or, better, security; a country which had – and, indeed, still has – no use for capital or labour at loggerheads with each other, preferring to obliterate, or at least reduce to a minimum, the unearned income; and, discarding the modern idea of socialism, even state socialism or state capitalism – two names for the same thing – in favour of free individualism 'within the law' – shall we call it communalism? Its national dynamic of peace would make possible the proper functioning of a League of Nations, for it would proceed to build from the parish – or foundation – up and not from the League – or roof – down. Co-operation, not domination, would be its aim. It would ruthlessly destroy the modern European state, which is essentially a warlike grouping of peoples thinking primarily in terms of armies, unable as at present constituted, to build up a peace organisation such as a League of Nations. And it would substitute states or nations of a size small enough to allow of the citizens in fact controlling the governments.[52]

Although notable for their lack of realism, these ideas were nonetheless significant because they located Scottish nationalism in a decentralising, participatory political lineage that was sceptical of the polarity between capitalism and socialism that dominated ideological debate in the mid-twentieth century.

Instead, the sources of these democratising impulses were attributed to the distinctiveness of Scottish constitutional development, which (nationalists argued) differed from English feudal traditions insofar as it rested on popular, perhaps even proto-democratic, foundations. Nationalist writers such as MacNeill and the novelist and historian (and some-time suffragette) Agnes Mure MacKenzie (1891–1955) delved deep into medieval and early modern Scottish history to draw a pioneering contrast between an English constitution founded on the authoritative command of the sovereign, later embodied in the unconstrained will of Parliament itself, and a Scottish political system that reflected a tradition of wider political cooperation between different sections of the community. This

---

[52] Duncan H. MacNeill, *The Scottish Constitution* (Glasgow, SNP, 1943), pp. 28–9. MacNeill's dates are from his obituary notice in the *University of Edinburgh Journal*, 30 (1981), p. 169.

Scottish tradition was even said to have prefigured the republican assertion of 'the rights of man' and prescribed a monarch subject to the law
and contractually bound to serve the community, as epitomised for
example in the 1320 Declaration of Arbroath and the political theory of
the great sixteenth-century Scottish humanist, George Buchanan.[53] In
MacNeill's evocative phrase, 'measured by a chronological table, the
Scots constitution is ancient; but measured by philosophical content
and humanitarian practice, it is modern among the moderns'.[54] The
pioneering labour historian William Marwick (1894–1982) observed
shortly after these words were published that MacNeill's notion of a
'"primitive democracy" in medieval Scotland' had 'a curiously eighteenth century flavour (as of a minor Rousseau or Scots Major Cartwright)', and firmly concluded that MacNeill's account 'has been
generally rejected by historians'.[55]

But, as we will see in Chapter 5, this constitutional narrative would in
fact become a widely disseminated and influential one. It achieved widespread attention because of two important legal cases fought by nationalists against the British state in the 1940s and 1950s. The first – and less
well known of the two – concerned Douglas Young, who had declined to
be conscripted into the armed forces or industrial work during the
Second World War on the grounds that Scots should only undertake
such national service under the command of a Scottish government with
equal status to the dominion governments of Australia, Canada and New
Zealand. In the ensuing prosecutions in 1942 and 1944, Young, who had
become the leader of the SNP in the course of his legal action, argued
that there was no legal basis under the Treaty of Union for Britain to
demand national service from Scots. His case was a detailed and multifaceted one, but a fertile part of his argument was that the Treaty of
Union functioned as a kind of written constitution that bound the new
British Parliament to protect certain basic rights of the Scots, notably a

---

[53] Agnes Mure MacKenzie, *Scotland in Modern Times 1720–1939* (London, W & R
Chambers, 1941), pp. 52–3; Agnes Mure MacKenzie, *Scottish Principles of Statecraft
and Government* (Glasgow, Scottish Convention, 1942), pp. 7–13; William Donaldson,
'Agnes Mure MacKenzie (1891–1955)', *Oxford Dictionary of National Biography* (online
ed., 28 September 2006), at https://doi.org/10.1093/ref:odnb/57342 (accessed 2 October
2019); MacNeill, *Scottish Constitution*, pp. 6–7, 10–16, 20–5; Duncan H. MacNeill, *The
Scottish Realm: An Approach to the Political and Constitutional History of Scotland* (Glasgow,
A. and J. Donaldson, 1947). This historical argument was adopted by other nationalists
such as McIntyre, 'Challenge of Today', p. 1.

[54] MacNeill, *Scottish Realm*, p. 283.

[55] William H. Marwick, *Scottish Devolution* (London, Fabian Society, 1950), p. 3. Major
John Cartwright was an eighteenth-century English campaigner for radical parliamentary
reform.

rather extensive right of personal liberty.[56] Young was in effect calling the bluff of the defenders of the Union, who presented it as a uniquely favourable deal for Scotland, since it integrated Scotland into a wider economic market while guaranteeing from English dominion the Scots' right to a distinctive society. Nationalists had long been sceptical of this claim, noting that there were in fact no legal mechanisms to enforce 'the rights of Scotland preserved to her at the time of Union', since Scotland was now subject to an 'omnipotent' Parliament in London.[57] Young sought to test this proposition – perhaps not entirely in good faith – by making the audacious counter-claim that the courts *should* view the Union as entailing legally enforceable rights for Scotland. In correspondence with one such trenchant critic of the Union, the nationalist legal scholar, Andrew Dewar Gibb (1888–1974), Young summarised his claim as that 'the British constitution rests upon a *foedus*, ie is federal, like the USA, Canada, etc, and its Constituent Law is adjudicable by Courts of every degree'.[58] Young added to this a related point, namely that parliamentary sovereignty should be seen as a specifically English constitutional tradition. With the creation of the new United Kingdom, Young argued, there was no reason to believe that this English model should straightforwardly trump 'the ancient Scots principle of the sovereignty of the people'.[59] Young was in close contact with other leading figures in the national movement throughout this litigation, including Robert McIntyre and Duncan MacNeill, and it is likely he developed his arguments in collaboration with them (on Young's own retrospective account, 'advocates and solicitors and others' had been advising him on how to prepare his case).[60]

---

[56] Douglas Young, *The Free-Minded Scot* (Glasgow, Scottish Secretariat, 1942), pp. 8–17; Douglas Young, *An Appeal to Scots Honour: A Vindication of the Right of the Scottish People to Freedom from Industrial Conscription and Bureaucratic Despotism under the Treaty of Union with England* (Glasgow, Scottish Secretariat, 1944), pp. 9–17.

[57] Dewar Gibb, *Scotland in Eclipse*, pp. 82–4; Andrew Dewar Gibb, *The Shadow on Parliament House: Has Scots Law a Future?* (Edinburgh, Porpoise Press, 1932), pp. 12–14; Pentland, 'Douglas Young', pp. 153, 155.

[58] Douglas Young to Andrew Dewar Gibb, 27 September 1944, Andrew Dewar Gibb Papers, National Library of Scotland, Acc. 9188/4. A more formal statement of this point is Young, *Appeal to Scots Honour*, pp. 17–19, 20–3.

[59] Douglas Young, *Quislings in Scotland* (Glasgow, Scottish Secretariat, 1942), pp. 3–32 (quote at p. 15); Young, *Free-Minded Scot*, pp. 2–7; Young, *Appeal to Scots Honour*, pp. 19–20, pp. 25–7.

[60] See the correspondence and drafts collected in the Robert McIntyre Papers, National Library of Scotland, Acc. 10090/15, especially Douglas Young to David Watson, 21 October 1944; see also Douglas Young to Duncan MacNeill, 4 April 1944, Douglas Young Papers, National Library of Scotland, Acc. 6419/40. Young cited MacNeill's work, for example in his *Fascism for the Highlands? Gauleiter for Wales?* (Glasgow, Scottish National Party, 1943), p. 3. Young's account is in his *Chasing an Ancient Greek* (London, Hollis & Carter, 1950), pp. 56–66, quote at p. 59.

Young's case was denied by all of the courts in which he was heard and he served two spells in prison as a result. Of course, amid the Second World War Young's contentions appeared eccentric – even frivolous – but he had set out the essentials of the argument that would later be prosecuted to greater effect by John MacCormick in 1953, when he contended that the decision to style the new Queen Elizabeth II was a violation of the Treaty of Union (since Elizabeth I had not been Queen of Scotland). This case was also unsuccessful legally, but, as we will discuss in greater detail in Chapter 5, it produced a slow-burning publicity coup for Scottish nationalists when the presiding judge, Lord Cooper of Culross (1892–1955), expressed some sympathy for MacCormick's contention that the Treaty of Union had a quasi-constitutional status that in theory ought to constrain the British Parliament, though Cooper doubted that in practical terms any court was competent to do so. However, Cooper agreed outright with Mac-Cormick that parliamentary sovereignty was an English rather than a Scottish constitutional principle (curiously, this was in spite of the fact that Cooper had previously ruled against Douglas Young's earlier case along the same lines without making this point).[61] Cooper's remarks were eagerly seized upon by nationalists as on the one hand a vindication of their stance on Scotland's distinctive constitutional development and on the other as demonstrating the legal impotence of the protections that had purportedly been written into the Treaty of Union.[62] This was therefore a line of argument that would thrive in subsequent nationalist political thought and represents an important ideological continuity between early Scottish nationalism and its later iterations towards the end of the twentieth century.

Class and the State

Overall, the early nationalist vision of a new Scottish state was counter-cultural to the dominant intellectual trends of the mid-twentieth century. Scottish nationalists did not support a more expansive role for a large public sector in managing an industrial economy (though some state activism was to be directed towards developing rural areas) and were even at times ambivalent about what nationalists regarded as the over-expansion

---

[61] MacCormick, *Flag in the Wind*, pp. 46–8, 189; Colin Kidd, *Union and Unionisms: Political Thought in Scotland, 1500–2000* (Cambridge, Cambridge University Press, 2008), pp. 293–5.

[62] 'Court Decision Warning to All Those Who Would Be Free', *Scots Independent*, No. 322, June 1953, p. 1; 'Scotland's Dilemma Posed Again by Judicial Opinion', *Scots Independent*, No. 325, September 1953, pp. 5–6; Finlay, 'Robert McIntyre', pp. 191–3.

of social services into state monopolies.[63] Nationalists argued that standard political ideologies such as socialism, liberalism and conservatism were ephemeral and unstable when compared to the fundamental national distinction between Scotland and England, with the English point of view inevitably destined to win out in a British political system where Scots formed a numerical minority.[64] Most revealing was a notable reluctance to identify class divisions within Scotland as a source of political concern or as offering a potential base of social support – whether working or middle class – for the independence cause, on the grounds that internal social divisions within Scotland were merely a distraction from the national interest. As Charles Stewart Black (1887–1963), a prolific nationalist writer (and by profession a doctor), put it: 'Class antagonism is a thing quite foreign to the Scottish spirit. It was unknown here until it was imported from England.'[65]

A further counter-cultural tendency among early Scottish nationalists was that they deployed a libertarian rhetoric of freedom from state interference. Robert McIntyre stressed that 'the Scottish nation is dependent for its existence on the home and the individual, rather than the state' and urged nationalists to pursue policies that focused on strengthening the family and civil society rather than 'the glorification of the state'.[66] 'We do not appeal to any particular sectional interest or self-interest', McIntyre said in a later speech, 'we appeal to the nation as a whole, to the loyalty of the people, to their love of freedom. Make this your stand – "Freedom and Scotland".'[67] Douglas Young, who for a time combined his membership of the SNP with membership of the Labour Party, even praised Friedrich Hayek's 'valuable volume *The Road to Serfdom*' for demonstrating the damaging effects on individual liberty of forms of state planning that pursued full employment through '*industrial conscription* and *delegated legislation*'. Young argued that 'the slogan of *full employment* is appropriate only to a servile state' and that the true 'Scottish principles of government are freedom, security and responsibility'.[68] As Malcolm Petrie has

[63] Maxwell, 'Social Justice and the SNP', pp. 120–1; Petrie, 'Anti-socialism, Liberalism and Individualism', p. 215; SNP, *Statement of Aim and Policy*, pp. 14–16.

[64] Tom Gibson, 'The Reasons for a National Party', *Scots Independent*, No. 13, November 1927, p. 5.

[65] Charles Stewart Black, *Scottish Nationalism: Its Inspiration and Aims* (Glasgow, National Party of Scotland, 1933), p. 29; Obituary of C. Stewart Black, *British Medical Journal*, 27 April 1963, p. 1168.

[66] McIntyre, *Some Principles for Scottish Reconstruction*, p. 12.

[67] McIntyre, 'Challenge of Today', p. 2.

[68] Douglas Young, *British Invasion of Scottish Rights: Douglas Young's Speech in Paisley Sheriff Court on 12th June* (Glasgow, Scottish Secretariat, 1944), p. 19; emphasis in the original; F. A. Hayek, *The Road to Serfdom* (London, Routledge, 1944).

observed, this libertarian language echoed the critique of Labour socialism articulated around the same time by the Conservatives and the
Liberals, positioning the SNP to appeal to the substantial portion of the
Scottish electorate that felt alienated by the new regime of economic
planning that had emerged in London in the 1940s and which was largely
preserved intact by the Conservative government of the 1950s.[69]

Later Scottish nationalists were to take a different view of class and the
state, aligning the objective of Scottish independence with the quest for a
stronger social democracy, but also questioning the extent of the conflict
between the individual and the state that McIntyre had identified. This
subsequent generation of nationalists – born between the 1930s and the
early 1950s – came less from business or traditional professional backgrounds and more from what one of their number, Stephen Maxwell
(1942–2012), described as 'the new middle class – academics, media
people, employees of pressure groups or of the public sector, the technical middle class'. Maxwell saw the SNP leadership of the 1960s and
1970s as bringing together this rising social group with a still 'significant
admixture of small businessmen, farmers, solicitors in private practice
and representatives of the private "service" sector'.[70] These new exponents of Scottish independence – from whose ranks the major figures in
this book are drawn – tended to be more secular than their predecessors
and more comfortable with the economic and social responsibilities
assumed by the state after the Second World War. However, as Maxwell
observed, they also retained a conviction that the modern state should be
made more democratic and accountable, favouring measures such as
electoral reform, a bill of rights, and the decentralisation of power to
local government. Where the nationalist pioneers had sought a new
sovereign Scottish state to depart from an era of bureaucratised industrial
politics and economics, their political successors sought a modernising
state that would enable Scotland to resemble other Western European
polities in its democratic constitution and in its power to shape economic
outcomes and centrally redistribute resources.

---

[69] Petrie, 'Anti-socialism, Liberalism and Individualism', pp. 212–17.
[70] Stephen Maxwell, 'The Implications of Prospective Independence: The Problem of
State Power', *Nevis Quarterly*, No. 2, January 1979, pp. 14, 18–20.

2   A Democratic Nation

Scottish nationhood does not rest on constitutional history alone. It is supported by a culture reaching back over centuries and bearing European comparison in depth and quality, nourished from a relatively early stage by an education system once remarkable by European standards. Since the Union, the strength of that culture has fluctuated but there is no ground for any claim that, overall or even at any particular time, it has benefitted from the Union. On the contrary the Union has always been, and remains, a threat to the survival of a distinctive culture in Scotland.   *A Claim of Right for Scotland*, 1988[1]

Scottish nationalists have long had mixed feelings about how far independence was necessary to safeguard Scotland's distinctive culture. As we saw in Chapter 1, support for 'Scottish culture' understood in linguistic, literary or artistic terms was certainly a recognisable strand of nationalist argument from the mid-twentieth century onwards but it was never central to the pro-independence case. However, 'Scottish culture' could also be construed in a more general sense, as a reference to the norms and social institutions of Scotland that set it apart from England and which were critical to the formation of a distinctive Scottish identity. From the mid-twentieth century onwards, some nationalists did regard this broader notion of Scottish culture as an increasingly important political priority and argued that a new state was essential to resist the Anglicising trends that threatened to envelop modern Scotland.[2]

---

[1] Campaign for a Scottish Assembly, *A Claim of Right for Scotland*, July 1988, reprinted in Owen Dudley Edwards (ed.), *A Claim of Right for Scotland* (Edinburgh, Polygon, 1989), p. 14.

[2] As Scott Hames has shown, this also holds true for the wider late twentieth-century political mobilisation in favour of devolution, where a discourse of cultural difference was nurtured as a powerful rhetoric in favour of greater Scottish political autonomy (*The Literary Politics of Scottish Devolution* [Edinburgh, Edinburgh University Press, 2019]). Although note that Hames chiefly examines literature and the arts as the vehicle of this cultural movement whereas my focus in this chapter is on debates about the institutions of Scottish national life.

Over the centuries of union with England, Wales and, later, Ireland and Northern Ireland, a distinctive Scottish identity has chiefly been shaped and transmitted through a set of autonomous national institutions, the preservation of which was thought to constitute one of the basic protections for Scotland written into the 1707 Acts of Union. Indeed, one strand of unionist political argument has always maintained that it was precisely through a negotiated political union with England that Scotland avoided the drastic cultural assimilation to English norms that would have followed a more coercive political settlement.[3] The expression of Scottishness through Scotland's separate religious, legal and educational institutions has therefore been a commitment shared by supporters of the Union and independence alike.

However, it is certainly possible to give this Scottish identity a specifically nationalist inflection, in two ways. First, by drawing such a sharp contrast between the character of this Scottish institutional culture and its English counterpart as to imply an irreconcilable ideological mismatch between Scotland and England. And, second, by suggesting that the Union, far from guaranteeing the rude health of Scottish institutions, in fact poses a grave threat to their distinctive national characteristics. In some formulations, this latter claim can even offer a 'declinist' account of recent Scottish history, which sees the Union as facilitating a creeping process of Anglicisation that is slowly snuffing out the flickering flames of Scottish national life. Both of these lines of argument have been widely used by the exponents of Scottish independence, but the classic and most influential version of them was expressed by the Edinburgh philosopher George Davie (1912–2007) in his remarkable book, *The Democratic Intellect* (1961).

Educational Independence

Davie completed a DLitt at Edinburgh University in 1953 on the Scottish school of common-sense philosophy in the eighteenth and nineteenth centuries. He was pressed by potential publishers of the thesis to preface his philosophical analysis with an initial chapter placing it in its historical context. This historical chapter grew in scope – or as Davie put it 'unsuspected dramas were revealed' – and it eventually became *The Democratic Intellect* (Davie's original philosophy thesis was only published in 2001 as *The Scotch Metaphysics: A Century of*

---

[3] Richard Finlay, 'Controlling the Past: Scottish Historiography and Scottish Identity in the 19th and 20th Centuries', *Scottish Affairs*, no. 9 (1994), pp. 133–6; Christopher Harvie, *Scotland and Nationalism* (London, Routledge, 2004 [1977]), p. 17.

Enlightenment in Scotland.[4] Although Davie came from an older generation than the other protagonists of this book, *The Democratic Intellect* had a formative impact on many younger nationalists. It was published, as the leading nationalist thinker Stephen Maxwell observed, at approximately the same time as the first edition of the collected poems of Davie's close friend, Hugh MacDiarmid. Reading both these books as a student in the early 1960s, Maxwell later recalled, 'had the force of revelation' in opening up new vistas on Scottish cultural history.[5] (MacDiarmid himself referred to *The Democratic Intellect* as 'the most important book on any Scottish subject published in my lifetime'.)[6] Neil MacCormick (1941–2009), John MacCormick's son and as we will see another important theorist of Scottish nationalism, likewise recalled reading *The Democratic Intellect* as a student. Its publication, he said, was 'a momentous event', which enabled students at Scottish universities 'to appreciate in an informed way the remaining if emasculated virtues of the tradition and intellectual heritage to which we belonged'.[7]

Davie's work focused on the threat posed by English cultural and political influences to the Scottish education system, but it is intriguing that around the same time a similar set of arguments began to be elaborated by Scottish jurists about the deleterious Anglicising effects of English legal hegemony on Scots law. Figures such as Andrew Dewar Gibb, Lord Cooper of Culross and Thomas B. Smith (1915–88) contrasted the distinctive character of Scotland's legal tradition with its English counterpart. Scots law, they argued, mixed civil law and common law elements and relied on deductive reasoning and principled argument rather than induction and the authority of precedent. Smith's *British Justice: The Scottish Contribution*, like *The Democratic Intellect* published in 1961, presented Scotland's legal tradition as more European, cosmopolitan and outward-looking than the insular English common law. Yet the character of Scots law, Smith thought, was threatened by

---

[4] George Davie, *The Democratic Intellect* (Edinburgh, Edinburgh University Press, 2013 [1961]), p. xvii; George Davie, *The Scotch Metaphysics: A Century of Enlightenment in Scotland* (London, Routledge, 2001). Some of Davie's earlier philosophical work was published as 'Hume and the Origins of the Common Sense School', *Revue internationale de philosophie*, 6 (1952), pp. 213–21; 'Common Sense and Sense-Data', *Philosophical Quarterly*, 4 (1954), pp. 229–46.

[5] Hugh MacDiarmid, *Collected Poems* (Edinburgh, Oliver and Boyd, 1962); Stephen Maxwell, 'The Crisis of the Democratic Intellect', *Radical Scotland*, no. 23, October/November 1986, p. 16. For MacDiarmid's friendship with Davie, see Hugh MacDiarmid, *The Company I've Kept* (London, Hutchinson, 1966), pp. 237–55.

[6] Hugh MacDiarmid, *A Political Speech* (Edinburgh, Reprographia, 1972), p. 12.

[7] Neil MacCormick, 'The Idea of Liberty: Some Reflections on Lorimer's Institutes', in Vincent Hope (ed.), *Philosophers of the Scottish Enlightenment* (Edinburgh, Edinburgh University Press, 1984), p. 233.

the unthinking importation of English legal culture into Scotland by 'certain southern mandarins' who 'have sought to subvert valued and valuable Scottish institutions'.[8] This emergent 'legal nationalism' (as it became known) had an important influence on Scottish public life, but its political impact was not straightforwardly pro-independence or left-wing. Instead, much of it reflected a libertarian anxiety about the growth of the British state in the mid-twentieth century and a desire to shore up the authority of the Scottish legal elite in the face of an apparently unappealing democratisation of British society. Of the three leading thinkers associated with legal nationalism, only one (Dewar Gibb) supported Scottish independence and he combined this advocacy with an unabashed imperialism and anti-Catholicism that places him some distance from later Scottish nationalist thought.[9]

George Davie's own outlook was not entirely free of the mid-twentieth-century anxieties about the rise of the welfare state that characterised legal nationalism, but he offered an interpretation of Scottish national institutions that could be more easily adapted to a left-wing agenda. While Davie's ideas were often technical and obscure in detail, at a general level they were more vivid and politically salient than the inevitably more specialised legal discourse. Davie's significance for nationalist thought is that he presented Scottish national values, as expressed through the history of Scotland's educational system, as democratic ones (in a way that ran parallel to the characterisation of Scottish constitutional development as embodying the ideal of popular sovereignty which we encountered in Chapter 1 and will explore further in Chapter 5). Most importantly, he was thought to have shown that more egalitarian and communitarian Scottish schools and universities had been threatened by, and ultimately succumbed to, an elitist, hierarchical

---

[8] T. B. Smith, *British Justice: The Scottish Contribution* (London, Stevens & Sons, 1961), p. 3. Hugh MacDiarmid even recommended to his readers that they complement *The Democratic Intellect* by perusing Smith's *British Justice: Company I've Kept*, p. 243.

[9] Ian D. Willock, 'The Scottish Legal Heritage Revisited', in John Grant (ed.), *Independence and Devolution: The Legal Implications for Scotland* (Edinburgh, W. Green & Sons, 1976), pp. 1–14; Lindsay Farmer, 'Under the Shadow Over Parliament House: The Strange Case of Legal Nationalism', in Lindsay Farmer and Scott Veitch (eds.), *The State of Scots Law: Law and Government After the Devolution Settlement* (London, Bloomsbury, 2001), pp. 151–64; Hector MacQueen, 'Legal Nationalism: Lord Cooper, Legal History and Comparative Law', *Edinburgh Law Review*, 9 (2005), pp. 395–406; Hector MacQueen, 'Two Toms and an Ideology for Scots Law: T. B. Smith and Lord Cooper of Culcross', in Elspeth Reid and David Carey Miller (eds.), *A Mixed Legal System in Transition: T. B. Smith and the Progress of Scots Law* (Edinburgh, Edinburgh University Press, 2005), pp. 44–72; Colin Kidd, *Union and Unionisms* (Cambridge, Cambridge University Press, 2008), pp. 198–210.

Anglicising tendency that had little time for more inclusive Scottish educational traditions. As we will see, Davie's argument was in fact more ambiguous than that, although this description captures accurately enough the spirit if not the letter of Davie's panoramic vision of Scottish intellectual history after 1707.

Walter Elliot (1888–1958), the Conservative politician and Secretary of State for Scotland 1936–8, is widely credited with coining the phrase 'democratic intellectualism' in a 1932 essay that reflected on 'the Scottish heritage in politics'. Significantly, the 'democratic intellectualism' that Elliot referred to in this essay was associated with the distinctive church government of Presbyterianism, which he glossed as entailing 'a fierce egalitarianism, and a respect for intellectual pre-eminence, and a lust for argument on abstract issues'.[10] Elliot found little evidence of a secular Scottish political tradition, evocatively concluding that 'the "polis" of Scotland, the "city" with which our politics really concern themselves, is a city not made by hands'.[11] Davie appropriated (or perhaps misappropriated) the term 'democratic intellect' from Elliot but one of the less remarked upon features of Davie's book was that he was sceptical about the importance of religious institutions as in themselves bearers of Scottish national distinctiveness, a more radical stance to adopt in 1961 than today.[12] He aimed in particular to correct what he saw as a mistaken historiographical emphasis on post-Reformation Scottish culture as dominated by a particular kind of sectarian Protestantism. Davie argued that the Union of 1707 was most profitably seen not as the housing of 'two state-churches in one state but rather as a unity in politics combined with a diversity in what may be called social ethics', the latter encompassing a much wider field than religious life. Indeed, Davie noted that Presbyterian egalitarianism was by no means absent from English culture. Instead, it was the secular Scottish institutions – the law and education – which, in combination with the church, created 'the distinctive code regulating the Scottish way of life':

---

[10] Walter Elliot, 'The Scottish Heritage in Politics', in the Duke of Atholl (ed.), *A Scotsman's Heritage* (London, A. Maclehose, 1932), pp. 53–65, quotes at pp. 59, 63; Catriona M. M. MacDonald, 'Alba Mater: Scottish University Students, 1889–1945', in Robert Anderson, Mark Freeman and Lindsay Paterson (eds.), *The Edinburgh History of Education in Scotland* (Edinburgh, Edinburgh University Press, 2015), pp. 287–8. The phrase 'democratic intellect' was used before Elliot. In 1874, for example, the American novelist Henry James described the Russian novelist Ivan Turgenev as uniting 'an aristocratic temperament with a democratic intellect'. Henry James, 'Ivan Turgenev', in his *Literary Criticism: French Writers, Other European Writers* (New York, Library of America, 1984), p. 992.

[11] Elliot, 'Scottish Heritage', p. 64.   [12] Davie, *Democratic Intellect*, pp. 75, 286–7, 289.

the ratiocinative approach of Parliament House, looking as it did to Roman and Continental law, was out of line with the inherited English practice; and still more alien and uncongenial was an educational system which, combining the democracy of the Kirk-elders with the intellectualism of the advocates, made expertise in metaphysics the condition of the open-door of social advancement.[13]

For Davie, it was these interlocking institutional features of Scottish life that preserved a measure of 'independence' for Scots even after the Union.

A second neglected aspect of Davie's book is that it was saturated by the language of independence. Davie deployed this vocabulary at regular intervals as he related the story of how an 'independent' Scottish tradition of education had been repeatedly threatened and eroded by English cultural influences and heavy-handed, unsympathetic union-state management. With the Union, 'Scots virtually gave up their political and economic independence', but retained their other separate institutions, maintaining at least until the mid-nineteenth century 'their national independence in this spiritual and cultural realm'.[14] But (Davie continued) there was a basic instability in the Union settlement. The combination of 'social dependence on England with educational independence' constituted an insecure basis for the preservation of Scottish traditions.[15] As the pressure to Anglicise became more profound during the nineteenth century, on Davie's telling there emerged defenders of Scottish educational traditions who formed a 'patriotic party' that sought to maintain 'the national tradition' against the 'pro-English party', who were more favourably disposed to reform and aligned with 'the cause of the Auld Enemy'.[16] Indeed, Davie argued, 'education became the chief forum of resistance to Southern encroachment, and provided a rallying-point for national principle'. The stakes were high: 'what was being decided by the struggle was no less than the fate of the distinctive sort of society developed by the Scots'.[17]

This was, however, a declinist story. Davie broadly saw the nineteenth century as a period of retreat on the part of the intellectual patriots. Before the Universities Commission Report of 1889, which introduced new specialised honours courses into Scottish universities alongside the existing generalist ordinary degrees, 'the Scots still clung to their old ideal of national independence in education, but,

---

[13] Davie, *Democratic Intellect*, pp. xviii–xxi, quotes at xviii, xix. Parliament House is the collective name of the buildings that house the Supreme Courts of Scotland.

[14] Davie, *Democratic Intellect*, pp. 3, 261; see also pp. 242, 310.

[15] Davie, *Democratic Intellect*, p. 3.

[16] Davie, *Democratic Intellect*, pp. 324, 78, 234; see also p. 71.

[17] Davie, *Democratic Intellect*, p. 4.

subsequently, they have shown a decided preference for subordination above initiative'. Later generations of Scots formed by these reforms, said Davie, have lost interest in the distinctive values of Scottish education: 'The Scots of today are too deeply imbued with English or rather semi-English values to be able to take seriously the fierce spirit of intellectual independence which until recently animated the higher institutions of their country'.[18] Although in *The Democratic Intellect* Davie's historical narrative was pessimistic about the prospects for a renewed Scottish intellectual or perhaps even political independence, in the wake of the 1960s nationalist revival he did observe with satisfaction that 'a re-assertion of independent sovereignty' could still appeal to the Scottish public at moments of political stress such as during Winnie Ewing's victory for the SNP at the 1967 Hamilton by-election under the slogan 'Put Scotland Back on the Map'. Davie thought this indicated a persisting sense of 'national pride and aspirations in Scottish life', which was expressed, among other ways, through a struggle 'to keep alive the tradition of distinctive Scottish universalism in research' in spite of living in a time when 'an apparently alien set of values complacently attempt to over-look it'.[19]

What did Davie mean by a distinctive tradition of 'Scottish universalism in research'? The focus of *The Democratic Intellect* was the 'independence' of the Scottish universities (and their relationship with secondary schooling). The Scottish system, Davie argued, had historically offered an open, democratic model of higher education. Davie referred in particular to 'the traditional Scottish machinery designed to neutralise the inequalities of scholastic and family backgrounds', which enabled promising students from a variety of social classes to receive higher education, so that 'careers were opened to talents'. But in addition to this democratic, or, more precisely, meritocratic, characteristic of Scottish schools and universities, Davie emphasised the importance of the particular intellectual content of a Scottish university degree: 'Lest this selection and fostering of talents would produce a flood of one-sided experts and bureaucratic specialists, general studies of a non-utilitarian kind were

---

[18] Davie, *Democratic Intellect*, pp. 8–9. In a similar vein, Davie later sympathetically reconstructed the 'intellectual Anglophobia' of James Steuart's defence of Scotland's 'economic independency' against 'English hegemony', which he contrasted with the 'Scoto-English' approaches of Adam Smith and James Mill: George Davie, 'Anglophobe and Anglophil', *Scottish Journal of Political Economy*, 14 (1967), pp. 291–302, quotes at pp. 299, 300, 301.

[19] George Davie, 'Discussion', in J. N. Wolfe (ed.), *Government and Nationalism in Scotland: An Enquiry by Members of the University of Edinburgh* (Edinburgh, Edinburgh University Press, 1969), pp. 204–5. This piece was later reprinted as 'Nationalism and the Philosophy of the Unthinkable', in *Edinburgh Review*, no. 83, 1990, pp. 38–9.

given pride of place in the curriculum'.[20] The degree syllabus was thus organised around generalist rather than specialist principles, offering a broad-based introduction to a variety of disciplines. Intellectually, averred Davie, 'the Scots had an almost religious attachment to their inherited ideal of a culture in which the general should take precedence over the particular and the whole over the parts'.[21]

But at the heart of this traditional Scottish university education, argued Davie, was the discipline of philosophy, which formed a compulsory part of this generalist curriculum. Writing against the background of the rise of Anglo-American analytical philosophy, a trend which Davie deprecated, *The Democratic Intellect* sought to defend not just the place of philosophy as a compulsory element in the Scottish university curriculum but also the importance of a particular school of philosophy that Davie saw as distinctively Scottish in character. Common sense philosophy, as a sort of epistemological third way between the extremes of radical English empiricism and continental rationalism, offered a democratic model of knowledge ultimately indebted, Davie thought, to the Calvinist tradition.[22] 'Common sense', in Davie's view, referred not just to a set of true ideas inherent in each individual, but also included knowledge acquired socially, 'through mutual communication':

Scottish democracy develops on the basis of a two-world view of man as a creature whose cognitive equipment depends on a sort of balance between an instinctive a priori, revealed by introspection and reflection to learned and unlearned alike, on the one hand, and the a posteriori facts revealed to the systematic observation and experimentation of the experts, on the other.[23]

Knowledge, Davie said, therefore requires 'social-intellectual communication with "other minds"'; the danger of a highly specialised society was that it prevented the necessary clear communication between different sections of society.[24] Such a democratic social dialogue in Davie's view formed a system of checks and balances on the power of experts and leaders, just as 'the minister's theological supervision of the congregation was checked and balanced by the congregation's common sense scrutiny

---

[20] Davie, *Democratic Intellect*, p. xxiv.   [21] Davie, *Democratic Intellect*, p. 4.

[22] For the philosophical and political provenance of 'common sense', including its incubation in Scotland, see Sophia Rosenfeld, *Common Sense: A Political History* (Cambridge, MA, Harvard University Press, 2011).

[23] George Davie, *The Crisis of the Democratic Intellect* (Edinburgh, Polygon, 1986), p. 259; George Davie, 'The Social Significance of the Scottish Philosophy of Common Sense' [1972], in George Davie, *The Scottish Enlightenment and Other Essays* (Edinburgh, Polygon, 1991), p. 63.

[24] Davie, 'Social Significance', p. 66.

of the minister'.[25] A constructive dialogue between widely held ideas and rational expertise was the fruit of this philosophical school but it was, Davie suggested, ultimately pushed aside, in the first place by the rise of evangelical religion after the Disruption of 1843, which bowdlerised common sense into an unreflective defence of basic intuitions, and subsequently by the philosophical influence of utilitarianism and idealism, both of which Davie saw as foreign imports to Scottish culture.[26] Indeed, he audaciously remarked in passing that 'seen in a Scottish context, idealism was not so much the opponent of positivistic utilitarianism but rather its ally in a common struggle against the traditions of common sense dualism'.[27]

Unquestionably a milestone in Scottish cultural and intellectual history, the narrative presented in *The Democratic Intellect* has nonetheless been widely criticised, not least by Davie himself, who in later work appeared (without much explicit acknowledgement) to have changed his mind on certain points. In particular, Davie extended his periodisation of crisis and decline from the nineteenth century into the twentieth century. His sequel, *The Crisis of the Democratic Intellect* (1986), claimed that in fact philosophy returned to the centre of Scottish higher education as a compulsory subject for ordinary degree students in 1927,[28] and argued that a set of debates about philosophy and the Scottish universities in the 1920s formed an important context for the Scottish literary renaissance of the same period. The writings of Hugh MacDiarmid were critical to this story and Davie developed a penetrating account of the philosophical background to MacDiarmid's poetry and of MacDiarmid's own interventions in the debate over the Scottish universities. This fecund age for Scottish culture also featured its own clash with a utilitarian Anglicising state, this time in the guise of the Scottish Education Department, which sought to imbue Scottish universities with a more professional, scientific and technocratic ethos. Shortly afterwards, Davie related, the continued vitality of a generalist, common-sense philosophy, represented by intellectuals such as the classicist, John Burnet (1863–1928)

---

[25] Davie, 'Social Significance', p. 59; quoted in Lindsay Paterson, 'George Davie and the Democratic Intellect', in Gordon Graham (ed.), *Scottish Philosophy in the Nineteenth and Twentieth Centuries* (Oxford, Oxford University Press, 2015), p. 242.

[26] Davie, *Democratic Intellect*, pp. 286–338. The 1843 Disruption was the major schism within the Church of Scotland over whether the state had jurisdiction over church affairs.

[27] Davie, *Democratic Intellect*, p. 354, n. 40.

[28] Robert Anderson pointed out that in fact this was not true: after a curriculum reform in 1908 compulsory philosophy for ordinary degree students had been retained at Glasgow and St. Andrews but removed at Edinburgh and Aberdeen; it was then restored at these institutions in 1919 and 1914 respectively ('Democracy and Intellect', *Cencrastus*, no. 25, spring 1987, p. 3).

and the philosophers, Norman Kemp Smith (1872–1958) and John Anderson (1893–1962), petered out. Influenced by philosophical developments in Oxford and Cambridge, the grander ambitions of this style of philosophy were displaced by a more technical analytical form of the discipline, a development that Davie regarded as in its essentials one of Anglicisation.[29]

Leaving aside Davie's periodisation and the historical accuracy of his account of Scottish education (both points that have been contested by his critics), for our purposes a more significant aspect of Davie's work relates to the central concept of democracy. As Robert Anderson, Davie's most trenchant critic, pointed out, Davie offered what appeared at first sight to be a narrative of a broadly egalitarian Scottish educational tradition, and it is indeed this understanding of Davie's argument that passed into wider public culture in Scotland. But a closer investigation of Davie's argument, Anderson continued, revealed it to be more merito-cratic than egalitarian: 'the "democratic intellect" of Davie's title is the intellect of the nation's elite, not of the masses'.[30] This Scottish national elite could be understood as democratic, Davie thought, because it was recruited from a variety of social backgrounds and Scottish common sense philosophy was methodologically committed to cultural leaders engaging with wider currents of public opinion. In many ways, then, Davie's subtle, multilayered arguments were a modernisation of the historic memory of the Scottish education system as facilitating social mobility, opening the way for the 'lad o'pairts' to ascend to a professional career from a modest family background.[31] But this is a social ideal that, while clearly an important component of a just society, is by no means straightforwardly egalitarian in terms of its economic and social out-comes, and in its origins was characterised by significant gender inequality (the place of women in the Scottish educational tradition was not discussed by Davie). In spite of Davie's efforts to distance Scottish identity from its religious roots, Anderson pointed out that Davie was essentially offering a secularisation of an ancient religious ideal, in which the leadership of the clergy was replaced with 'a secular clerisy' of Scottish origins, formed by distinctive Scottish philosophical traditions and thus immune to the charms of Oxbridge philosophy and

---

[29] Davie, *Crisis*; Paterson, 'George Davie', pp. 240–1, 245–50.
[30] Robert Anderson, 'The Scottish University Tradition: Past and Future', in Jennifer Carter and Donald Withrington (eds.), *Scottish Universities: Distinctiveness and Diversity* (Edinburgh, John Donald, 1992), p. 71.
[31] David McCrone, *Understanding Scotland: The Sociology of a Nation* (2nd ed., London, Routledge, 2001), pp. 93–100.

the English social values that came with it.[32] Interestingly, Stephen Maxwell had offered a similar, although more sympathetic, reading of Davie at the time of the publication of *The Crisis of the Democratic Intellect*. Maxwell concluded his review of the book by posing the question of whether the idea of 'democratic intellectualism' can

be extended beyond the bourgeois perspectives of Scottish Enlightenment thinkers, nineteenth-century metaphysicians and inter-war innovators to encompass an alternative vision of a secularised democracy – founded on a moral idealism free of utopian illusions about human perfectibility, individualist in its respect for individual conscience, collectivist in its insistence on the right of the majority to organise public institutions in accord with strenuously debated values, scornful of the pretensions of the worldly powerful *sub specie aeternitas*?[33]

Maxwell offered the possibility of a more egalitarian, and social democratic, version of Davie's historic tradition, but it was not clear if Davie himself would have endorsed this. As he wrote at the end of *The Crisis of the Democratic Intellect*, Davie's own concern was with how elites and experts should relate to mass opinion in modern societies: should the few control the many or the many the few? Davie believed that the tradition of Scottish 'democratic intellectualism' offered a third way, in which the elite and the masses can together share control, because collective deliberation would generate a critical dialogue between mass and expert opinion, preventing one from exerting unilateral power over the other.[34] Aside from the difficult practical issues raised by this formulation, it demonstrates that Davie was sceptical of radical movements that would ultimately undermine authoritative elites – seeing such radicals, from his secularised Calvinist perspective, as neglectful of human fallibility. This set him apart from the insurgent participatory democracy that animated the New Left movements of the 1960s and which, as we will see in Chapters 3 and 4, played an important role in shaping other strands of nationalist thought. Davie coupled this with a dismissive posture towards the philosophical schools that had dug the intellectual foundations of the

---

[32] Anderson, 'Scottish University Tradition', pp. 71–7, quote at p. 72; Robert Anderson, 'Education and Society in Modern Scotland: A Comparative Perspective', *History of Education Quarterly*, 25 (1985), p. 478; Jean Barr, 'Re-framing the Democratic Intellect', *Scottish Affairs*, no. 55 (2006), pp. 23–46. Anderson disagreed with both Davie's overall argument, and the empirical detail (or lack of it) in Davie's historical narrative, as set out in Robert Anderson, *Education and Opportunity in Victorian Scotland* (Oxford, Oxford University Press, 1983), pp. 358–61.

[33] Maxwell, '*Crisis*', p. 17. Maxwell had earlier written about the importance of such a secularised Presbyterianism in the work of key interwar Scottish figures such as John Reith, John Grierson and A. D. Lindsay: 'The Secular Pulpit: Presbyterian Democracy in the Twentieth Century', *Scottish Government Yearbook*, 1982, pp. 181–98.

[34] Davie, *Crisis*, p. 262.

British welfare state – the radicalism of J. S. Mill's utilitarianism; the left idealism of T. H. Green and his followers – but which were not as distinct as Davie believed from Scottish traditions.[35] Davie's intellectual history was Manichean in its segregation of these 'English' ideas from authentically Scottish thought. But the liberal and socialist strands that were woven together into the ideology of British social democracy in the mid-twentieth century also wrestled with the reconciliation of democracy and expertise, and had been articulated, and exchanged, by both English and Scottish thinkers.[36] Neither of the main political options offered by the democratic left could therefore be easily accommodated by Davie, leaving his own constructive political position elusive. In a rare later foray into public debate, Davie defended Scottish comprehensive schools from reforms initiated by the Thatcher government in the 1980s, but in doing so highlighted some of his own ambivalence about the left's egalitarianism. Davie accepted that, in spite of his initial reservations, the Scottish comprehensive system had been able to accommodate and perhaps even advance the concept of the democratic intellect. But in addition to the defence of the comprehensive system, he argued that it was necessary for the Scottish education system as a whole, and particularly the universities, to return to 'a situation in which cultural egalitarianism is no longer opposed (as it has been in Scotland this century) to the intellectual distinction of the few'. Davie looked back instead to the nineteenth century as a period in which 'egalitarianism did not exclude intellectualism and elitism'.[37]

At one level Davie therefore offered a resonant lament for the dissolution of Scottish traditions. Unprotected from 'the characteristically English refusal to take a serious interest in the question of philosophical foundations', Davie concluded, 'a nation noted educationally both for social mobility and for fixity of first principles gradually reconciled itself to an alien system in which principles traditionally did not matter and a rigid social immobilism was the accepted thing'.[38] But the eloquence and originality of Davie's analysis stirred some of his most attentive readers to develop their own variations on the thesis of *The Democratic Intellect* and

---

[35] Jose Harris, 'Political Thought and the Welfare State 1870–1940', *Past and Present*, 135 (1992), pp. 116–41; Michael Freeden, 'The Coming of the Welfare State', in Terence Ball and Richard Bellamy (eds.), *Cambridge History of Twentieth Century Political Thought* (Cambridge, Cambridge University Press, 2003), pp. 5–44; Ben Jackson, *Equality and the British Left* (Manchester, Manchester University Press, 2007).

[36] A searching critique of Davie along these lines has been made by Paterson, 'George Davie', pp. 250–64.

[37] George Davie, 'The Threat to Scottish Education', *Edinburgh Review*, no. 83, 1990, pp. 35–7, quotes at p. 37.

[38] Davie, *Democratic Intellect*, pp. 263, 106.

to view the book as a resource for contemporary political thought. As Robert Anderson put it, Davie had created 'a poetic vision, or inspirational myth, of "metaphysical Scotland"', which he combined with a taste for 'scenarios of cultural catastrophe and prophets who preach in the wilderness'. It was precisely this juxtaposition that was to prove appealing to certain later nationalist writers and activists.[39]

After Davie

In spite of Davie's own political ambiguity, then, he served as an inspiration to subsequent writers in search of an explicitly nationalist political philosophy. One reason for this is that the politics of the 1970s and 1980s provided a context in which Davie's style of nationalist argument could acquire a fresh relevance. The immediate background to the writing and reception of *The Democratic Intellect* had been the pressing debates of the 1950s and 1960s about the introduction of comprehensive secondary schooling and university expansion, notably the 1963 Robbins Report, rather than the question of Scottish national identity, a topic which only gradually became the subject of serious political scrutiny as the 1960s progressed.[40] The notion that a distinct set of Scottish values and institutions was under threat from the Union rose in salience during the economic upheavals of the 1970s before reaching a fever pitch during the Thatcher years. In this climate, Scottish nationalists were scathing about what they saw as the failure of Scotland's core national institutions to stand up for Scottish interests. Stephen Maxwell, in particular, criticised the lack of national consciousness promoted by the Scottish universities. This was a grievous blow to national aspirations, he argued, since the Scottish universities were in fact the only one of Scotland's important pre-1707 institutions to have grown in social significance in

[39] Anderson, 'Democracy and Intellect', pp. 3, 4. On Davie's work as a mobilising myth, see Lindsay Paterson, *Scottish Education in the Twentieth Century* (Edinburgh, Edinburgh University Press, 2003), pp. 5–7; Michael Gardiner, *The Cultural Roots of British Devolution* (Edinburgh, Edinburgh University Press, 2004), pp. 57–77.

[40] Lindsay Paterson, 'Democracy or Intellect: The Scottish Educational Dilemma of the Twentieth Century', in Robert Anderson, Mark Freeman and Lindsay Paterson (eds.), *The Edinburgh History of Education in Scotland* (Edinburgh, Edinburgh University Press, 2015), p. 241. Initial reviews of *The Democratic Intellect* usually viewed it in terms of contemporary debates about education policy or philosophy, notably C. P. Snow, 'Miasma, Darkness and Torpidity', *New Statesman*, 11 August 1961, pp. 186–7. See also the reviews by Brian Simon, *Victorian Studies*, 5 (1961), pp. 168–9; D. B. Horn, *Scottish Historical Review*, 41 (1962), pp. 82–3; H. J. Paton, *Hibbert Journal*, 60 (1962), pp. 268–9; G. P. Henderson, *Philosophical Quarterly*, 13 (1963), pp. 89–91; D. M. Tulloch, *Philosophy*, 38 (1963), pp. 373–4. Richard Storr's review in *Journal of Modern History*, 35 (1963), pp. 188–9 did emphasise the nationalist dimensions of Davie's book.

the wake of the Union. He lamented the loss of the distinctive Scottish tradition of higher education detailed by George Davie and the extent to which the Scottish university system had become integrated into a British framework. Although the Scottish universities had been critical of devolution in the late 1970s (and had sought to be excluded from the purview of any new devolved Scottish government), Maxwell hoped that the hostility of the British state to universities in the 1980s would ultimately lead to Scottish higher education seeking greater autonomy from London and a concerted attempt to retrieve the 'democratic intellectualism' Davie had recounted.[41]

As we will see, Maxwell eventually played a key role in conceptualising Scottish nationalism in socialist terms but in the 1970s he was not averse to describing his support for independence as in a broad sense cultural. Responding to the New Left theorist Tom Nairn (b. 1932), whose early interventions in Scottish politics were sceptical about the cultural resources available for Scottish nationalism, Maxwell argued:

The nationalist case rests, first, on the recognition that every society has its inheritance of problems and preoccupations, some of which are shared with other societies, some of which may be peculiar to it; and, second, that every society has an obligation to equip itself to talk, think, write, dance, sing and *act* (both representationally and politically) its way through these problems.[42]

Maxwell believed at this stage that Scottish culture possessed sufficient resources to build such a nationalism, but that Scotland currently lagged behind other nations in the opportunities that existed to do so, not least because of the weakness of Scottish cultural institutions. One of Maxwell's hopes was that the emergence of a Scottish state would in fact advance Scottish cultural life insofar as it would create a new focus of Scottish identity that could relieve Scottish writers and artists from 'the burden of national assertion', thus freeing them from the political pressure to address the state of the Scottish nation that Maxwell thought had had an inhibiting effect on the quality of recent Scottish literature in particular.[43] Maxwell and Nairn both changed their minds in significant

---

[41] Stephen Maxwell, 'Treason of the Clerks', *Scottish International*, vol. 5, no. 6, August 1972, pp. 18–20; Stephen Maxwell, 'Treason of the Clerks II', *Scottish International*, vol. 5, no. 7, September 1972, pp. 14–17; Stephen Maxwell, 'The English in Scotland', *New Edinburgh Review*, no. 37, spring 1977, pp. 44–5; Stephen Maxwell, 'Scottish Universities', *Radical Scotland*, no. 7, February/March 1984, pp. 12–13.

[42] Stephen Maxwell, letter to the editor, *Scottish International*, vol. 6, no. 5, May/June/July 1973, p. 9; emphasis in the original. Maxwell was replying to 'Culture and Nationalism: An Open Letter from Tom Nairn', *Scottish International*, vol. 6, no. 4, April 1973, pp. 8–9.

[43] Stephen Maxwell, 'Politics and Culture', *Question*, no. 25, 1 April 1977, p. 5.

respects after this early exchange, converging on a political case for Scottish independence based on popular sovereignty and the pursuit of socialism.[44] But other writers on the Scottish question remained convinced that the core of the case for Scottish independence was a cultural one and they looked to George Davie's account of educational Anglicisation as a source of inspiration for this argument.

The most prominent exponents of such a case were Craig Beveridge and Ronald Turnbull, by training a historian and a philosopher respectively. Beveridge and Turnbull had been activists in the Scottish Labour Party (SLP), the new party founded in 1976 by the then Labour MP Jim Sillars (b. 1937) to take on the SNP by synthesising the politics of socialism and nationalism.[45] After the SLP fizzled out, they became influential contributors to the leading Scottish cultural magazines of the 1980s and 1990s, both serving at various times on the editorial boards of *Cencrastus* and the *Edinburgh Review*. Beveridge and Turnbull argued for the reconstruction of a Scottish cultural nationalism along the lines suggested by George Davie in a series of articles in the 1980s and then in their books *The Eclipse of Scottish Culture* (1989) and *Scotland after Enlightenment* (1997).

Beveridge and Turnbull added a postcolonial dimension to this debate by suggesting that Scottish intellectuals, even those who were sympathetic to Scottish nationalism, suffered from what the influential theorist of anti-imperialism Frantz Fanon had called 'inferiorisation', the process by which colonised peoples were led to believe that their own culture was backward and provincial compared to the more sophisticated culture of the imperial metropole. In the Scottish case, they argued, the unstoppable influence of English ideology had undermined Scottish self-knowledge:

English culture, or to be more precise, the public-school, Oxbridge, 'Home Counties' formation is steeped, to a singular degree, in the bizarre belief that its own history, institutions and practices are paradigms for other less favoured peoples.[46]

---

[44] See Chapters 3 and 4 for a detailed discussion of the political ideas of Nairn and Maxwell.

[45] For their activism in the SLP, see the Scottish Labour Party Edinburgh Branch Papers, National Library of Scotland, for example SLP Edinburgh Bulletins for April 1976, January 1977, February 1978, Acc. 7472/5 and SLP Edinburgh membership list, Acc. 7472/4; Ronald Turnbull, 'Letter to the Editor: Hardie's Home Rule', *Scotsman*, 16 December 1977. The SLP will reappear in each of the subsequent chapters of this book – but see Chapter 4 for the most extended discussion of its ideological significance.

[46] Craig Beveridge and Ronald Turnbull, *The Eclipse of Scottish Culture* (Edinburgh, Polygon, 1989), pp. 4–15, 112. Beveridge and Turnbull introduced the concept of 'inferiorisation' into Scottish debate in their 'Inferiorism', *Cencrastus*, no. 8, spring

Scottish nationalist currents of the 1960s and 1970s, Beveridge and
Turnbull argued, had taken too pragmatically political a stance and
deliberately eschewed any serious engagement with cultural nationalism,
with the result that this first significant wave of Scottish nationalist
mobilisation had run aground intellectually on some deeply entrenched
negative ideological assumptions about the nature of Scottish culture.[47]
Beveridge and Turnbull were particularly dissatisfied with the work of
Tom Nairn, which they saw as offering a merely instrumental form of
Scottish nationalism that was ultimately interested in using Scotland to
destabilise British capitalism, rather than endorsing the intrinsic value
of an independent Scottish nation. As we will see in Chapter 3, Nairn
had famously railed against what he saw as the kitsch 'tartan monster' of
Scottish popular culture: a sentimental, mawkish and ultimately highly
conservative construct that offered little in the way of resources for any
putative national movement.[48] Such views, Beveridge and Turnbull
argued, were ultimately based on dismissive English interpretations of
Scottish culture and thus marginalised some highly significant strands of
intellectual and artistic achievement.[49] One example was the literary
fluorescence of the interwar period, and the associated debates about
Scottish literature and the indigenous Scottish languages, but for Beveridge and Turnbull the most significant case was drawn from the work of
George Davie. Davie had 'laid the groundwork for a decolonised understanding of Scotland', they argued, because he had unearthed a distinctive Scottish philosophical tradition that could be counterposed to the
'Anglo-American', 'British' or 'Oxbridge' style of philosophy dominant
in both Scottish and English universities. Taking the proper measure of
Scottish educational and philosophical traditions would thus begin the
process of establishing a more autonomous understanding of Scottish
identity and thus 'the formation of a sophisticated opposition to the
intellectual discourses which underwrite Scotland's subordination'.[50]

1982, pp. 4–5; and in 'The Myth of Scottish Inarticulacy', *Bulletin of Scottish Politics*,
no. 2, spring 1981, pp. 134–8 (the latter article did not mention Fanon by name but
invoked instead Paulo Freire's *Pedagogy of the Oppressed* [1970]).

[47] Beveridge and Turnbull, *Eclipse*, pp. 4–5.

[48] Tom Nairn, *The Break-up of Britain* (London, New Left Books, 1977), pp. 162–3; Tom
Nairn, 'Dr Jekyll's Case: Model or Warning?', *Bulletin of Scottish Politics*, no. 1, autumn
1980, pp. 136–42.

[49] Ronald Turnbull an Craig Beveridge, 'Scottish Nationalist, British Marxist: The Strange
Case of Tom Nairn', *Cencrastus*, no. 13, summer 1983, pp. 2–5; Beveridge and
Turnbull, *Eclipse*, pp. 51–61; Ronald Turnbull, 'Nairn's Nationalisms', in Eleanor Bell
and Gavin Miller (eds.), *Scotland in Theory* (Edinburgh, Rodopi, 2004), pp. 35–48.

[50] Beveridge and Turnbull, *Eclipse*, pp. 112, 63, 113; see also Ronald Turnbull and Craig
Beveridge, 'Philosophy and Autonomy', *Cencrastus*, no. 3, summer 1980, pp. 2–4.

In their view, the reception of Davie's *Democratic Intellect* had missed this fundamental cultural aspect of Davie's work by becoming distracted by '*sociological* questions about access to the Scottish universities in the nineteenth century'.[51]

Precisely how to characterise the political philosophy of Davie's work was, as we have seen, a difficult question. Bob Tait (1943–2017), the founder editor of the cultural magazine *Scottish International* and by background a philosopher, observed that Davie's account underestimated the extent to which the twentieth century was a period in which earlier philosophical foundations and models of rationality had come into question internationally. Philosophers in Scotland were not the only ones who found themselves cast adrift from previous intellectual traditions after the Second World War – Tait mentioned the Frankfurt School as another case where 'there were more than casual reasons for mistrust of normative models and philosophy's contributions to them. Of course, as the work of Habermas and others has since shown, that need not be the end of the story. Even in Scotland.'[52] During the 1980s and 1990s some of Davie's colleagues and students at Edinburgh University argued that in spite of Davie's own determination to present common sense philosophy as distinctively Scottish in fact it could profitably be brought into constructive dialogue with precisely those left Hegelian and Marxist intellectual currents that Tait had mentioned. This group, led by the political theorist Richard Gunn (b. 1947), and including the sociologist John Holloway (b. 1947), along with others such as the art historian Murdo Macdonald (b. 1955), founded a journal of social critique in a broadly Marxist vein, *Common Sense*, which was also inspired by (and took its name from) Davie's account of the Scottish generalist intellectual tradition. The journal ran from 1987 to 1999.[53] Gunn in particular made the case that the tradition of critical theory that emphasised uncoerced social dialogue, mutual recognition and reciprocity shared many features

---

[51] Ronald Turnbull and Craig Beveridge, 'The Historiography of External Control', *Cencrastus*, no. 23, June/August 1986, p. 43; emphasis in the original.

[52] Bob Tait, 'Scottish Education in Dubious Battle', *Cencrastus*, No. 25, spring 1987, p. 5; for Tait's background and career, see David Gow, 'Obituary: Bob Tait, Writer and Intellectual', *Scotsman*, 2 January 2018.

[53] See opening statement in *Common Sense*, no. 1, May 1987, pp. 1–2 (and the website archive of the journal at http://commonsensejournal.org.uk) (accessed 2 October 2019); Richard Gunn, 'Common Sense: A Presentation', background paper for talk at the Ragged University, Edinburgh, June 2013, pp. 4–5, at www.thiswasnottheplan.com/wp-content/uploads/2016/05/9_common_sense_a_presentation.pdf (accessed 2 October 2019); Richard Gunn, 'Common Sense, Scottish Thought and Current Politics', *Bella Caledonia*, 26 July 2014, at https://bellacaledonia.org.uk/2014/07/26/common-sense-scottish-thought-and-current-politics (accessed 2 October 2019). I am grateful to Murdo Macdonald for his help with understanding the origins of *Common Sense*.

with common-sense philosophy. Common-sense philosophy, on Gunn's reading of Davie, was in large measure about the formation of individual identity, including the capacity to make sense of one's own experiences, which was only possible by participating in a community in which the individual interacts with – and recognises – others and engages in dialogue with them about the character of that experience. In Gunn's view, this took common-sense philosophy a long way towards the idea of mutual recognition found in Hegel (and then later in critical theorists such as Jürgen Habermas). Gunn added that Scottish common-sense philosophers, rather like Hegel and Marx, saw the division of labour under capitalism as socially damaging insofar as it resulted in a highly specialised society unable to achieve political cooperation and mutual recognition. The difference was that the Scottish tradition's scepticism about human perfectibility led it away from ideas about social revolution towards Davie's emphasis on education.[54]

While this Hegelian-cum-Marxist approach injected a Jacobin note into the politics of Davie's democratic intellectualism – and largely sidestepped its nationalist implications – Beveridge and Turnbull were more interested in taking Davie's work in a resolutely anti-modernist direction. They warmly cited Davie's emphasis in *The Crisis of the Democratic Intellect* on a form of secularised Calvinism that focused on human fallibility and hence, they judged, expressed a welcome scepticism about progressivism in education and politics.[55] Such a position led Beveridge and Turnbull to extend Davie's work by reference to another Scottish philosophical critic of modernist hubris, Alasdair MacIntyre (b. 1929).[56] One of the most important moral and political philosophers of his generation, MacIntyre had been born in Glasgow and pursued his university education and academic career in England and the United States. An early participant in the revisionist debates about Marxism associated with the New Left, MacIntyre's intellectual agenda eventually resolved itself into a far-reaching critique of contemporary liberalism and what he saw as its failure to offer a satisfactory alternative to Nietzschean relativism.

---

[54] Richard Gunn, 'George Davie: Common Sense, Hegelianism and Critique', *Cencrastus*, no. 27, autumn 1987, pp. 48–51; Richard Gunn, 'Marxism and Common Sense', *Common Sense*, no. 11, winter 1991, pp. 79–100; Richard Gunn, 'Scottish Common Sense Philosophy', *Edinburgh Review*, no. 87, winter 1991, pp. 117–40; Richard Gunn, review of Davie, *The Scottish Enlightenment and Other Essays*, *Common Sense*, no. 12, summer 1992, pp. 101–5.

[55] Beveridge and Turnbull, *Eclipse*, pp. 93–4.

[56] Turnbull and Beveridge introduced MacIntyre's project to a Scottish audience in their 'Towards Postmodernism: An Introduction to MacIntyre', *Cencrastus*, no. 26, autumn 1988, pp. 1–3. An early reference to MacIntyre in their writing is their 'Philosophy and Autonomy', p. 2.

MacIntyre's iconoclastic book *After Virtue* (1981) concluded by recommending a return to an older Aristotelian tradition of ethics that embedded moral conduct in an account of the realisation of the virtues, rather than the approaches to ethics recommended by the more familiar modern philosophical schools of utilitarianism (in which moral behaviour is determined according to whether it produces good consequences) or Kantianism (in which moral behaviour is determined by obedience to ethical rules).[57] In the sequel to *After Virtue*, *Whose Justice? Which Rationality?* (1988), MacIntyre contended that concepts of justice, and the standards of rationality that inform our choice between these views, each have to be seen as emerging from particular moral traditions, in

> which the standards of rational justification themselves emerge from and are part of a history in which they are vindicated by the way in which they transcend the limitations of and provide remedies for the defects of their predecessors within the history of that same tradition.[58]

MacIntyre identified three such moral traditions that he examined in some detail: the ancient Greek view of justice and practical rationality which culminated in the works of Aristotle; an Augustinian theology that was synthesised with Aristotelianism by Thomas Aquinas; and a Calvinist version of Augustinianism that was combined with Aristotelian ideas in the Scottish Enlightenment, concluded in the work of Frances Hutcheson, and ultimately subverted and Anglicised by David Hume.

It was this latter aspect of MacIntyre's work that appealed to Beveridge and Turnbull because it presented a sophisticated portrait of the philosophical distinctiveness of Scotland in contrast with England. MacIntyre was interested in the sociological context of philosophical doctrines and he located the emergence of this Scottish philosophical tradition in the particular character of Scottish institutional life. He argued that the survival of Scottish religious, legal and educational systems after the Union cultivated a 'peculiarly Scottish ethos' in which 'the tasks of rational justification by appeal to principles with an authority independent of the social order were central'.[59] MacIntyre distinguished this view from the contemporary English conception of social organisation in which individual passions and interests were granted primacy over rational justification and the standard of justification in, for example, the law emerged through established practice rather than logical enquiry.[60]

---

[57] Alasdair MacIntyre, *After Virtue* (Notre Dame, University of Notre Dame Press, 1981).
[58] Alasdair MacIntyre, *Whose Justice? Which Rationality?* (Notre Dame, University of Notre Dame Press, 1988), p. 7.
[59] MacIntyre, *Whose Justice?*, pp. 219–21, quotes at p. 220.
[60] MacIntyre, *Whose Justice?*, pp. 215–19, 228–9.

MacIntyre had also been influenced by George Davie and he drew on Davie's work in presenting a historical account of the place of philosophy in Scottish public life.[61] In eighteenth-century Scotland, MacIntyre argued, philosophy achieved a 'cultural hegemony' that extended beyond formal university instruction. Private classes given by professors, student societies and philosophical clubs all gave a social salience to philosophy unmatched elsewhere:

> The effect was to create that very rare phenomenon, an educated public, in this case a philosophically educated public, with shared standards of rational justification and a shared deference to a teaching authority, that of the professors of philosophy and especially of moral philosophy.[62]

This philosophical culture was sociologically possible in Scotland, MacIntyre believed, because 'the peculiar and distinctive principles of Scottish law, Scottish education, and Scottish theology depended for their survival on the elaboration of philosophical theories and theses which could underpin those principles'.[63] MacIntyre dated the decline of this Scottish philosophical culture much earlier than Davie, in the work of David Hume, which MacIntyre argued constituted a monumental subversion of the Scottish tradition and prescribed an assimilation of Scottish culture to a more 'modern' English one. Hume's *Treatise of Human Nature* (1739–40) was thus a philosophical articulation of 'the concepts and theses embodied in the thought and practice of the dominant English social and cultural order'.[64]

What does any of this have to do with Scottish nationalism? Beveridge and Turnbull said comparatively little about the contemporary implications of MacIntyre's history of ideas. But it appears that they read MacIntyre as (like Davie) showing how powerful indigenous Scottish cultural currents had been Anglicised, with Anglicisation understood to entail an ideology of possessive individualism. For example, Beveridge and Turnbull drew on MacIntyre's gloss on Hume's account of pride and love as principally concerned with pride in the ownership of property. In doing so, MacIntyre argued, Hume thought he had described human nature as such 'but what he in fact offers is a description of the eighteenth-century English propertied classes – and, we might add, their

[61] Alasdair MacIntyre, 'The Idea of an Educated Public', in Paul Hirst (ed.), *Education and Values* (London, Institute of Education, 1987), pp. 29–30; MacIntyre, *Whose Justice?*, pp. 240, 249, 257; Alasdair MacIntyre, *Three Rival Versions of Moral Enquiry* (Notre Dame, University of Notre Dame Press, 1990), p. 3.

[62] MacIntyre, *Whose Justice?*, pp. 247–8.   [63] MacIntyre, *Whose Justice?*, p. 258.

[64] MacIntyre, *Whose Justice?*, p. 295.

contemporary spiritual heirs'.[65] As that last remark indicates, Beveridge and Turnbull saw MacIntyre as essentially revealing the ideological foundations of capitalism: 'a society dedicated to the achievement of consumer satisfaction'. Hume's social order, they said, was one saturated by greed and acquisitiveness.[66] One implication of the work of Beveridge and Turnbull was that this sort of cultural history provides a deeper foundation for a Scottish nationalist politics than the more instrumental political nationalism of figures such as Nairn. Although sceptical of socialism as an offshoot of a now discredited 'Enlightenment project', Beveridge and Turnbull nonetheless suggested that egalitarian and communitarian values have a cultural authenticity in Scotland that they lack in England and might perhaps be recuperated following a return to the Scottish philosophical and educational tradition.[67] Following MacIntyre, Turnbull later presented his positive political position as an anti-capitalist Aristotelianism, offering a fundamental critique of contemporary bureaucratic managerialism and economic individualism on the grounds that they are inimical to the pursuit of justice and non-commercial values, including in the latter category the democratic educational philosophy that George Davie had highlighted.[68]

Whose Scottish Tradition?

These attempts to characterise an authentic Scottish cultural tradition associated with the peculiar institutional structures of Scottish life were only indirectly presented as arguments for Scottish independence. Yet there can be little doubt that they painted a rather dark picture of the impact of the Union on Scottish traditions, to the extent that for some readers they called into question the compatibility of England and Scotland in a single political union. Beveridge and Turnbull's recourse to postcolonial language such as Fanon's notion of 'inferiorisation' offered a powerful nationalist rhetoric: that Scotland had fallen victim to cultural colonisation, its way of life denigrated even by Scottish elites, who had been lured into offering fealty to dominant English norms. One of the reasons this analysis held some appeal was that it seemed to offer a

---

[65] As summarised by Beveridge and Turnbull, *Scotland After Enlightenment: Image and Tradition in Modern Scottish Culture* (Edinburgh, Polygon, 1997), p. 109.

[66] Beveridge and Turnbull, *Scotland*, p. 110; see MacIntyre, *Whose Justice?*, pp. 294–6.

[67] Beveridge and Turnbull, *Scotland*, pp. 121–6; Turnbull, 'Nairn's Nationalism', pp. 39–40, 46–7.

[68] Ronald Turnbull, 'Reviving Critique', *Irish Review*, no. 28, winter 2001, pp. 98–107.

plausible explanation for the widely discussed cultural phenomenon of a Scottish lack of self-confidence.[69]

But the Scottish 'culture' that these nationalists sought to protect was not a linguistic or even literary one (although the latter did play some part in the argument). It was fundamentally about the retrieval of the distinctive character of Scottish institutional life and the values that it represented, values which were taken to be democratic, egalitarian and communitarian, in contrast to what was understood to be the hierarchical, elitist and individualist values of England. This contrast was personified institutionally in the differences between the apparently socially inclusive, generalist degree programmes of the ancient Scottish universities and the elitism and narrow specialism that was said to be involved in studying at Oxbridge. The authentic Scottish tradition was therefore, in spite of what Beveridge and Turnbull said, fundamentally a political one, and it was this understanding of Scottishness that appeared increasingly persuasive during the 1980s. Davie published *The Democratic Intellect* at the high tide of the British welfare state, just after the Conservative Party had topped the poll in Scotland in the general election of 1959, winning 47 per cent of Scottish votes (Labour won slightly more seats but on a lower share of the popular vote). In such a context, Davie's historical argument had comparatively little political traction. But when read at a time of rapid deindustrialisation and a fundamental restructuring of the post-war settlement, debates about apparently obscure nineteenth-century educational reforms could achieve a much wider resonance.

Although this vision of an authentic Scottish tradition of democratic intellectualism has proved to be widely appealing, and not only to full-blooded supporters of Scottish independence, it has also attracted significant criticism. One important line of critique concerned the place of class in this discourse. The literary scholar Cairns Craig has pressed this point in relation to MacIntyre – and his point could be extended to George Davie as well. As Craig noted, MacIntyre's presentation of Hume as ultimately endorsing English values by connecting pride with the ownership of property misses that Hume might instead be read as articulating bourgeois, rather than national, values. Indeed, Craig added, MacIntyre's treatment of Hume had the curious effect of classifying the greatest philosopher ever produced in Scotland as fundamentally 'unScottish'.[70]

---

[69] For a popular cultural history of this, which engages with Beveridge and Turnbull, see Carol Craig, *The Scots' Crisis of Confidence* (Glendaruel, Argyll Publishing, 2011 [2003]). Like Beveridge and Turnbull, Craig was also a former member of the Edinburgh Branch of the SLP.

[70] Cairns Craig, *The Modern Scottish Novel* (Edinburgh, Edinburgh University Press, 1999), pp. 24–30.

The association between Englishness, social elitism and inequality, which is present in most of the texts discussed in this chapter, remained an untested assumption, a representation of an 'other', rather than a fully realised analysis. It is certainly possible to offer alternative, more democratic accounts of Englishness and English culture.[71] As Lindsay Paterson has observed, for example, Davie's focus on the contrast between the Scottish universities and Oxbridge left undiscussed the important English civic universities and their traditions of social inclusion, universities which were themselves sometimes explicitly influenced by Scottish higher education.[72] Likewise, the popular understanding of Davie's ideas of democratic intellectualism usually overlooked the significant social hierarchies that were, on Davie's own account, an integral part of this Scottish tradition.

A second line of criticism of this form of nationalist argument was that it constructed an essentialist model of Scottish culture that on the one hand isolated only one strand of a more multifaceted Scottish national story and on the other dismissed a priori any influence of English culture as neocolonial.[73] The issues at stake here can be demonstrated by considering the case of Alasdair MacIntyre. Beveridge and Turnbull were critical of discussions of MacIntyre's work that failed to locate him in a Scottish context. In their view, MacIntyre was most accurately seen as an inheritor of a Scottish tradition of communitarian moral theory and not as an offshoot of what they called 'English New Leftism'.[74] Yet MacIntyre's philosophical education and political and religious formation took place in England. MacIntyre was at various points a member of the Communist Party of Great Britain, a communicant in the Church of England, an active Trotskyist in the Socialist Labour League and International Socialism, and a participant in the emergent British New Left of the 1950s.[75] Indeed, there is a lot to be gained by locating MacIntyre as one of the great intellectuals produced by the anti-Stalinist Marxism of

---

[71] Arthur Aughey, *The Politics of Englishness* (Manchester, Manchester University Press, 2007); Michael Kenny, *The Politics of English Nationhood* (Oxford, Oxford University Press, 2014).

[72] Paterson, 'George Davie', p. 253. Davie himself saw these English universities as embodying a professional rather than philosophical ethos. In his view, Scottish universities became more like English 'Redbrick' universities in the late twentieth century as part of the erosion of the distinctive Scottish tradition of generalism in this period ('The Importance of the Ordinary MA', *Edinburgh Review*, no. 90, 1993, p. 69).

[73] See for example Eleanor Bell, *Questioning Scotland: Literature, Nationalism, Postmodernism* (Basingstoke, Palgrave, 2004), pp. 70–80; Laurence Nicoll, 'Philosophy, Tradition, Nation', in Bell and Miller (eds.), *Scotland in Theory*, pp. 211–28.

[74] Beveridge and Turnbull, *Eclipse*, p. 100.

[75] Paul Blackledge, 'Freedom, Desire and Revolution: Alasdair MacIntyre's Early Marxist Ethics', *History of Political Thought*, 26 (2004), pp. 696–720; Neil Davidson, 'Alasdair

the early British New Left, alongside other outstanding figures such as E. P. Thompson (1924–93), Stuart Hall (1932–2014), Charles Taylor (b. 1931), Raymond Williams (1921–88) and (more tangentially) Eric Hobsbawm (1917–2012).[76] Of those five, Thompson was the only born and bred Englishman among them. Taylor was Canadian; Hall brought up in Jamaica; Williams was Welsh; and Hobsbawm raised in Vienna and Berlin. A comparison with Taylor is particularly apt: like MacIntyre, Taylor moved from a humanistic Marxism to a more fundamental reappraisal of the foundations of modern political theory, plotting a path towards a communitarian politics and ultimately Catholicism via a deep historical critique of contemporary liberalism. Taylor, who is a Québécois, was also an active participant in the debates over Quebec sovereignty in the 1970s and 1980s, though he opposed Quebec departing from the Canadian federation (in contrast MacIntyre, based by then in North America, made no public comment on Scottish constitutional debates).[77] MacIntyre's focus on 'the threat posed to the moral life' by 'currents which present moral beliefs as based on individual choices and preferences' was not in fact distinctively Scottish but rather formed one strand of a communitarian critique of liberalism that absorbed a great deal of intellectual energy in Anglo-American political philosophy during the 1980s and 1990s.[78]

One riposte to this criticism of Beveridge and Turnbull – pressed in particular by the aforementioned Cairns Craig in a later guise – is that this was indeed the point that Beveridge and Turnbull were making: that a liberal public philosophy leads to a dysfunctional individualism and should be replaced, or at least augmented, by a revival of authentic national communitarian traditions. In the Scottish case, that would involve attending to the reinforcement of Scotland's institutions and the distinctive educational, legal and philosophical culture that they generated. From this perspective, what was significant about MacIntyre's work was not that he was born in Scotland but that he had helped, along

---

MacIntyre as a Marxist', in Neil Davidson, *Holding Fast to an Image of the Past* (Chicago, Haymarket, 2014), pp. 129–81.

[76] Michael Kenny, *The First New Left* (London, Lawrence & Wishart, 1995); Dennis Dworkin, *Cultural Marxism in Post-War Britain* (Durham, NC, Duke University Press, 1997).

[77] Charles Taylor, *Sources of the Self* (Cambridge, MA, Harvard University Press, 1989); Charles Taylor, *Reconciling the Solitudes: Essays on Canadian Federalism and Nationalism* (Quebec City, McGill-Queens University Press, 1993); Mark Redhead, *Charles Taylor: Thinking and Living Deep Diversity* (Lanham, MD, Rowman & Littlefield, 2002).

[78] Beveridge and Turnbull, *Eclipse*, p. 100; on the wider debate in political theory, see Stephen Mulhall and Adam Swift, *Liberals and Communitarians* (Oxford, Wiley-Blackwell, 1996).

with Davie, in disinterring and dusting off a neglected Scottish philosophical and educational culture.[79] This was certainly a more convincing
reconstruction of the cultural nationalist case, and in some ways similar
to the points made by Stephen Maxwell in response to Tom Nairn in
1973. But if this *was* the central argument made by Beveridge and
Turnbull, they had in truth found it hard to restrain themselves from
fighting on several other fronts at the same time. Meanwhile their proposed ideological route map for Scottish nationalism involved an ambitious project of cultural retrieval that relied on some contentious
philosophical claims about the historical arc of liberal modernity. From
a political perspective, this looks like more philosophical freight than a
popular democratic nationalism could bear and indeed few later nationalists have prosecuted precisely the kind of long-range cultural case for
independence that Beveridge and Turnbull outlined.

MacIntyre's own view was that his critique of modernity led to an
endorsement of Christianity, in his case an Augustinian Thomism. But
perhaps the most practically applicable aspect of the vision of Scottish
institutional life articulated by Davie and his followers was that it showed
that, on the contrary, a distinctive Scottish identity need not be synonymous with Presbyterianism and the specific democratic culture of the
Church of Scotland, a version of Scottish identity that inevitably
excluded Scotland's large Catholic population. Instead, the 'democratic'
elements of Calvinism could be given a secular form, rooted in the
history of Scottish education and in Scottish philosophical and legal
debate. This was a vision of Scottishness that, suitably popularised, could
form the basis of a wider national appeal than one that invoked the
sectarian connotations of what Davie called the 'dismal denominational
obsessions which have done so much to discredit Scotland and its
history'.[80] As we have seen, the related line of argument that Davie
prompted in his readers was therefore a sense that it was this democratic
Scottish culture that the Union had eroded, a point that could be readily
associated with the claim that Scotland was in fact the victim of cultural
or intellectual colonialism. Murdo Macdonald, who had been Davie's
student at Edinburgh, a member of the editorial collective of *Common
Sense*, the editor of the *Edinburgh Review*, and by 2014 was a professor of
the history of art at Dundee University, explained on the website of
National Collective his reasons for voting 'yes' to Scottish independence
in precisely these terms. He recounted that working with Davie had led

[79] Cairns Craig, *Intending Scotland: Explorations in Scottish Culture since the Enlightenment* (Edinburgh, Edinburgh University Press, 2009), pp. 56–74.
[80] Davie, *Democratic Intellect*, p. xxi.

him to realise the 'everyday international significance of Scotland's intellectual culture' and its neglect within Scotland:

Davie made me aware of Westminster's treatment of Scotland as a subaltern culture, that is to say a culture not in control of its own standing either nationally or internationally. Such subaltern patterns have been evident recently as we see adherents of the sad remains of the Labour Party and the Liberal Democrats trotting about doing the will of the old imperial Tories, like trusty servants. They don't seem to realise that they are perpetuating the forms of a long-dead empire.[81]

This more vernacular defence of Scottish culture demonstrated how such an argument could complement and reinforce a second preoccupation of Scottish nationalists in this period: the decline of British imperial power and its implications for Scottish self-government. The next chapter turns to examine this strand of Scottish nationalist thought in more detail.

---

[81] Murdo Macdonald, 'I'm Voting Yes because I'm an Internationalist', *National Collective*, 26 February 2014, at www.nationalcollective.com/2014/02/26/murdo-macdonald-im-voting-yes-because-im-an-internationalist (accessed 2 October 2019). National Collective was an organisation that brought together independence supporters from the arts and culture to argue for a 'yes' vote in the 2014 referendum.

3　Britain in Decline

'Wha's like us?' Damned few, and all dead. Well, yes, actually we killed
most of them off in our North British uniforms.　　Tom Nairn, 1975[1]

One of the most surreal spectacles of the 2014 independence referendum
was the sight of Yes campaigners on a rickshaw pursuing a group of
Labour MPs who had recently arrived from England along the streets
of Glasgow while playing 'The Imperial March' from *Star Wars*. Matt
Lygate, seated in the rickshaw, shouted over the music: 'Say hello to your
imperial masters. These lovely people, they have travelled all the way
from England to tell us that they are better to rule us than anybody else'.[2]
Although a demotic rhetoric of English imperialism has been irresistible
to certain advocates of Scottish independence, the relationship between
Scottish nationalism and empire has in fact been a complex one.[3] As we
saw in Chapter 1, some of the earliest Scottish nationalists in the 1920s
and 1930s were themselves imperialists, seeking to claim equality for
Scotland as an independent mother nation to the empire alongside
England.[4] While later Scottish nationalists took a more anti-imperialist
line, some of the most reflective and influential figures in the making of
modern Scottish nationalism were conscious of the distinctiveness of
Scotland's history under the Union and were correspondingly reluctant
to claim straightforwardly that Scotland had itself been a colony of the
empire. Instead, they argued that the British state – and Britishness – had
been irretrievably shaped by imperialism. The loss of empire had therefore been a mortal blow to the identity of Britain, undercutting its

---

[1] Tom Nairn, 'Old Nationalism and New Nationalism', in Gordon Brown (ed.), *The Red
Paper on Scotland* (Edinburgh, EUSPB, 1975), p. 41.
[2] Ned Simons, 'Scottish Independence: Darth Vader Music Chases Labour MPs around
Glasgow', *Huffington Post*, 12 September 2014, at www.huffingtonpost.co.uk/2014/09/11/
scottish-independence-darth-vader-music_n_5804224.html (accessed 2 October 2019).
[3] Colin Kidd and Gregg McClymont, 'Say No to Colony Myth', *Scotsman*, 6 August 2014.
[4] Richard Finlay, '"For or against?" Scottish Nationalists and the British Empire,
1919–39', *Scottish Historical Review*, 71 (1992), pp. 184–206; Colin Kidd, *Union and
Unionisms* (Cambridge, Cambridge University Press, 2008), pp. 275–93.

prestige and demolishing its economic foundations, while leaving the British state a decrepit, unreformed relic from an earlier historical epoch.

As Jimmi Østergaard Nielsen and Stuart Ward have pointed out, leading figures in the SNP deployed a rhetoric along these lines during their electoral rise in the 1970s, presenting Scottish independence not as about 'casting off the "shackles" of dominion' but as 'an exercise in cutting the losses of empire', with Scots 'electing to rule themselves once more now that ruling the world was no longer an option'.[5] Østergaard Nielsen and Ward cite as a vivid example the remarks of George Reid (b. 1939) during the second reading of the Scotland and Wales Bill in 1976. Reid was a former member of the Labour Party, SNP MP for Clackmannan and East Stirlingshire from 1974 to 1979, and would later become the Presiding Officer of the Scottish Parliament between 2003 and 2007:

we have come to the end of the Empire and the United Kingdom is currently in a state of economic decline. No one here would deny that. I may be making a point against myself, but we Scots had a privileged position in the days of Imperial grandeur. We were both Scots and British. We ran the docks in Hong Kong, the judicial system in the Punjab and held Burns suppers in temperatures of 102 degrees in India. Those days are gone and those options are no longer open to us. We stay at home. The young Scots in Scotland today, looking at the obvious degradation and neglect, are not prepared to tolerate these conditions. They are back in our country for keeps and wish to do something about the situation – usually by joining the SNP.[6]

For a more analytical discussion of the relationship between Scotland and empire, Scottish nationalists have usually turned to the writings of Tom Nairn, whose work has been pivotal in defining modern Scottish nationalism as a language of anti-imperialism. Nairn's political thought is therefore the focus of this chapter. Through a reconstruction of Nairn's intellectual trajectory, the chapter identifies a transition in the work of Nairn and other like-minded radical critics of the British state as we move from the 1960s to the twenty-first century: a shift from an initial critique of British nationalism that was Marxist and economistic in character to one that relied more heavily on what figures such as Nairn might once have regarded as bourgeois conceptions of sovereignty and democracy.

---

[5] Jimmi Østergaard Nielsen and Stuart Ward, 'Three Referenda and a By-Election: The Shadow of Empire in Devolutionary Politics', in John MacKenzie and Bryan Glass (eds.), *Scotland, Empire and Decolonisation in the Twentieth Century* (Manchester, Manchester University Press, 2015), pp. 204–9, quote at p. 205.

[6] George Reid, Hansard, H. C. Debates, fifth series, vol. 922, col. 1359 (14 December 1976), quoted in Østergaard Nielsen and Ward, 'Three Referenda', p. 206.

English Questions

The pages of *New Left Review* might seem an unlikely location for the intellectual origins of modern Scottish nationalism, yet this journal of rigorous Marxist analysis has a good claim to such a title. In the 1960s writings of Perry Anderson (b. 1938) and Tom Nairn, later to be collectively immortalised as the 'the Anderson–Nairn thesis', lie some of the foundational assumptions of later Scottish nationalist rhetoric. Anderson and Nairn were leading figures in what has become known (somewhat misleadingly) as the 'Second New Left', the cohort of intellectuals and activists who obtained control of *New Left Review* and the broader theoretical direction of the movement in the early 1960s from the initial architects of the New Left such as E. P. Thompson, Stuart Hall and Raymond Williams. This earlier New Left, which we touched on in Chapter 2, had emerged from the crisis of Marxism engendered by the 1956 Soviet invasion of Hungary and from the initial stirrings of the youthful revolt and countercultural politics that were to be such a marked feature of the succeeding two decades. In books and articles of dazzling creativity, Thompson, Hall, Williams, Charles Taylor, Richard Hoggart (1918–2014), Alasdair MacIntyre and an array of other luminaries set out an anti-Stalinist, humanist Marxism that sought to catalyse the possibilities for radical change latent within a Britain seemingly frozen into the cosy welfare politics of the 1950s.[7] A distinctive feature of this early work was that it aimed to renovate a British – or, at times, English – radical tradition that had seemingly fallen into abeyance as the Labour Party began to compromise with the new consumer capitalism of the 1950s. These ideas were most famously expressed in E. P. Thompson's *The Making of the English Working Class* (1963), but were also powerfully evoked in Raymond Williams's *Culture and Society* (1958) and, less directly, in Richard Hoggart's *Uses of Literacy* (1957).

---

[7] Michael Kenny, *The First New Left* (London, Lawrence & Wishart, 1995); Lin Chun, *The British New Left* (Edinburgh, Edinburgh University Press, 1993); Madeleine Davis, 'The Marxism of the British New Left', *Journal of Political Ideologies*, 11 (2006), pp. 335–58; Madeleine Davis, 'Arguing Affluence: New Left Contributions to the Socialist Debate 1957–1963', *Twentieth Century British History*, 23 (2012), pp. 496–528; Madeleine Davis, 'Reappraising British Socialist Humanism', *Journal of Political Ideologies*, 18 (2013), pp. 1–25; Madeleine Davis, '"Among the Ordinary People": New Left Involvement in Working Class Mobilisation 1956–68', *History Workshop Journal*, 86 (2018), pp. 133–59; Holger Nehring, '"Out of Apathy": Genealogies of the British "New Left" in a Transnational Context, 1956–1962', in Martin Klimke, Jakko Pekelder and Joachim Scharloth (eds.), *Between Prague Spring and French May: Opposition and Revolt in Europe, 1960–1980* (New York, Berghahn Books, 2013), pp. 15–31.

Whether there was a clear and systematic break between two distinct New Lefts is questionable – since there was in fact significant continuity across this divide in terms of both personalities and ideas – but the rise of Anderson, Nairn and like-minded colleagues such as Robin Blackburn (b. 1940) did signal a conscious departure from this specifically British focus in the pages of *New Left Review*.[8] These new voices were scathing about what they regarded as the insular and provincial character of British radical culture, indeed of British society more generally, and sought instead to expose the British left to a more rigorous schooling in continental European Marxism. From this perspective they sought a rupture with the indigenous British left rather than a resumption of neglected earlier socialist traditions. It was in this context that Nairn and Anderson set out to construct a systematic analysis of the historical trajectory of England and of English radical politics, one that would offer a more forensic understanding of the political problems of the 1960s and a sobering view of what might be expected from the English working classes and labour movement.

In this enterprise they were chiefly inspired by the writings of Antonio Gramsci. Nairn, who had spent time in Italy and was connected to the Italian communist movement, was an important figure in the transmission of Gramsci's ideas to Britain (as was another leading Scottish leftist, Hamish Henderson [1919–2002]).[9] As Anderson later recalled, it was Nairn who first highlighted the fertility of a Gramscian analysis of British society. Gramsci's importance to Nairn and Anderson was twofold. First, Gramsci had pioneered the idea that the distinctive character of a capitalist society should be understood in relation to the particular bourgeois revolution that had generated it. Second, Gramsci argued that revolutionary strategy in advanced industrialised democracies in the West would require a different approach from the one adopted by the Bolsheviks, since it would be necessary to pay attention to the way in which capitalism had entrenched itself ideologically as well as coercively.[10] These considerations inspired Nairn and Anderson to undertake a panoramic historical

---

[8] For justified scepticism about the first/second New Left distinction, see Davis, 'Marxism of the British New Left'; Wade Matthews, *The New Left, National Identity and the Break-up of Britain* (Chicago, Haymarket, 2014), pp. 12–19; Alexandre Campsie, 'A Social and Intellectual History of British Socialism from New Left to New Times' (unpublished PhD thesis, Cambridge University, 2017).

[9] William Thompson, 'Tom Nairn and the Crisis of the British State', *Contemporary Record*, 6 (1992), pp. 308–10; Neil Davidson, 'Antonio Gramsci's Reception in Scotland', in Neil Davidson, *Holding Fast to an Image of the Past* (Chicago, Haymarket Books, 2014), pp. 261–2, 267–72.

[10] Perry Anderson, *English Questions* (London, Verso, 1992), pp. 2–3; David Forgacs, 'Gramsci and Marxism in Britain', *New Left Review*, no. 176, 1989, pp. 75–6.

sociology of England in a Gramscian vein, seeking to understand Britain's malaise in the early 1960s as the culmination of a deeper structural crisis at the heart of the British polity. It was the picture of Britain, and in particular England, that emerged from this analysis that was subsequently to become an important ideological resource for the political thought of Scottish nationalism.

Anderson's classic 1964 article 'Origins of the Present Crisis' provided the fundamental premises of this account. In a corrective to what he regarded as the ahistorical and non-sociological analyses of Britain's economic decline placed at the heart of political debate by publicists such as the economic journalist Andrew Shonfield, Anderson argued that Britain's decay was fundamentally the product of its unusual histor- ical development.[11] England was exceptional, he argued, because it had been the first country to industrialise but also because it had never enjoyed a full-blooded bourgeois revolution. The seventeenth-century revolution certainly 'shattered the juridical and constitutional obstacles to rationalised capitalist development' but it also 'left almost the entire social structure intact'.[12] The failure of the English bourgeoisie to over- throw fully the aristocracy and assume the modernising leadership of the state led instead to the formation of a partnership between the upper and middle classes which decisively excluded the working classes from polit- ical power: '*There was thus from the start no fundamental, antagonistic contradiction between the old aristocracy and the new bourgeoisie. English capitalism embraced and included both. The most important single key to modern English history lies in this fact.*'[13] In Anderson's view, the subsequent history of the eighteenth and nineteenth centuries continued this pattern, with the fusion of the upper and middle classes into one hegemonic class while the numerically dominant working class arrived on the scene too early because 'its maximum ardour and insurgency coincided with the minimum availability of socialism as a structured ideology'; the writing of the *Communist Manifesto*, Anderson noted, was two months before the end of Chartism.[14]

Imperialism was central to Anderson's analysis. The British Empire was in the first place a critical element in the take-off and rise of British capitalism. But more specifically, Anderson argued that the intense and militaristic imperialism of the late nineteenth and early twentieth

---

[11] Anderson, 'Origins of the Present Crisis', *New Left Review*, no. 23, 1964, pp. 26–7. On the 'declinism' of this period, see Jim Tomlinson, *The Politics of Decline: Understanding Post-War Britain* (London, Routledge, 2014).

[12] Anderson, 'Origins', pp. 29–30.   [13] Anderson, 'Origins', p. 31; emphasis in original.

[14] Anderson, 'Origins', pp. 32–4, quote at p. 33.

centuries was decisive in shaping the hierarchies of British society and the dominant model of British leadership – 'aristocratic, amateur, and "normatively" agrarian'. In case any readers in 1964 needed further prompting, Anderson made clear that he had in mind here 'the governing class which has at length found its final, surreal embodiment in the fourteenth Earl of Home'.[15] In Anderson's view, social imperialism had one further consequence: it moulded working-class consciousness into a national-imperial alliance with the upper classes, distracting the workers from confrontation with their exploiters. The contemporaneous, and comparatively late, rise of the Labour Party – and the absence of Marxist influence on its ideology – was merely a further indicator of the political weakness of the British working class.[16] Anderson highlighted British victories in both world wars as a final explanatory factor, since these had insulated British institutions and social structures from any radical reconstruction that might have otherwise been undertaken in the wake of occupation or defeat.[17]

On this account, then, the British state and economy were essentially imperial and unmodernised, suffused with the hierarchies and fripperies of empire rather than the norms of democratic equality and citizenship. The British labour movement, meanwhile, was likewise channelled down an exceptional historical path because it emerged too early in the nineteenth century to benefit from the insights of Marxist theory. The result was what the New Left, following Ralph Miliband (1924–94), dubbed 'Labourism': a conservative form of working-class politics that unquestioningly accepted British parliamentary traditions and pursued gradual reforms rather than radical social change.[18] It was this point that was driven home by Tom Nairn in his early contributions to *New Left Review*. Nairn, born and brought up in Fife, had studied philosophy at Edinburgh and Oxford before heading to Italy. On his return to Britain he had moved to Birmingham and then London and was put into contact with the circles around the *New Left Review* by Ralph Miliband.[19] Nairn was to become one of the greatest writers on Scottish politics, but at this stage in his career he wrote about England rather than Scotland, devoting his energies to a critical analysis of the English working class and labour movement. Drawing on Ralph Miliband's *Parliamentary Socialism*

---

[15] Anderson, 'Origins', pp. 34–5. A reference to the then prime minister, Alec Douglas-Home.

[16] Anderson, 'Origins', pp. 35–7.   [17] Anderson, 'Origins', pp. 37–8.

[18] Ralph Miliband, *Parliamentary Socialism* (London, Allen & Unwin, 1961).

[19] For Nairn's biography, see Thompson, 'Tom Nairn', pp. 308–10; Rory Scothorne, 'From the Outer Edge', *London Review of Books*, vol. 40, no. 23, 6 December 2018, pp. 35–8; Neal Ascherson, *Tom Nairn: 'Painting Nationalism Red'?* (Dundee, Democratic Left Scotland, 2018).

(1961), Nairn analysed the conservative character of the Labour Party as the logical outgrowth of English working-class life and culture rather than as simply the result of a right-wing leadership that betrayed authentic Labour values. Departing from E. P. Thompson's *Making of the English Working Class*, Nairn argued that the apparently attractive working-class consciousness that Thompson depicted had significant political limits. The potent sense of working-class solidarity that emerged during the eighteenth and nineteenth centuries, thought Nairn, while in many respects an inspiring story of proletarian resistance, nonetheless embedded within working-class life a deference to the dominant social order rather than a universal notion of civic equality and participation. Ultimately, this left the English working class vulnerable to assimilation into 'bourgeois ideas and customs'. Liberation from this state, Nairn concluded, would have required not just access to Marxist theory but a systematic application of Marxist ideas to the peculiarities of English society, which would in turn have required a 'radical, disaffected intelligentsia to even undertake it'.[20] The Labour Party, from this perspective, could be nothing other than a conservative organisation that reflected the character of its social base, in essence trade unionists who faithfully imitated Victorian notions of respectability. Ideologically, Labour 'adapted and transformed third-rate bourgeois traditions into fourth-rate socialist traditions, imposing upon the working class all the righteous mediocrity and worthless philistinism of the pious Victorian petty bourgeois'.[21] It was therefore idle to appeal to authentic Labour traditions and principles that had been betrayed by compromising parliamentarians – no return to founding ideals was possible, Nairn commented, since it was precisely the founding principles and strategic assumptions of Labour that had led to its unimpressive record in challenging British capitalism.[22]

Extraordinary as it might seem now, in 1964 Perry Anderson (although not Nairn) believed that the rise of Harold Wilson might open

---

[20] Tom Nairn, 'The English Working Class', *New Left Review*, no. 24, 1964, pp. 43–57, quotes at pp. 55, 57.
[21] Tom Nairn, 'The Nature of the Labour Party I', *New Left Review*, no. 27, 1964, pp. 39–48, quote at p. 44.
[22] Tom Nairn, 'The Nature of the Labour Party II', *New Left Review*, no. 28, 1964, pp. 44–5. Famously E. P. Thompson himself issued a magisterial reply to both Nairn and Anderson, including a note of dissent over their treatment of the British labour movement: 'The Peculiarities of the English', *Socialist Register*, 2 (1965), pp. 311–62; see e.g. pp. 347–9 on their treatment of the British left. For further discussion of this debate, see Scott Hamilton, *The Crisis of Theory: E. P. Thompson, the New Left and Postwar British Politics* (Manchester, Manchester University Press, 2011), pp. 93–132.

the way to a new departure in British socialist politics.[23] Although
certainly not uncritical of Wilson, Anderson thought Wilson's agenda
(and his winning of the Labour leadership from the left of the party)
indicated a structural opening in the 1960s for a radical socialism that
sought to tackle the fundamental weaknesses Anderson and Nairn had
identified in the British state and economy.[24] But after Wilson took office
in 1964 it soon became clear that the Anderson–Nairn thesis could
instead serve as a deeper diagnosis of the arrested development of England, Britain and the Labour Party, purveying an unflinchingly critical
portrait of a society that had failed to modernise and was trapped within a
mystifying imperial ideology. This in turn lent support to the proposition
that, as Nairn later remarked, it was only through 'a political break: a
disruption at the level of the state' that this ideology could be shattered,
'allowing the emergence of sharper antagonisms and a will to reform the
old order root and branch'.[25] The break-up of the imperial British state
into its constituent nations could therefore be presented as one such
exogenous shock to the complacency of the British political system.
Nairn in particular was to build on these themes in his later work, and
as he did so he engaged more directly with the Scottish question.

The Peculiarities of the Scots

Nairn returned to live in Scotland in 1975 but well before this, while
spending much of the 1960s in London and then in Amsterdam working
for a radical think tank, the Transnational Institute, Scottish nationalism,
and nationalism more generally, became a central theme of his writing.
However, as Stephen Maxwell observed in a review of Nairn's *The Break-
up Britain* (1977), which collected together Nairn's essays on the national
question from these years: 'The development of Nairn's views on Scottish nationalism has something of an epic quality.'[26] The initial impetus
for Nairn to write about Scotland was the SNP's dramatic electoral
breakthrough in the 1967 Hamilton by-election, as we have seen a
hitherto safe Labour seat won for the SNP by Winnie Ewing, and which
Nairn was commissioned to write about for *New Left Review*. His
response was a powerful polemic that turned Nairn's caustic wit against
the SNP and sentimental nationalist myths about Scottish culture.

---

[23] On Nairn's dissent from this position, see Thompson, 'Tom Nairn', p. 312; Tom Nairn,
'Labour Imperialism', *New Left Review*, no. 32, 1965, pp. 3–15.
[24] Perry Anderson, 'Critique of Wilsonism', *New Left Review*, no. 27, 1964, pp. 3–27.
[25] Tom Nairn, 'Twilight of the British State', *New Left Review*, no. 101/102, 1977, p. 28.
[26] Stephen Maxwell, 'Review: *The Break-Up of Britain*', *Question*, no. 31, 24 June 1977, p. 7.

He identified two earlier 'dreams' that had shaped Scottish national identity: an austere, philistine Calvinism and a sentimental, clichéd romanticism (ultimately leading to 'Sporranry, alcoholism, and the ludicrous appropriation of the remains of Scotland's Celtic fringe as a national symbol'), both of which had laid the groundwork for a third dream, the modern nationalism that sought Scottish independence.[27] Nairn was unimpressed by the distinctively Scottish bourgeois social attitudes that he thought were influential in the SNP:

This evil mélange of decrepit Presbyterianism and imperialist thuggery, whose spirit may be savoured by a few mornings with the Edinburgh *Scotsman* and a few evenings watching *Scottish Television*, appears to be solidly represented in the Scottish National Party . . . This rough-hewn sadism – as foreign to the English as anything in New Guinea – will surely be present in whatever junta of corporal-punishers and Kirk-going cheese-parers Mrs. Ewing might preside over one day in Edinburgh.[28]

Nairn argued that Scottish nationalism as currently constituted offered a bourgeois nationalism, of a sort broadly similar to that found elsewhere around the globe: 'The SNP Nationalists are merely lumpen-provincials whose parochialism finds its adequate expression in the asinine idea that a bourgeois parliament and an army will rescue the country from provincialism; as if half of Europe did not testify to the contrary.'[29]

Socialist support for nationalism, Nairn noted, could be forthcoming in two kinds of case. Nationalism could legitimately serve as either a mechanism for economic modernisation and breaking free of the fetters of feudalism, or as a weapon against Western imperialism for non-European peoples. Nairn was famously sceptical about this second reason: 'Scotland is not a colony, a semi-colony, a pseudo-colony, a near-colony, a neo-colony, or any kind of colony of the English. She is a junior but (as these things go) highly successful partner in the general business enterprise of Anglo-Scots Imperialism.'[30] He therefore offered a sobering disenchantment of any Scottish nationalism grounded on escaping from imperial decline: 'it may be quite reasonable for the Scots to want out. But there is really no point in disguising this desire with heroic ikonry. After all, when the going was good for Imperialism, the world heard very little indeed for the Scots' longing for independence.'[31]

---

[27] Tom Nairn, 'The Three Dreams of Scottish Nationalism', *New Left Review*, no. 49, 1968, pp. 4–11, quote at p. 9.

[28] Nairn, 'Three Dreams of Scottish Nationalism', pp. 15–16.

[29] Nairn, 'Three Dreams of Scottish Nationalism', p. 18.

[30] Nairn, 'Three Dreams of Scottish Nationalism', pp. 12–13, quote at p. 13.

[31] Nairn, 'Three Dreams of Scottish Nationalism', p. 13.

Nairn's treatment of the first reason for socialist support of nationalism was more muted. Perhaps this was because the more general Anderson–Nairn argument could in fact be construed as lending support for a national modernising project aimed at breaking up the archaic economic and political structures holding Britain back. Nairn noted that places such as Scotland had certainly been the victims of capitalist underdevelopment but stressed that in world-historical terms the Scots were not 'Fanon's *The Wretched of the Earth*' but rather 'had belonged to the conquerors', and that the economic disparities between industrial Scotland and the South-East of England, though striking, were not comparable to the more serious issue of global underdevelopment.[32] Nonetheless, Nairn's broad position at this stage seemed to be that cautious, unillusioned support for Scottish independence was on balance worthwhile, since it would be a powerful blow against the British state and decentralise political power, enabling greater popular participation in political decision-making.[33] But he added that it would only be through the creation of a better, socialist Scottish nationalism that true emancipation could be achieved and an escape effected from the 'garrulous, narcissistic windbaggery' that so often gripped the Scottish intelligentsia when wrestling with the myths of Scottish culture.[34]

The kind of socialist nationalism that Nairn had in mind became clearer when he published a revised version of 'The Three Dreams of Scottish Nationalism' in 1970. Enthused by the radical energies of 1968 and the student movement, Nairn added a new conclusion to the essay, including this evocative passage:

In the same years in which nationalism again became a force in Scotland, the western world was shaken by the first tremors of a new social revolution, from San Francisco to Prague. I for one am enough of a nationalist, and have enough faith in the students and young workers of Glasgow and Edinburgh, to believe that these forces are also present in them. I will not admit that the great dreams of May 1968 are foreign to us, that the great words on the Sorbonne walls would not be at home on the walls of Aberdeen or St Andrews, or that Linwood and Dundee could not be Flins and Nantes. Nor will I admit that, faced with a choice between the spirit of the *Mouvement du 22 mars* and Mrs Ewing, we owe it to 'Scotland' to choose the latter. On the contrary, in a country poisoned by stale authoritarianism, the universal revolt of youth against authoritarianism should have a quite special sense and value.[35]

---

[32] Nairn, 'Three Dreams of Scottish Nationalism', pp. 13–14.
[33] Nairn, 'Three Dreams of Scottish Nationalism', p. 16.
[34] Nairn, 'Three Dreams of Scottish Nationalism', pp. 17–18, quote at p. 17.
[35] Tom Nairn, 'The Three Dreams of Scottish Nationalism', in Karl Miller (ed.), *Memoirs of a Modern Scotland* (London, Faber and Faber, 1970), pp. 53–4.

In retrospect Nairn was correct to see a connection between the shifting cultural tides symbolised by 1968 and Scottish nationalism – rising demands for greater Scottish autonomy were a local expression of the rebellions against authority that flared up across the globe in the late 1960s and 1970s.[36] But the contrast between the spirit of 1968 and the actually existing SNP was not as stark as Nairn suggested. Although by no means socialist at this stage, the SNP's electoral appeal in the 1960s was a youthful and dynamic one, which sought to contrast distant and alien British political structures with a more authentic form of democratic government than would be possible in an independent Scotland.[37]

Nairn's essay signalled the arrival of an influential voice in the debate on Scottish independence, a writer whose theoretical depth set a new standard for analysing the national movement. But, as Stephen Maxwell pointed out, Nairn's position was not a static one – this essay was only the beginning of a complex intellectual journey characterised above all by an increasingly sympathetic interpretation of Scottish nationalism. Nairn subsequently began to relate the case of Scotland more explicitly to the set of arguments about Britain that he and Anderson had pursued in the early 1960s. Scotland, it transpired, was itself an exceptional nation. Unlike other European nations, Nairn argued, Scotland had not produced a nationalist movement in the classic nineteenth-century mould, with Scottish nationalism only emerging for the first time in the late 1920s with the foundation of the National Party of Scotland in 1928 and the publication of Hugh MacDiarmid's poem *A Drunk Man Looks at the Thistle* in 1926. Drawing on the modernist theory of nationalism that had been pioneered by Ernest Gellner (1925–95), and on the work of another Czech historian, Miroslav Hroch (b. 1932), Nairn interpreted the European nationalisms of the nineteenth century as modernising ideologies, used by a middle-class intelligentsia to mobilise mass populations against the uneven economic development of capitalism.[38] Viewing this as a suitably materialist starting point for analysis,

---

[36] Gerd-Rainer Horn, *The Spirit of '68: Rebellion in Western Europe and North America, 1956–76* (Oxford, Oxford University Press, 2007); Richard Vinen, *The Long '68: Radical Protest and its Enemies* (London, Allen Lane, 2018).

[37] James Mitchell, *Hamilton 1967: The By-Election that Transformed Scotland* (Edinburgh, Luath Press, 2017), pp. 40–8, 131–7.

[38] Tom Nairn, 'Scotland and Europe', *New Left Review*, no. 83, 1974, pp. 59–65; Nairn drew on Ernest Gellner, 'Nationalism', in his *Thought and Change* (London, Weidenfeld & Nicolson, 1964), pp. 147–78; and on Miroslav Hroch, *Die Vorkämpfer der nationalen Bewegung bei den kleinen Völkern Europas* (Prague, Universita Karlova, 1968) (later revised and translated as *Social Preconditions of National Revival in Europe* [Cambridge, Cambridge University Press, 1985]). Gellner's theory was later fully set out in his *Nations and Nationalism* (Ithaca, Cornell University Press, 1983).

Nairn argued that this modernist account deepened the mystery of Scotland's absent nationalism. Scotland had all the necessary ingredients – national folklore and culture; a recently lost national independence; and a separate and distinctive civil society, including an upwardly mobile middle class and an outstanding intelligentsia. Crucially, though, just as the English working class had matured before the arrival of Marxism, Scotland had achieved economic development *before* the rise of nationalism.[39] Its nineteenth-century culture was therefore – in Nairn's account – one in decline, made up of Walter Scott's elegiac romanticism and 'the great tartan monster' of mawkish Scottishness Nairn had castigated in his earlier work.[40] Nairn's point was that this absence of a vibrant nationalism was the product of material circumstances, of a Scotland that had industrialised and been integrated into the British economy and of a Scottish intelligentsia that had been drawn into an imperial British culture.[41] In turn, it was material circumstances that were reviving Scottish nationalism in the 1970s. The emergence of this 'neo-nationalism' was once again triggered by the uneven development of capitalism, but in the case of Scotland it was a symptom of a more general decline of imperial Britain after the Second World War. The failure of both of the major British political parties to address Britain's stagnating economy, Nairn said, had left the British state adrift in the 1960s and 1970s, unable to cope with the scale of the challenge it faced. Nairn believed that this delicate equipoise had been decisively upended by the discovery of North Sea oil and the arrival of multinational companies in Scotland to exploit it. This had created a situation analogous to the rise of nationalism in earlier periods – a perception of a nation's economic development falling under foreign control that must be resisted through a national mobilisation.[42]

In Defence of Nationalism

While Nairn had never hidden his sympathy with Scottish nationalism, by the mid 1970s the nationalist aspects of his thought had begun to eclipse his socialism. He was straightforward about this at one level. As he wrote in 1975: 'My main past mistake lay in assuming that the

[39] Nairn, 'Scotland and Europe', pp. 69–71.
[40] Nairn, 'Scotland and Europe', pp. 74–5, quote at p. 75.
[41] Nairn, 'Scotland and Europe', pp. 75–82.
[42] Nairn, 'Old Nationalism and New Nationalism', pp. 23–5, 45–7. This argument could also be broadened to encompass the rise of multinational capital in Scotland more generally and not just in the North Sea oil sector: see Stephen Maxwell (ed.), *Scotland, Multinationals and the Third World* (Edinburgh, Mainstream, 1982).

question of effective Scottish self-government would never be posed on this side of socialism.'[43] Socialists, he noted, had simply paid too much attention to 'the rationality of the working class based social struggle (understood as a potentially international force)' and not enough to 'the non-rational strengths of nationalism'.[44] In terms of his immediate political prescriptions, Nairn now argued that the left should accept that it would be necessary to support rising neo-nationalisms in Scotland, Wales, Quebec, the Basque Country and so on as broadly progressive forces. But he acknowledged the complexity of the social character of this nationalism:

The question is really not at all whether new nationalism has, or has not, a 'positive' side to it. No intellectual from a repressed or destroyed nationality has doubts about this, if he is honest with himself. Return from oblivion, the reassertion of identity, adult control of one's own affairs – it does not matter what terminology is used, the value of national liberation is plain enough.[45]

The problem, as Nairn saw it, was how to achieve such a 'national liberation' without also unleashing chauvinism and xenophobia. He did not believe that it was possible to distinguish different sorts of nationalism 'into the clean and the dirty, the "progressive" and the "reactionary" (or imperialist)' since all nationalisms were inevitably a mix of both.[46] On the contrary, Nairn argued, nationalism was Janus-faced, looking both forward and backward: a modernising ideology that plundered the past for usable political resources for the present. It was therefore by its very nature characterised *'by a certain sort of regression* – by looking inwards, drawing more deeply upon their indigenous resources, resurrecting past folk-heroes and myths about themselves and so on'.[47] The psychoanalytic language in this passage was not accidental. Going all the way back to his earliest writings on nationalism, Nairn had drawn on psychoanalytic concepts. His initial piece on Scottish nationalism, for example, was a study of 'the dream-psychology (which has very often been a dream-pathology) of Scottish history'.[48] Nairn believed that there was a sense in which nationalism's summoning of the 'irrational' to cope with the social

---

[43] Nairn, 'Old Nationalism and New Nationalism', p. 49.

[44] Nairn, 'Old Nationalism and New Nationalism', p. 49.

[45] Nairn, 'Old Nationalism and New Nationalism', p. 49.

[46] Nairn, 'Old Nationalism and New Nationalism', p. 50.

[47] Tom Nairn, 'Modern Janus', *New Left Review*, no. 94, 1975, p. 18; emphasis in original. Jim Sillars subsequently drew on Nairn's argument about nationalism's mixture of progressive and regressive elements in his *Scotland: The Case for Optimism* (Edinburgh, Polygon, 1986), pp. 84, 88–90, 92.

[48] Nairn, 'Three Dreams of Scottish Nationalism', pp. 4–5. On this aspect of Nairn's writing, see Cairns Craig, *Out of History* (Edinburgh, Polygon, 1996), pp. 87–98.

trauma of uneven development was analogous to a psychological
trauma – in both cases the forces unleashed from either the collective
or individual unconscious would not necessarily be susceptible to
rational control.[49]

With respect to Scotland, Nairn did not therefore spring to the defence
of Scottish nationalism as a distinctively civic or left-leaning patriotism.
He thought that, like any other national movement, Scottish nationalism
necessarily combined progressive and regressive elements and that it
could not be assumed a priori that in an independent Scotland the left
would become a hegemonic force. Instead, Nairn argued that it was
important to reflect on the international context in which Scotland would
achieve independence, since new nations were usually forced down
unappetising chauvinistic paths because they had to build a new state
in the face of fierce international competition or even outright hostility.[50]
Here Nairn should be credited as one of the first to perceive that
European integration offered an escape route from this dilemma and a
structure within which nationalist energies could be channelled in their
most constructive direction.[51] He had earlier mounted a ferocious critique of the British left's insularity on the question of British membership
of the EEC, supporting Britain's entry as a step towards a broader
Western European polity, the decomposition of the traditional British
state, and stronger working-class collaboration across national boundaries.[52] Excoriating the British nationalism of Labour Eurosceptics, Nairn
argued that for any progressive or leftist, 'no fate could be worse than
national isolation in the grip of an unreformed UK state'. Europe was 'a
modern, voluntary, genuinely multi-national organisation, capable of
farther progress and influence'; in contrast, said Nairn, the United
Kingdom was none of those things.[53]

---

[49] Nairn, 'Modern Janus', pp. 18–19.
[50] Nairn, 'Old Nationalism and New Nationalism', pp. 50–1. In the 1970s Nairn often
pressed on nationalists the importance of reflecting on an independent Scotland's place
in the international order: see Tom Nairn, 'The Radical Approach', *Question*, no. 10,
July 1976, p. 11; Tom Nairn, 'Scotland the Misfit', *Question*, no. 13, 8 October 1976,
pp. 3–4 (a reply to Stephen Maxwell, 'Scotland's Foreign Policy', *Question*, no. 12,
September 1976, pp. 5–7).
[51] Strictly speaking Robert McIntyre and Douglas Young were the first leading Scottish
nationalists to articulate such a vision in the 1940s and 1950s: Douglas Young, *The
International Importance of Scottish Nationalism* (Glasgow, Scottish Secretariat, 1947),
pp. 16–17; Robert McIntyre, 'European Union', *Scots Independent*, no. 260, April
1948, pp. 1–2; Robert McIntyre, 'England Turns Back: The National Idea', *Scots
Independent*, no. 287, July 1950, p. 3.
[52] Tom Nairn, *The Left against Europe?* (London, Pelican, 1973); Matthews, *New Left,
National Identity*, pp. 260–3.
[53] Nairn, 'Twilight of the British State', pp. 34, 52.

Nairn's support for Scottish independence in Europe built on this analysis. In part, it deployed similar reasons to the ones developed by later Scottish nationalists – which we will examine in more detail in Chapter 5 – namely that growing international economic interdependence made an autarchic vision of Scottish independence seem unattractive and unrealistic. But Nairn added a further dimension to this case, in that he believed that it was only through economic and political cooperation at a European level that the dangers of nationalist self-assertion could be evaded. Nairn speculated that in the new era of European integration Scotland's absence of cultural nationalism would prove to be an advantage by giving it a shortcut to novel forms of transnational cooperation and convergence.[54] Indeed, drawing on George Davie, Nairn argued that Scottish history offered valuable resources for fostering a federal or confederal Europe insofar as Scotland's Enlightenment legacy inclined it towards a wider universalism rather than a narrow nationalism: 'towards a new interdependence where our nationhood will count, rather than towards mere isolation; towards Europe, as well as towards self-rule; towards that new, more democratic and socialist Enlightenment which Marxism prefigured, but will never realise until nationality ceases to be nationalism and becomes a more direct contribution to the universal'.[55]

While this conclusion suggested that a residual Marxist aspiration remained part of Nairn's thinking in the mid 1970s, the core of his thinking had in fact moved some distance from Marx. Nairn had seized on the modernist theory of nationalism as effectively offering a materialist account that was compatible with Marxism, but this underestimated the differences between the two. As Neil Davidson has observed, in spite of some similarities, Gellner's modernisation theory is not in the end quite the same as a theory about capitalism as an exploitative mode of production.[56] Ernest

---

[54] Tom Nairn, 'Culture and Nationalism: An Open Letter from Tom Nairn', *Scottish International*, vol. 6, no. 4, April 1973, pp. 7–9. As we saw in Chapter 2, Nairn's rather casual dismissal of the nationalist possibilities of Scottish culture was vigorously contested by Stephen Maxwell, 'Letter to the Editor', *Scottish International*, vol. 6, no. 5, May/June/July 1973, p. 9. Nairn later recollected that such exchanges with Maxwell had 'put me right about both the causes and the likely character of Scottish nationalism, in a period when I remained over-attached to the fossilised remains of "Internationalism"': Tom Nairn, 'Preface' to Stephen Maxwell, *The Case for Left-Wing Nationalism* (Edinburgh, Luath Press, 2013), p. 9.

[55] Nairn, 'Old Nationalism and New Nationalism', pp. 50–4, quote at p. 54. Nairn drew here on Davie's summary of the argument of *The Democratic Intellect* in 'Discussion', in J. N. Wolfe (ed.), *Government and Nationalism in Scotland: An Enquiry* (Edinburgh, Edinburgh University Press, 1969), pp. 204–5. Nairn had also referred to Davie in 'Scotland and Europe', pp. 68–9. See Chapter 2 for further discussion of Davie.

[56] Neil Davidson, 'Tom Nairn and the Inevitability of Nationalism', in Neil Davidson, *Holding Fast to an Image of the Past* (Chicago, Haymarket Books, 2014), p. 29.

Gellner himself had made a similar point. Amid an otherwise positive review of Nairn's *Break-up of Britain*, Gellner nonetheless pronounced himself glad that the book's blurb told him it was a 'Marxist reflection on the United Kingdom' since 'I would have had some difficulty in deciding on internal evidence just what the author's attitude to Marxism is'.[57] In the course of trying to make amends for what Nairn regarded as Marxism's historical neglect of the national question, he had in fact drifted away from a Marxist explanatory framework towards a sociological modernisation theory that postulated modern bureaucratic states and markets as the final resting point of history.[58]

In contrast, a more precisely Marxist engagement with the rise of Scottish nationalism was offered in 1981 by George Kerevan (b. 1949), later to be a Labour councillor; a prominent economic commentator at the *Scotsman*; and briefly SNP MP for East Lothian (2015–17), but at that time an active member of the Trotskyist International Marxist Group (IMG). Like Nairn, Kerevan interpreted the rise of a politicised form of Scottish nationalism as the product of the growing failure of the British imperial state to deliver economically for Scotland or, as he put it, to ensure 'the reproduction of civil society in Scotland'. But Kerevan's argument was that this nationalism was an illusory 'mass populist attempt to solve the alienation of the bourgeois (state) power by bourgeois political methods, ie by setting up another bourgeois state'. For Kerevan the rising tension between the nature of the British state and the weakening Scottish economy could only be properly resolved by the creation of 'a new society where the division between civil society and political life will be eliminated in a workers' democracy. If necessary, north of the Border alone.'[59]

Nairn was more cautious about using this sort of socialist language and was politically committed to a more conventional model of Scottish independence where the distinction between the state and civil society

---

[57] Ernest Gellner, 'Nationalism, or the New Confessions of a Justified Edinburgh Sinner', *Political Quarterly*, 49 (1978), p. 103. Eric Hobsbawm was also doubtful about the Marxist credentials of Nairn's arguments: 'Some Reflections on *The Break-Up of Britain*', *New Left Review*, no. 105, 1977, pp. 8–23.

[58] Nairn, 'Modern Janus', p. 3. In his later work Nairn remained committed to the idea that Gellner's modernisation theory was 'a version of philosophical materialism' that was 'surprisingly similar' to historical materialism and Marxism, though he also noted that Gellner himself was politically on the right: Tom Nairn, *Faces of Nationalism* (London, Verso, 1997), p. 11; Tom Nairn, 'Twenty-First Century Hindsight: *Break-Up* Twenty-Five Years on', in Tom Nairn, *The Break-Up of Britain* (3rd ed., Altona, Common Ground, 2003), p. xviii.

[59] George Kerevan, 'Arguments within Scottish Marxism', *Bulletin of Scottish Politics*, no. 2, spring 1981, pp. 111–33, quotes at pp. 131, 132. For discussion of Kerevan's later career, see Chapter 4.

was preserved, at least to begin with. Kerevan, like Nairn (and Craig Beveridge and Ronald Turnbull), had been a member of the short-lived SLP, which as we saw in Chapter 2 broke away from the Labour Party in 1976 under the leadership of Jim Sillars to propound a socialism that favoured Scottish independence. The SLP was riven by factional conflict, notably over the acceptability of the involvement of the IMG and the far left more generally, and eventually collapsed in 1981.[60] Although Nairn saw fault on both sides of these internal debates, he was scornful of the 'strugglist rhetoric and paleozoic left-wing commonplaces' that the IMG had adopted, in particular the framing of the key strategic choice for the SLP as between a revolutionary or a parliamentary route to power. Nairn argued that in the absence of a Scottish parliament it made no sense to be either 'parliamentarist' or 'anti-parliamentarist' since the central issue for Scottish socialists for the moment was rather how to establish and entrench a new Scottish state that would be governed as a parliamentary democracy. Such a state, Nairn pointed out, would of course have to be markedly different from its British predecessor. The aim of the left should therefore be 'an advanced social constitution, and a democratic politics whose spirit and functioning is the inverse of the English model'. Such a constitution would not be socialist but would 'be the precondition of whatever "socialism" can be made in this nation'. In Nairn's view, attempts by the Scottish radical left to prioritise class struggle over this project of state formation were therefore mistaken since 'a tactic of ultra-constitutionalism and pro-nationalism would be far more effective' at building an alliance between social and national struggles.[61] Although in the late 1970s Nairn remained open to the possibility of 'a radical, left-directed break-through at the centre' that could lead to 'a new, fairer, more federal British order', Nairn argued that if there was no such development then the Scots, the Welsh and perhaps even the Northern Irish should be entitled to go their own way. Retaining a Marxist confidence about the structural inevitability of the demise of the British state, Nairn thought it 'certain' that 'the British regime will finally founder' in the next few decades, probably bringing to the fore a new form of

---

[60] George Kerevan, 'Local Perspectives in Edinburgh: Some Personal Notes Towards a Discussion', SLP Edinburgh Area Bulletin, September 1976, p. 6, in Scottish Labour Party Edinburgh Branch Papers, National Library of Scotland, Acc. 7472/5; Thompson, 'Tom Nairn', pp. 316–17; Tom Nairn, 'The SLP: Report on the First Year of a New Party', Planet, no. 37/38, May 1977, pp. 14–17; Henry Drucker, Breakaway: The Scottish Labour Party (Edinburgh, EUSPB, 1978), pp. 60–1, 91, 102–3, 106, 124. For further discussion of the SLP, see Chapter 4.

[61] Tom Nairn, 'Revolutionaries Versus Parliamentarists', Question, no. 16, 19 November 1976, pp. 3–4; see also Tom Nairn, 'The National Question', Scottish Worker, vol. 3, no. 10, December 1976, p. 11.

'conservative reaction', and hence making the independence of Scotland and Wales 'an urgently necessary, practical step'.[62]

A Junior Partner

Throughout his journey towards Scottish nationalism, Nairn had consistently warned that it was a fundamental misconception to view Scotland as a victim of imperialism. On the contrary, as we have seen, Nairn emphasised that Scotland had played a fundamental role in the colonial exploitation and atrocities that built Britain into the leading world power in the nineteenth century. However, in spite of Nairn's strictures, the language of imperialism and colonialism has always been hard to resist for Scottish nationalists, since it offers a powerful rhetoric for the legitimation of nationalist politics.[63] As we saw in Chapter 2, one way of substantiating this interpretation of Scottish history has been to switch from an economic to a cultural register and to use Frantz Fanon to argue that English dominance over Scotland has become colonial at a psychological and intellectual level. But whether Scotland might be viewed as a colony in an economic sense is also a question that has been fiercely debated among nationalists. Nairn's own writings provided an important stimulus to this discussion by placing the political economy of Scotland at the heart of the debate about Scottish nationalism.

Nairn's economic ideas drew on the world systems theory of the American sociologist, Immanuel Wallerstein (1930–2019), who depicted global capitalist development as highly uneven and divided between advanced nations in the capitalist core and an exploited dependent periphery, whose economic progress was effectively constrained or even sabotaged by the power of the wealthy core to design the terms of international trade in its favour.[64] Nairn did not suggest that Scotland should be seen as a peripheral nation in Wallerstein's terms, but an influential argument along these lines was developed around the same time by another American sociologist, Michael Hechter (b. 1943), whose PhD at Columbia University had been supervised by Wallerstein. Hechter recalled beginning his graduate research in 1968 and situated his academic interest in the integration of national minorities in Britain in the broader political currents in the United States at that time, notably

---

[62] Nairn, 'Twilight of the British State', p. 61.
[63] Østergaard Nielsen and Ward, 'Three Referenda', pp. 200–20.
[64] Immanuel Wallerstein, *The Modern World-System I* (New York, Academic Press, 1974); Nairn, 'The Modern Janus', p. 28. Nairn discussed Wallerstein at greater length in *Break-Up of Britain*, pp. 310–20.

the Vietnam War and the civil rights movement. The eventual book of the PhD, *Internal Colonialism: The Celtic Fringe in British National Development* (1975), was therefore an attempt to use the case study of the oldest industrial society to examine whether capitalism would 'level all ethnic and racial differences and bring about cultural unity'.[65] Hechter argued in the book that he hoped the study of the British case would shed some light on debates within African American politics about the relative merits of an assimilationist versus a nationalist strategy. The central concept that Hechter deployed to that end was 'internal colonialism', an idea that had originated with Marxist authors such as Lenin and Gramsci to describe the economic exploitation of particular regions within a state. It had then been adopted by Latin American development economists – most famously André Gunder Frank (1929–2005) – to characterise the economic and racial divisions between metropolitan and peripheral regions in Latin American nations, imbuing the concept with its later connotation of a combination of economic and cultural discrimination. It was this version of the idea that was subsequently employed by Black and Latino theorists and activists in the United States and which Hechter encountered in the radical student politics of the 1960s.[66]

Hechter argued that the uneven economic development pursued across the British Isles from the sixteenth century onwards had left Ireland, Scotland and Wales as internal colonies, a description that identified a cultural division of labour in which individual life chances were systematically constrained by membership of these subordinate nationalities. This provided local elites with an incentive to create a nationalist politics to escape from these material and symbolic inequalities. Hechter used sophisticated quantitative techniques to demonstrate the presence of nationalist sentiment – although not necessarily nationalist voting – in the 'Celtic fringe' between 1885 and 1966 (as measured for example by the propensity of the Celtic nations to vote against the Conservative Party).[67] While recognised immediately as a path-breaking work, Hechter's book was also greeted with scepticism, particularly with respect to his treatment of Scotland.[68] Hechter

---

[65] Michael Hechter, 'Introduction to the Transaction Edition' of *Internal Colonialism: The Celtic Fringe in British National Development* (New Brunswick, Transaction Publishers, 1999 [1975]), p. xiii.

[66] Hechter, *Internal Colonialism*, pp. xiii–xiv, xxvi–xxviii, 30–4; Ramón A. Gutiérrez, 'Internal Colonialism: An American Theory of Race', *Du Bois Review*, 1 (2004), pp. 281–95.

[67] Hechter, *Internal Colonialism*, pp. 39–43, 208–340.

[68] James Hunter, review of Hechter, *Internal Colonialism*, *Scottish Historical Review*, 56 (1977), pp. 103–5; Edward Page, 'Michael Hechter's Internal Colonial Thesis: Some

himself noted that his theory did not precisely fit the Scottish case; the integration of the central belt of Scotland (although not the Highlands) into the imperial British economy was underplayed in his book.[69] Tom Nairn observed that in pursuit of an abstract theory, Hechter had missed the extent to which external British colonialism had in fact enabled 'real integrative tendencies to outweigh those of "uneven development" for a prolonged period'.[70] Hechter later amended his treatment of Scotland to make it more consonant with Nairn's, observing that in the case of Scotland a 'segmental division of labour' could be observed rather than the hierarchical cultural division that Hechter had noted in his book. In the Scottish case, the institutional autonomy of large parts of Scottish society meant that occupational spaces existed which depended on the preservation of a distinctive Scottish culture. This therefore created 'a substantial material incentive for the reproduction of Scottish culture through history'.[71] Hechter's considered position was therefore somewhat more aligned with Nairn's view that one of the key differences between Scottish and Welsh nationalism was that Scottish identity had been in less need of renovation than in the Welsh case because of the immense durability of Scottish civil society.[72]

Yet the ideological frisson of the concept of 'internal colonialism' was simply too great for it to be ignored by Scottish nationalists. As David McCrone observed, the language of 'dependency' and 'colonialism' was transformed into a 'metaphor rather than [an] explanatory concept' in Scottish political argument.[73] The Marxist historian James D. Young (1931–2012), for example, enthusiastically embraced Hechter's work in his *The Rousing of the Scottish Working Class* (1979), which proceeded from the starting point (also influenced by George Davie) that Scotland was a victim of 'internal colonialism' and 'became an English cultural colony after the Reformation'.[74] Where Nairn saw the Scottish Enlightenment as the kernel of a rational and universalising progress,

---

Theoretical and Methodological Problems', *European Journal of Political Research*, 6 (1978), pp. 295–317; Michael Keating and David Bleiman, *Labour and Scottish Nationalism* (London, Macmillan, 1979), pp. 11, 22. For a later critique, see David McCrone, *Understanding Scotland: The Sociology of a Nation* (2nd ed., London, Routledge, 2001), pp. 64–7.

[69] Hechter, *Internal Colonialism*, pp. xviii–xix, 307–10, 342–3.
[70] Nairn, 'Twilight of the British State', p. 42; Nairn, *Break-up of Britain*, pp. 200–2.
[71] Michael Hechter, 'Internal Colonialism Revisited', *Cencrastus*, no. 10, autumn 1982, pp. 9–10, quote at p. 10.
[72] Nairn, *Break-up of Britain*, pp. 207–8.   [73] McCrone, *Understanding Scotland*, p. 67.
[74] J. D. Young, *The Rousing of the Scottish Working Class* (London, Croom Helm, 1979), p. 11.

Young argued that it succeeded because of 'the philosophes' willingness to ape the manners and the language of the English'.[75] It was left to the Scottish working class, said Young, in the face of very difficult constraints, to mobilise resistance to capitalism by blending the politics of nationalism and socialism. But in spite of some sporadic successes (he wrote in 1979), the radical potential of the Scottish workers had as yet to be fully realised.[76]

Wallerstein himself later entered the fray in response to a challenge from the eminent historian of Scotland, Christopher Smout (b. 1933), about the place of Scotland within world-systems theory. Smout observed that, if Wallerstein's view of economic development was correct, then Scotland should surely have been relegated to the economic periphery and the status of a dependent economy in thrall to England. Instead, the case of Scotland appeared to adhere to the very economic model that Wallerstein sought to disprove, namely that economic development can be diffused from core to periphery through standard capitalist growth.[77] Wallerstein's reply was that the Scottish case should be seen as an exceptional rather than a typical one – an example, he said, of 'development by invitation'. Scotland – or more precisely the Scottish lowlands – benefited from integration into the rising English economy simply because it suited England to acquire the 'wider economic and demographic base' that it gained from Scotland's incorporation into the Union. But this path, Wallerstein continued, was not open to other peripheral states and hence, like Nairn, Wallerstein regarded Scottish economic development in the eighteenth and nineteenth centuries as distinctive.[78] Nairn agreed with Wallerstein in his review of this exchange, but he also noted the paradoxical political effects of such historical debates. Nationalists, Nairn observed, find it difficult to look on the rise of Scottish capitalism and the achievements of the Scottish Enlightenment with much enthusiasm because of what they see as its assimilationism and complicity 'in the larger crimes and vulgarities of all-British imperialism'. Unionists, on the other hand, see Scotland's economic ascent as making the case against independence. The paradox, then, was that 'nationalists are unable to employ Scotland's greatest achievement in their ideology; the anti-nationalists use it

---

[75] Young, *Rousing*, pp. 29–31, quote at p. 30.   [76] Young, *Rousing*, pp. 134–6, 189–228.

[77] T. C. Smout, 'Centre and Periphery in History; with Some Thoughts on Scotland as a Case Study', *Journal of Common Market Studies*, 18 (1980), pp. 256–71; T. C. Smout, 'Scotland and England: Is Dependency a Symptom or a Cause of Underdevelopment?', *Review*, 3 (1980), pp. 601–30.

[78] Immanuel Wallerstein, 'One Man's Meat: The Scottish Great Leap Forward', *Review*, 3 (1980), pp. 631–40, quotes at pp. 633, 636.

to undermine and discredit the very notion of an independent Scottish achievement'.[79]

Writing in 1980, Nairn viewed some resolution of these historical questions as essential to generating a powerful Scottish socialism. But as we will see in Chapters 4 and 5 the absence of a resonant nationalist narrative about the Scottish past was compensated for during the 1980s by the experience of deindustrialisation and the attribution of this disturbing period of economic change to the actions of a Conservative government that had little democratic legitimacy in Scotland. Scotland's relatively privileged place in the rise of capitalism became less central to nationalist debates because more immediate and tangible experiences of economic exploitation, unemployment and poverty began to dominate Scottish public life during the Thatcher years. Although the language of colonialism was used only intermittently by nationalists, a clear perception of Scotland as a victim of economic injustice under Thatcherism became the central myth of Scottish nationalism and suggested to some commentators that Hechter's model applied to Scotland in the latter part of the twentieth century rather than the earlier period Hechter himself had scrutinised.[80] As Chapter 4 will document, this helped to generate a new model of Scottish nationalist ideology based on advancing egalitarian socialist principles. Stephen Maxwell, one of the key writers and activists who initiated this development, had already noted in his 1977 review of *The Break-Up of Britain* that Nairn's own work implicitly raised the question of whether in Scotland the way forward for supporters of independence would be in constructing 'a nationalism that discards nationalist myth':

Where such a wealth of evidence of nationality, ranging from the Scottish legal system to the Scottish football league, from the STUC and the Scottish National Orchestra to Andy Stewart, exists, the elaboration of myths about Wallace and Bruce is superfluous. A case for independence can be constructed which owes nothing to any of the traditional Nationalist categories, but which relies instead on the reasoned conviction that independence is as necessary to realise the full potential of Scotland in the latter part of the twentieth century as perhaps the Union – its problems and subsequent trauma notwithstanding – was to realise Scotland's potential in the eighteenth century.[81]

---

[79] Tom Nairn, 'Dr Jekyll's Case: Model or Warning?', *Bulletin of Scottish Politics*, no. 1, autumn 1980, pp. 136–42, quotes at p. 141.

[80] Ian Hepburn, 'I'll Say That Again', *Radical Scotland*, no. 1, February/March 1983, p. 22. As Jim Phillips has shown, this process built on an earlier convergence of national and industrial politics during the 1960s and 1970s: *The Industrial Politics of Devolution* (Manchester, Manchester University Press, 2008).

[81] Maxwell, 'Review: *The Break-Up of Britain*', p. 7.

From Marx to Rousseau

Maxwell's tentative suggestion was a fertile one. In many respects the subsequent history of Scottish nationalism consisted in the elaboration of the kind of case for independence that Maxwell identified, although it turned out that he had underestimated how important it would be to construct a different sort of nationalist myth, relating to deindustrialisation rather than the deep Scottish past. Tom Nairn himself played a less prominent role in the prosecution of this case during the 1980s than he had in the 1970s. There were contingent, professional reasons for this – he resigned from the *New Left Review* Editorial Board in 1982 (apparently largely because of procedural or personality differences rather than political disagreement) and later worked in television and as a journalist.[82] But the political situation in Scotland in the 1980s was also not very encouraging to figures such as Nairn who had endured the hope and the disappointment of the run-up to the 1979 devolution referendum. Nairn had been involved in two initiatives designed to foster a synthesis of socialist and nationalist politics, both of which fizzled out: the SLP, of which Nairn was a founding member, and the SNP's '79 Group, which Nairn, although not a member of the SNP, exerted some influence over.[83] Nairn's later wave of writings on Scotland and the theory of nationalism largely emerged into public view as the Conservative government disintegrated after the 1992 general election and Labour's devolution proposals moved into the realm of practical possibility.

However, there was a notable difference between Nairn's new work and his earlier writings on this topic: a perceptible loss of faith in socialism.[84] In effect, Nairn had now put Marx to one side in favour of a Rousseau-style nationalist republicanism. The political vision that Nairn offered was similar to the ideas advanced around the same time by the pressure group Charter 88, which was led by Nairn's erstwhile *New Left*

---

[82] Thompson, 'Tom Nairn', pp. 320–2.

[83] Stephen Maxwell, 'The '79 Group: A Critical Retrospect', *Cencrastus*, no. 21, 1985, p. 12; Tom Nairn, 'Scotland after the Elections', in *SNP '79 Group Papers No. 1*, papers discussed at founding meeting on 31 May 1979, Belford Hotel, Edinburgh (no publisher/date), pp. 5–7. For further discussion of the SLP and the '79 Group, see Chapter 4.

[84] This observation about Nairn has been made in different ways by Davidson, 'Tom Nairn and the Inevitability of Nationalism'; Joan Cocks, 'In Defence of Ethnicity, Locality, Nationality: The Curious Case of Tom Nairn', in her *Passion and Paradox: Intellectuals Confront the National Question* (Princeton, Princeton University Press, 2002), pp. 111–32; Matthews, *New Left, National Identity*, pp. 272–84; Scothorne, 'From the Outer Edge'.

Review colleague (and friend), Anthony Barnett (b. 1942), and which campaigned for constitutional reform in Britain in the run-up to Labour's return to office in 1997.[85] In this respect a key transitional work for Nairn was his searing analysis of the British state and monarchy, *The Enchanted Glass*, published in 1988 (the year that the eponymous Charter was issued to the public). Among other things, this book articulated the emerging Charter 88 view that Britain – or Ukania as Nairn now dubbed it – lacked an adequately democratic constitution and that the rise of absolute parliamentary sovereignty in place of absolute monarchy was at the heart of this democratic deficit, particularly when it came to the protection of individual rights.[86] This marked a return to some of the constitutionalist themes set out by the pioneering Scottish nationalist publicists of the mid-twentieth century (and explored in Chapter 1 of this book). More immediately, though, the influential journalist Neal Ascherson (b. 1932) – a close friend and colleague of Nairn, a fellow member of the SLP, and political correspondent at *The Scotsman* between 1975 and 1979 – had been a forceful recent proponent of this view. Ascherson devoted one of his *Scotsman* columns to it in 1977 (which Nairn approvingly quoted in *Break-Up of Britain*), and later used his 1985 John Mackintosh Memorial Lecture to develop a more extensive critique of what Ascherson now saw (in the light of Thatcherism) as the historic failure of British political culture to embrace the modernist politics of freedom and equality associated with Jacobin republicanism.[87] Nairn had been sympathetic to this analysis for some time and had for example joined Ascherson in *The Break-Up of Britain* by arguing that the archaic structures and feudal trappings of the 'Crown-in-Parliament' had

---

[85] See for example Nairn's tribute to Barnett in Tom Nairn, *After Britain* (London, Granta, 2000), p. ix. On the origins and work of Charter 88, see David Erdos, 'Charter 88 and the Constitutional Reform Movement: A Retrospective', *Parliamentary Affairs*, 62 (2009), pp. 537–51; Stephen Howe, 'Some Intellectual Origins of Charter 88', *Parliamentary Affairs*, 62 (2009), pp. 552–67; Stuart White, 'A Marquandian Moment? The Civic Republican Political Theory of David Marquand' and Ben Jackson, 'A Union of Hearts? Republican Social Democracy and Scottish Nationalism', both in Hans Schattle and Jeremy Nuttall (eds.), *Making Social Democrats: Citizens, Mindsets, Realities: Essays for David Marquand* (Manchester, Manchester University Press, 2018), pp. 139–59, 161–73.

[86] Tom Nairn, *The Enchanted Glass* (London, Radius, 1988), pp. 93–8, 144–50, 163–5. 'Ukania' was intended to evoke Robert Musil's characterisation of the Austo-Hungarian Empire as 'Kakania' in his novel, *The Man without Qualities* (1930–43).

[87] Neal Ascherson, 'Divine Right of Parliaments', *Scotsman*, 18 February 1977; Nairn, *Break-up of Britain*, p. 302; Neal Ascherson, 'Ancient Britons and the Republican Dream', John Mackintosh Memorial Lecture, Edinburgh University, 16 November 1985, *Radical Scotland*, no. 18, December/January 1986; reprinted in Ascherson's *Games with Shadows* (London, Radius, 1988), pp. 146–58.

led to a British nationalism that lacked the egalitarianism and democratic populism of other modern national forms.[88]

However, Nairn and like-minded colleagues from the New Left had previously seen such pathologies of the British state as ultimately rooted in material circumstances – in the distinctiveness of the development of British capitalism, its class structure, and its role as the leading imperial power of the nineteenth century – rather than in constitutional history.[89] During the 1980s this level of analysis receded into the background – when it was present at all. Nairn instead urged that the left should prioritise constitutional reform, since the Thatcherite offensive had been fundamentally enabled by Britain's winner-takes-all political system. He acknowledged that this 'new republicanism' to a large extent rested on what radicals of the 1970s used to call pejoratively 'the autonomy of the political' (though Nairn briefly noted that these constitutional tensions did reflect a decomposition of traditional British ideologies that was in an ultimate sense the result of economic decline). But in the circumstances of the 1980s, Nairn concluded, the traditional path of the British left – socialism through the Westminster system – 'looks more like a hearse every day'. 'The only way out or forward is via constitutional reform.'[90]

Nairn's writings differed from Charter 88's ideology by placing a stronger emphasis on nationalism as an ineradicable, indeed broadly progressive, phenomenon and a related commitment to the superiority of small, self-determining states as the optimal basis of political organisation.[91] This aspect of Nairn's thought became ever more important in the 1990s as he digested the collapse of Soviet communism and the resurfacing of nationalism in the formerly communist states. Nairn interpreted the post-1989 period as the start of a new era in which conflict between great imperial powers no longer held sway and instead new space existed in the global order for a plethora of independent small nations, linked together through trade and treaties of cooperation (he remained a firm supporter of European integration).[92] In a 2008 lecture Nairn argued that the global economic integration of the twenty-first century provided a favourable framework for small nations since it was no longer necessary to be part of a larger nation state for reasons of either national security or

---

[88] Nairn, *Break-up of Britain*, pp. 295–6, 302; reprised in Nairn, *Enchanted Glass*, pp. 181–9; Ascherson, *Tom Nairn*, p. 19.

[89] Nairn, *Break-up of Britain*, p. 297.

[90] Nairn, *Enchanted Glass*, pp. 378–91, quotes at p. 390.

[91] Anthony Barnett – later to come around to a more Nairn-like position on Scottish independence – initially registered some polite disagreement with Nairn on this point in his *This Time: Our Constitutional Revolution* (London, Vintage, 1997), pp. 186–93.

[92] Nairn, *Faces of Nationalism*, pp. 129, 134; Nairn, *After Britain*, p. 17.

market access.[93] As Ben Wellings and Michael Kenny have put it, where once Nairn had adhered to a Jacobin model of republican nationalism, in this later phase of his career 'all nations should normatively be something like Scotland rather than France'.[94]

Underpinning this analysis was Nairn's attempt to advance beyond Gellner's modernist explanation of nationalism. Aware of the force of the contrasting, so-called primordialist or ethno-symbolic theory of nationalism developed by Anthony Smith, Nairn now acknowledged that national sentiments had their roots in longer-range historical processes and 'deep-communal structures', and perhaps even reflected a more fundamental feature of 'human nature'.[95] The rise of nationalism could therefore no longer be as straightforwardly related to material causes as Nairn once believed.[96] In spite – or even because – of this, when Nairn recalled his view of nationalism as the 'modern Janus', he thought that by the 1990s 'on the whole, the forward-gazing side of the strange visage may be more prominent than it was in 1977. Perhaps because today the forward view is that much more open and more encouraging than it was then.'[97]

Nairn, who once referred to himself 'as a calloused veteran of declining-Britain horoscopes', still remained convinced that the political structures of the United Kingdom were doomed to collapse under the weight of their own contradictions.[98] But his case for this was now predominantly constitutional rather than economic. Where once Nairn had identified a decrepit state destined to fall because of post-imperial economic stagnation, he now said that Britain – or 'Ukania' – was riven by inescapable tensions over the locus of sovereignty in a multinational polity. Nairn had long supported devolution to Scotland as an important first step towards Scottish self-government, but his support was largely driven by his belief that devolution would prove to be a waystation en route to full independence. Like the opponents of devolution, Nairn

---

[93] Tom Nairn, 'Globalisation and Nationalism: The New Deal', Edinburgh Lecture, 4 March 2008, reprinted in Tom Nairn, *Old Nations, Auld Enemies, New Times: Selected Essays*, edited by Jamie Maxwell and Pete Ramand (Edinburgh, Luath Press, 2014), pp. 396–405.

[94] Ben Wellings and Michael Kenny, 'Nairn's England and the Progressive Dilemma: Reappraising Tom Nairn on English Nationalism', *Nations and Nationalism*, 25 (2019), p. 858.

[95] Nairn, *Faces*, pp. 1–17, quotes at p. 17. For an introduction to the debate between modernism and ethnosymbolism, and other cognate theories of nationalism, see Oliver Zimmer, *Nationalism in Europe, 1890–1940* (Basingstoke, Palgrave, 2003), pp. 4–26; Anthony Smith, *Nationalism* (2nd ed., Cambridge, Polity, 2010).

[96] Nairn, 'Twenty-First Century Hindsight', pp. xviii–xix.

[97] Nairn, *Faces of Nationalism*, p. 67.

[98] Tom Nairn, 'After the Referendum', *New Edinburgh Review*, no. 46, summer 1979, p. 5.

argued that once Scottish popular sovereignty was given an institutional form it would inevitably conflict with the parliamentary sovereignty of the British state. Nairn perceptively noted that the key fact about the new Scottish Parliament would not be the precise policy domains or fiscal powers it controlled, but rather its embodiment for the first time of a distinctively Scottish democratic will which would, inevitably, be able to address 'whether to try to alter the conditions of UK affiliation'.[99] While conversant with the increasing salience of debates about federal and 'post-sovereign' power-sharing arrangements between states and regions, Nairn's view was that in the British case there was little chance of such a comprehensive recasting of British constitutional practice (a view shared by Neil MacCormick, the leading theorist of 'post-sovereignty', as we will see in Chapter 5). For Scotland, the only path forward would ultimately have to be a fairly conventional model of independence rather than some more complex 'pooling or merging of statehood' within the United Kingdom.[100]

Nairn's case for Scottish independence was couched principally in terms of a right to democratic self-determination rather than in order to preserve Scottish distinctiveness – a common emphasis among Scottish nationalists from the 1980s onwards, which will be discussed in more detail in Chapter 5. But, as Nairn candidly recognised, this was not ultimately a purely non-nationalist case because it was premised on the assumption that democracy was currently only able to function effectively within a particular national community.[101] Indeed, at its most ambitious, Nairn's diagnosis of the emergent Scottish demos at the start of the twenty-first century offered a broader cultural critique of Scottishness under the Union. He was sceptical of the Scottish institutions that the Union had purportedly guaranteed, since in Nairn's view the crucial point about this associational life was that it was apolitical and conspicuously failed to offer any national leadership to the Scots (a point often made by Scottish nationalists about institutions such as the Scottish universities, as we saw in Chapter 2). Deploying language he had once sternly warned nationalists against, following the disappointment of the 1992 general election Nairn characterised Scottish identity as hobbled by a form of 'self-colonisation'. Since Scotland had not been coerced into the Union, Scots 'conquered and partly assimilated themselves', albeit for good reasons at the time, binding themselves into 'a chosen and sustained national servitude' in which the absence of an independent state had led to political passivity and a lack of national

---

[99] Nairn, *Faces of Nationalism*, p. 223.   [100] Nairn, *Faces of Nationalism*, p. 222.
[101] Nairn, *Faces of Nationalism*, pp. 223–4.

assertiveness. From Nairn's perspective this identity crisis could only be resolved by a national democratic constitutionalism that placed Scotland in a relationship of equality with England as fellow member states of the European Union.[102]

Notwithstanding the incident with the rickshaw recounted at the beginning of this chapter, reflective Scottish nationalists in the late twentieth and early twenty-first centuries would have rejected the notion that England has had a colonial relationship with Scotland, at least in the most common sense of that term. But imperialism is nonetheless an inescapable category in the political thought of Scottish nationalism. As the evolution of Tom Nairn's thinking demonstrates, and as we saw in Chapter 2, at one level this is because Scottish nationalists do generally believe that the loss of political autonomy after 1707 also led to some loss of cultural autonomy, which in turn created a Scottish ideological and even psychological assimilation into the metropolitan norms projected from London. This was what Nairn called 'self-colonisation' and Craig Beveridge and Ronald Turnbull had referred to – invoking Frantz Fanon – as 'inferiorisation'.

But in addition to this cultural meaning, imperialism has become a central concept in the Scottish nationalist critique of Britain. From the perspective of political thought, Jimmi Østergaard Nielsen and Stuart Ward are correct to suggest that historians have unduly neglected the way in which the 'discursive pressures of the end of Empire' corroded the case for Britain by bringing into question the ideology of Britishness.[103] For Scottish nationalists, it is the loss of empire that precipitated the decline of Britain both economically and as a coherent source of national identity. And they argue that it was imperialism that forged the British state into a distinctive neo-feudal relic, incapable of adapting to the demands of modern democratic values and managing economic change in an equitable fashion. Nairn himself placed less emphasis on the economic elements of this argument in his later work, seemingly influenced by the collapse of socialism as a systematic alternative to capitalism. But it was certainly possible to transfer his critique of the British state's failure to deal with the economic crisis of the 1970s to the economic restructuring

---

[102] Tom Nairn, 'Scottish Identity: A Cause Unwon', *Chapman*, 67, winter 1991/92, pp. 2–12, quote at p. 6; Nairn, *After Britain*, pp. 223–78; Nairn, *Faces of Nationalism*, pp. 73–89.

[103] Østergaard Nielsen and Ward, 'Three Referenda', pp. 216–20, quote at p. 220. They have made this point as a criticism of Tom Devine, 'The Break-Up of Britain? Scotland and the End of Empire', *Transactions of the Royal Historical Society*, 16 (2006), pp. 163–80; Tom Devine, *To the Ends of the Earth: Scotland's Global Diaspora* (London, Penguin, 2011), pp. 257–69.

of the 1980s, when it could be argued that a distant London government pursued a new quixotic image of national greatness at the expense of Scottish industrial development, with the Thatcher government now replacing American multinational companies as the agents of economic exploitation. It was this task of creating an explicitly socialist, anti-neoliberal case for Scottish independence that preoccupied many leading Scottish nationalists from the mid 1970s onwards and it is to that story that we will turn in the next chapter.

4   The Case for Left-Wing Nationalism

> Scotland rejects the values of Thatcherism because our country has a
> philosophy of egalitarianism.   Jim Sillars, 1988[1]

After the Second World War the Anglo-Scottish Union was renewed by
the arrival of the welfare state. As other popular bases of Britishness –
Protestantism, empire, even in due course the memory of the war
itself – faded away, it was the activist British state that was widely credited
with reviving Scotland's industrial economy after the depression and
opening up previously inaccessible life chances for the working classes
by guaranteeing access to education, healthcare, housing, pensions and
employment. This novel regime of economic security became, as Tom
Devine put it, 'the new anchor of the Union state'.[2] The corollary was that
this social democratic unionism would be vulnerable to attack if the
British state failed to maintain these social reforms and the egalitarian
goals that underpinned them.[3] The emergence of a state committed to
planning economic development played an important role in conceptualising and then popularising the Scottish economy as a distinct unit of
analysis with its own particular problems. 'Scotland' became one 'region'
among others that would receive state support aimed at maintaining
employment levels and economic growth. If the British state could not
in fact deliver on that commitment, then the case for a more autonomous
economic policy would gain a hearing.[4] There was indeed a correlation
between the decomposition of the British social democratic settlement in

---

[1] Jim Sillars, Hansard, HC Debates, sixth series, vol. 142, col. 165 (23 November 1988).
[2] Tom Devine, 'The Break-Up of Britain? Scotland and the End of Empire', *Transactions of
the Royal Historical Society*, 16 (2006), pp. 179–80, quote at p. 180.
[3] Nicola McEwen, *Nationalism and the State: Welfare and Identity in Scotland and Quebec*
(Brussels, Peter Lang, 2006).
[4] Jack Brand, *The National Movement in Scotland* (London, Routledge, 1978), pp. 68–88;
Michael Keating, *The Independence of Scotland* (Oxford, Oxford University Press, 2009),
pp. 8, 36; James Mitchell, *The Scottish Question* (Oxford, Oxford University Press, 2014),
pp. 132–48; Jim Tomlinson and Ewan Gibbs, 'Planning the New Industrial Nation:
Scotland 1931–79', *Contemporary British History*, 30 (2016), pp. 584–606.

the 1970s and the initial rise of Scottish nationalism as a popular political force. As we have seen, this led some nationalists to argue that the goal of independence should be supported less by arguments about Scottish cultural difference – however broadly construed – and more by mobilising Scotland as a politically distinctive community, which sought to conserve and deepen the social solidarity of the post-war settlement in the face of England's careless embrace of unfettered market capitalism. However, as this chapter will show, this argument was also a flexible one. The left-wing case for Scottish independence was itself carried along by the prevailing political tide of the 1990s until it occupied a political space that was significantly to the right of its initial iterations in the 1970s and 1980s.

Beyond Left and Right

Until the 1960s the position of Scottish nationalism on the left–right ideological spectrum was uncertain, in part because of a still skeletal SNP's necessarily limited resources for policy development but also, as we saw in Chapter 1, as a result of the political positioning chosen by the first generation of Scottish nationalists. As Scottish nationalism gathered support in the 1960s and 1970s, an invigorated SNP was able to devote greater thought to its ideological profile, which in turn generated further debate among supporters of independence who were not affiliated to the SNP. Drawing on the currents of participatory politics that emerged internationally during this period – and to an extent building on earlier nationalist thinking – Scottish nationalism began to present itself as a moderately social democratic ideology of community and decentralisation, commitments which nationalists argued had deep roots in Scottish history.[5] But this connection to a communitarian Scottishness also made key figures within the SNP reluctant to locate themselves too firmly on what they regarded as the British, or even English, left–right spectrum.

William Wolfe (1924–2010), one of the architects of the SNP's rise in this period and party leader from 1969 to 1979, sought to give the SNP a more consistently 'social democratic' image but he understood this term (rightly in the context of the 1970s) as signifying moderation and a judicious distance from the conventional ideological polarities that dominated British public life. He argued in his 1973 memoir that political analysts failed to understand how divergent the SNP was from this

---

[5] A useful overview of the crystallisation of SNP policy in this period is Gordon Wilson, *The SNP: The Turbulent Years 1960–90* (Stirling, Scots Independent, 2009), pp. 44–57. The ideological story has been summarised by Peter Lynch, 'From Social Democracy Back to No Ideology? The Scottish National Party and Ideological Change in a Multi-Level Electoral Setting', *Regional and Federal Studies*, 19 (2009), pp. 623–33.

framework: 'The vast majority of political observers of the SNP are trying to assess a fresh political and philosophical outlook which has had no counterpart in existing British politics within the experience or under-standing of the people designing the surveys and making the observa-tions.'[6] Wolfe had drafted *The SNP and You*, the party's 1964 manifesto, in this spirit, striking a social democratic note with an emphasis on social welfare provision but pitching Scottish nationalism as a cause that should draw together all Scots in a democratic struggle for national freedom: 'The National Party stands for the nation; all sections, all people in it; welded in a common purpose; devoted, dedicated to the social and economic improvement of all.'[7] The 'SNP Democrats' (Wolfe hoped around that time to restyle the party as the 'Scottish Democrats Party') aimed for Scotland to achieve 'freedom through unity – freedom and power to rule herself, reform herself, respect herself'.[8] Furthermore, 'SNP Democrats' understood popular participation in an expansive fashion, 'vesting responsibility and initiative in society wherever possible rather than in state bureaucracy' and seeking 'maximum possible demo-cratic devolution in all spheres of human activity'.[9] Wolfe built on these themes in his address to the SNP conference in 1970, characterising the party in lyrical terms as:

radical and egalitarian, in accordance with Scottish humanitarian traditions which have little to do with British party labels. The mainspring of our dedication is love of humanity in general and of Scotland in particular. Any love which is pure, any love which lifts the heart and soul must inevitably contain an element of sacrifice. Something has to be given up in order to achieve what is seen to be a greater and worthier goal. The lesser has to be absorbed in the greater. That is why being conservative, liberal or socialist is of secondary importance within the Scottish National Party. Once we have our own Parliament with Scottish general elections, people will have a choice of voting for whatever Scottish political parties are in existence at that time, but until then, we must put Scotland first and vote for independence.[10]

The roots of Wolfe's nationalism were cultural. On his own account it was reading Lewis Grassic Gibbon's novel, *Sunset Song* (1932) and publications of the Saltire Society on Scottish literature, poetry and song that led him to worry that Scotland's distinctive traditions were under

---

[6] Billy Wolfe, *Scotland Lives* (Edinburgh, Reprographia, 1973), p. 101. For an account of Wolfe's background and career, see Christopher Harvie, 'William Wolfe', in Gerry Hassan and James Mitchell (eds.), *Scottish National Party Leaders* (London, Biteback, 2016), pp. 247–64.

[7] SNP, *The SNP and You: Aims and Policy of the Scottish National Party* (Edinburgh, SNP, 1964), p. 1.

[8] SNP, *SNP and You*, p. 5.   [9] SNP, *SNP and You*, p. 19.

[10] Quoted in Wolfe, *Scotland Lives*, p. 149.

threat of assimilation into a larger English culture.[11] He was also later influenced by reading *The Fraternal Society* (1962) by Richard Hauser and Hephzibah Menuhin, a work of sociology that detected a (desirable) social trend towards cooperative and participatory, rather than state or paternalistic, forms of organisation.[12]

Like his predecessors in the SNP, Wolfe's view was that Scottish culture could be historically distinguished from its English counterpart by its 'collective fraternalism', a theme he elaborated on in support of the Upper Clyde Shipbuilders (UCS) work-in of 1971–2, which had successfully pressured Edward Heath's Conservative government into rescuing the company from liquidation.[13] Wolfe had previously helped Tom McAlpine (1929–2006), later a prominent SNP activist and councillor, to set up a producer cooperative, the Rowen Engineering Company (named after the utopian socialist Robert Owen), in Glasgow in 1963. The enterprise had emerged from the campaign for nuclear disarmament as a 'factory for peace' that sought to combine economic democracy and non-military industrial production, with any profit earmarked for the peace movement.[14] Wolfe and the SNP were therefore broadly supportive of moves to establish new forms of industrial democracy and participation. But Wolfe also saw the UCS and other moves to encourage cooperative production as expressive of Celtic traditions of fraternity:

> To me it is no accident that the desire for experiment in industrial democracy in order to find a new formula, particularly for productive industry, should show itself in Scotland and Wales. In both countries, the roots of this embryo movement are fraternal, whereas the origins of such factories as exist in England appear to be paternal and authoritarian, and rather more empirical than the developments in Wales and Scotland.[15]

At UCS, he argued, 'it was Scottish tradition, Scottish principles, Scottish determination and Scottish community spirit which won the day'.[16] This cultural nationalism even shaded into a more ethnic vision when Wolfe described 'the essence of Scottish existence' as 'its roots in the Celtic origins of the vast majority of the people of Scotland'.[17] Wolfe argued that 'a Scottish Parliament would safeguard the indefinable

---

[11] Wolfe, *Scotland Lives*, pp. 10, 26–7, 132.

[12] Richard Hauser and Hephzibah Menuhin, *The Fraternal Society* (London, Bodley Head, 1962).

[13] On UCS and the national question, see Jim Phillips, *The Industrial Politics of Devolution* (Manchester, Manchester University Press, 2008), pp. 79–116.

[14] Wolfe, *Scotland Lives*, pp. 33–5; Christopher Hill, 'Nations of Peace: Nuclear Disarmament and the Making of National Identity in Scotland and Wales', *Twentieth Century British History*, 27 (2016), pp. 40–1.

[15] Wolfe, *Scotland Lives*, p. 35.   [16] Wolfe, *Scotland Lives*, pp. 153–5, quote at 155.

[17] Wolfe, *Scotland Lives*, p. 161.

qualities of Scottish community life, which are endangered by the threat of wholesale uncontrolled immigration from England and elsewhere'.[18] Wolfe feared that the discovery of North Sea oil 'will allow the English government to foster the migration of hundreds of thousands of people to Scotland and thus effectively overwhelm the Scottish nation. This is the most serious threat to Scotland today.'[19]

Such nativist tendencies aside, Wolfe's political thought demonstrated that the New Left-inspired participatory radicalism of the 1960s and 1970s could be synthesised with the long-standing nationalist arguments about Scotland's traditions of decentralised government discussed in Chapter 1. On this account, independence could take its place as a local solution to the worldwide anxiety 'about the gap between those who govern and those who are governed', offering the opportunity to foster a more democratic Scotland in which citizens have 'a greater share in decision-making than merely voting in a parliamentary election every five years'.[20]

By the October 1974 general election, the SNP had officially adopted the label 'social democratic' to describe its political outlook, a label that indicated the party's stance was a moderate, centre-left one, supportive of full employment and the welfare state, but distinguished from the two larger parties by its participatory and decentralist commitments, as well as by its strong support for unilateral nuclear disarmament.[21] The leading public proponent of this 'social democratic' ideological profile was the SNP MP George Reid. Reid maintained that the central purpose of the SNP was 'to see a genuine return of social justice to the people of Scotland'. But he emphasised that the distinctive political argument the party sought to prosecute was 'that we shall never get genuine social justice and the creation of a compassionate, caring, egalitarian Scots society without control of our own affairs by Scots, for Scots, in Scotland'.[22] Reid also thought Scottish politics was divided between social democrats and socialists and contrasted the SNP's commitment to social justice with those further to the left. He distinguished

Between those pragmatists who believe in a mixed economy, and who are neither for nor against nationalisation ideologically, and those who want a return to a purer, more fundamental socialism in the old ILP tradition. Between those who are primarily concerned with individual rights, and emphasise classlessness, and those who adopt a fundamental class approach to politics.[23]

---

[18] Wolfe, *Scotland Lives*, p. 160.   [19] Wolfe, *Scotland Lives*, p. 160.
[20] SNP, *The New Scotland – Your Scotland* (Edinburgh, SNP, 1970), p. 3.
[21] Wilson, *Turbulent Years*, pp. 119–21; Hill, 'Nations of Peace', pp. 26–50.
[22] George Reid, Hansard, HC Debates, fifth series, vol. 870, cols. 596, 598 (15 March 1974).
[23] George Reid, 'A State of Flux', *Question*, no. 5, February 1976, p. 4.

In Reid's view, the SNP occupied this social democratic space and stood ready to build alliances in a putative Scottish parliament with social democrats in Labour and the Liberals against socialists such as Jim Sillars, who Reid suspected 'wants to build the sort of Scotland you won't find this side of Yugoslavia'.[24] To some extent the positioning of the SNP as 'social democratic' masked the ideological heterogeneity of the party's membership and its newly enlarged parliamentary group, but it formally placed Scottish nationalism somewhere near the centre of the left–right debate in Britain at that time.[25] Neal Ascherson, a close ally of Jim Sillars as well as one of *The Scotsman*'s political correspondents, described the 1975 SNP conference as revealing a party that was 'mildly' social democratic but also 'prevailingly middle-class in its general perception of society'.[26]

Radical Scotland

More radical ideas were also coursing through Scottish political debate during the 1970s and they exercised a decisive influence on the nascent discourse of Scottish nationalism. This influence was in fact a reciprocal one, since the emergence of a radical socialist analysis of Scottish politics was itself an attempt to understand the surprising revival of Scottish nationalism as a popular force during the late 1960s. A number of important writers, artists and intellectuals rallied to this task, many of them operating within a broadly Marxist or New Left framework.[27] Much of this work sought to interrogate whether – as the SNP claimed – 'the independence movement is a revolution of rising expectations rather than a mere support against economic deprivation', a framing that was

---

[24] Reid, 'State of Flux', p. 4.

[25] These ideological tensions and their consequences are carefully discussed by Ian O. Bayne, 'The Impact of 1979 on the SNP', in Tom Gallagher (ed.), *Nationalism in the Nineties* (Edinburgh, Polygon, 1991), pp. 46–65. The ideological space occupied by the SNP was roughly similar to the positioning of the Liberal Party at the same time: Thomas Stewart, '"A Disguised Liberal Party Vote?" Third Party Voting and the SNP under Gordon Wilson in Dundee in the 1970s and 1980s', *Contemporary British History*, 33 (2019), pp. 357–82. For comparison, see Tudor Jones, *The Revival of British Liberalism* (Basingstoke, Palgrave, 2011), pp. 52–88.

[26] Neal Ascherson, 'The Day the SNP Became a "Normal" Political Party', *Scotsman*, 2 June 1975.

[27] Ewan Gibbs and Rory Scothorne, '"Origins of the Present Crisis?": The Emergence of "Left-Wing" Scottish Nationalism, 1956–79', in Evan Smith and Matthew Worley (eds.), *Waiting for the Revolution: The British Far Left from 1956* (Manchester, Manchester University Press, 2017), pp. 163–181; Rory Scothorne, 'Nationalism and the Radical Left in Scotland, 1968–92' (PhD thesis, Edinburgh University, in progress).

intriguingly congruent with the wider radical politics of the era.[28] This confluence of Scottish nationalism with the New Left in the late twentieth century is important evidence for Madeleine Davis's wider contention that the political impact of the British New Left has been underestimated by a scholarship that has neglected the diffusion of New Left ideas and activism at a grass-roots level (as opposed to the metropolitan intellectual circles that form the subject matter of much existing research).[29] As we saw in Chapter 3, Tom Nairn was the most prominent example of a New Left figure who had journeyed, both intellectually and physically, from the New Left scene in London back to Scotland to offer a coruscating historical critique of the British state that inspired generations of activists. But Nairn himself had less to say in practical terms about how to construct a positive nationalist appeal that could claim independence for the left. Such a task ultimately fell to those more directly engaged in electoral politics than Nairn, but they did so by drawing on a number of key texts of the 1970s that significantly deepened the left's analysis of Scottish nationalism.

An influential starting point for much of this debate was an article on Antonio Gramsci by Ray Burnett (b. 1946) in the journal *Scottish International* in 1972. Burnett was at that time a member of the Trotskyist International Socialists and had recently been active in the Northern Irish civil rights movement.[30] For Burnett – as for many other radicals at the time – Gramsci's theoretical breakthrough was that he had identified the importance of civil society in entrenching capitalist power structures in Western Europe.[31] The density and complexity of these mature capitalist civil societies was such that they provided a robust defence against the economic crises that Marxists had traditionally regarded as the catalyst of revolution. This reading of Gramsci implied that advanced capitalism could most effectively be challenged through a 'war of position' that strategically advanced through the institutions of civil society rather than a 'war of manoeuvre' that simply sought to capture the state. In Burnett's view, the particular relevance of this point to Scotland was

---

[28] SNP, *The New Scotland*, p. 12.
[29] Madeleine Davis, '"Among the Ordinary People": New Left Involvement in Working Class Mobilisation 1956–68', *History Workshop Journal*, 86 (2018), pp. 133–59.
[30] Ray Burnett, 'When the Finger Points at the Moon', in James D. Young (ed.), *Scotland at the Crossroads: A Socialist Answer* (Glasgow, Clydeside Press, 1990), pp. 98–104. Burnett had been involved in the so-called Battle of the Bogside in August 1969, working with the Derry Citizens' Defence Association: 'Derry: Fighting under the Flag of the Citizens' Army: An Interview with Eamon McCann and Ray Burnett on the Barricades', *Socialist Worker*, 21 August 1969.
[31] See also Chapter 3 for further discussion of the influence of Gramsci on Perry Anderson and Tom Nairn.

that existing British socialist strategies did not recognise that Scottish civil society – and thus the 'external façade' of the state – was quite different from England. A successful Scottish socialism would therefore need to reckon with the specificities of the way in which capitalist dominance was achieved in Scotland – including through bourgeois nationalisms of both the British and Scottish varieties – and draw on radical elements of Scottish culture to contest hegemonic capitalist values:

> Indeed I believe that if the new social order we strive for is to be a worthwhile and fitting signification of the past and future history of the Scottish people then the left *must* uphold and expound the merits of past achievements and the richness of our inheritance. Just as Engels lamented the scantiness of surviving Irish bardic tradition – 'Their names are lost, of their poetry only fragments have survived, the most beautiful legacy they have left their enslaved, but unconquered, people is their music' – so we must cherish the diverse contributions of the flowering Makar and the rantin' ploughboy, the radical weaver, the passionate Gael, and the rovin' tinker. If we do not, then what price 'the revolution'?[32]

Burnett viewed this analysis as contributing to a radical socialist rather than straightforwardly nationalist politics and was dismissive of the SNP as a possible vehicle for his Gramscian strategy since he thought 'the SNP are no different from any other bourgeois parliamentary party'. In their version of an independent Scotland, Burnett said, political life 'will continue to be a false plurality masking the influence and power of one economically and politically dominant class over its subordinate'.[33] Burnett tried to advance his own vision of a Scottish socialism by founding and editing a short-lived periodical, *Calgacus*, between 1975 and 1976 (it was named after the chieftain who, according to Tacitus, had led the Caledonians against the Romans at the Battle of Mons Graupius). Edited from the village of Dornie near Kyle of Lochalsh in Wester Ross, *Calgacus* boasted an editorial advisory board that included the poet, folklorist and songwriter Hamish Henderson; the Gaelic poet Sorley McLean (1911–96); the long-standing Marxist activist (and friend of John Maclean) Harry McShane (1891–1988); and Tom Nairn. But the contents of the journal offered less than might have been expected on an industrially oriented Scottish socialism and focused more on what Neil Williamson termed an 'alliance between the folk revivalists of the

---

[32] Ray Burnett, 'Scotland and Antonio Gramsci', *Scottish International*, vol. 5, no. 9, November 1972, pp. 14–15 (emphasis in the original); Neil Davidson, 'Antonio Gramsci's Reception in Scotland', in Neil Davidson, *Holding Fast to an Image of the Past* (Chicago, Haymarket Books, 2014), pp. 263–8; Ray Burnett, 'Gramsci and Scotland Revisited', *Scottish Left Review*, no. 99 (2017), pp. 25–6.

[33] Ray Burnett, 'Socialists and the SNP', in Gordon Brown (ed.), *The Red Paper on Scotland* (Edinburgh, EUSPB, 1975), pp. 113, 117.

Edinburgh literati and the Celtic populists of Wester Ross', taking an approach to Scottish culture that was predominantly agrarian and attracted to a pan-Celtic radicalism that also encompassed Ireland and Wales.[34] Burnett's Gramscianism could in effect shade into a more straightforwardly nationalist politics insofar as it could be construed as offering theoretical warrant for upholding a distinctively Scottish populist radical tradition rather than a more orthodox class-based analysis. A similar observation might be made about John McGrath's (1935–2002) influential play, *The Cheviot, the Stag and the Black, Black Oil,* which Burnett had advised on and which began touring in 1973. Burnett later recalled that Gramsci had been an influence on McGrath's work, and though the political intent behind the play was socialist, it was certainly possible to construe its tale of successive waves of exploitation of the Highlands by capital and the British state in more nationalist terms.[35]

The confluence of socialist and nationalist ideas in the 1970s – and the tension between them – reached its most celebrated expression in *The Red Paper on Scotland,* published in 1975 and edited by the then rector of Edinburgh University, Gordon Brown (b. 1951).[36] Though some on the left felt that it was 'more "peely-wally" than red', this landmark volume was nonetheless an important exercise in socialist pluralism, bringing together supporters of Labour, more radical left parties and the SNP to debate the Scottish question and its intersection with the politics of socialism.[37] A central dilemma that preoccupied many contributors to the book was the basic strategic question – which has remained at the heart of the debate on Scottish independence ever since – of whether the politics of Scottish nationalism represented a distraction from socialist objectives or on the contrary the means by

---

[34] Neil Williamson, 'Ten Years After – The Revolutionary Left in Scotland', *Scottish Government Yearbook,* 1979, pp. 74–5; see the editorial masthead and contents pages of *Calgacus,* vol. 1, nos. 1–3, 1975–76. Burnett responded to Williamson's critique in 'When the Finger Points at the Moon', p. 100.

[35] John McGrath, *The Cheviot, the Stag and the Black, Black Oil* (London, Bloomsbury, 2015 [1974]), p. xvi; Burnett, 'Gramsci and Scotland Revisited', pp. 25–6; John Herdman, *Another Country: An Era in Scottish Politics and Letters* (Edinburgh, Thirsty Books, 2013), pp. 63–4. McGrath quoted from Gramsci in his 'Scotland: Up against It', in Brown (ed.), *Red Paper on Scotland,* p. 139; see also 'From Cheviots to Silver Darlings: John McGrath interviewed by Olga Taxidou', in Randall Stevenson and Gavin Wallace (eds.), *Scottish Theatre since the Seventies* (Edinburgh, Edinburgh University Press, 1996), pp. 153–4.

[36] The rector of Edinburgh University is elected by staff and students to represent their interests in university decision-making (at other ancient Scottish universities the office is elected only by students).

[37] John MacBean, review of *The Red Paper on Scotland, Scottish Worker,* vol. 2, no. 2, May 1975, p. 2.

which socialism might be advanced. As Tom Nairn recognised some years later, Gordon Brown's own introduction to the book was an artful synthesis of this debate that sought to reframe it as less about constitutional issues and more about how to secure popular control over economic development, a commitment that Brown argued should lead the left to reject both the SNP's vision of independence and an unvarnished unionism, since neither of these options offered meaningful change to the inequalities of wealth and power that bore down on the Scottish working class.[38] Some contributors were indeed highly sceptical of the SNP, notably Ray Burnett and John McGrath. Both observed that the true class character of the SNP was revealed by the absence of any strong internal socialist organisation seeking to win the party over to radical policy stances and to mobilise the working class behind it. But their clear sympathy for a distinctive form of Scottish socialism left them somewhat evasive in their ultimate tactical conclusions – the formation of a separate, probably pro-independence, Scottish socialist party appeared to be their recommendation.[39]

Other contributors were less dismissive of the SNP as the natural home for a radical nationalism. Tom Nairn, for example, expressed less overt antipathy to the SNP than in his previous interventions on Scottish politics. As we saw in Chapter 3, he now espoused a resigned acceptance of the irreversibility of the SNP's rise and the need to progress Scottish self-government under capitalist rather than socialist conditions. Nairn had been inspired by Burnett's earlier article on Gramsci to dissect the distinctive characteristics of Scottish civil society and national culture, ultimately recommending that Scottish autonomy should be achieved in the context of a federal or confederal system of European states in order to constrain the regressive nationalistic impulses that would otherwise come to the fore in an independent Scotland.[40] Bob Tait argued that the SNP should be positively supported as a progressive force and engaged with by socialists. In his view, the Scottish labour movement was constrained by its subordinate status within Britain; more radical accomplishments would be possible in an independent Scotland. Tait added

---

[38] Gordon Brown, 'Introduction: The Socialist Challenge', in Brown (ed.), *Red Paper on Scotland*, pp. 7–19; Tom Nairn, *Gordon Brown: Bard of Britishness* (Cardiff, Institute of Welsh Affairs, 2006), pp. 15–16.

[39] Burnett, 'Socialists and the SNP', pp. 124–5; McGrath, 'Scotland', p. 137.

[40] Tom Nairn, 'Old Nationalism and New Nationalism', in Brown (ed.), *Red Paper on Scotland*, pp. 22–57; see also Nairn's earlier remarks on Burnett in 'Culture and Nationalism: An Open Letter from Tom Nairn', *Scottish International*, vol. 6, no. 4, April 1973, pp. 8–9. See Chapter 3 for a more detailed account of Nairn's thinking in this period.

that it was *The Cheviot, the Stag and the Black, Black Oil* that expressed this politics best by showing

that a combination of analysis of Scottish history and the inspiration to revolt and seize control is a *sine qua non* of the reappropriation of assets, rights, dignity and of the revitalisation of a radical socialist spirit in Scotland. It seems to me that it has been in these recognitions that socialists and nationalists have found much common ground in their responses to the play.[41]

The strategy of Burnett and McGrath – of a party that sought to marry together socialism and nationalism – was to some extent tested empirically by the formation of the breakaway SLP by Jim Sillars in January 1976, a party that Bob Tait, in spite of his earlier support for the SNP, joined.[42] The SLP was a famously quixotic enterprise that failed to find that elusive political space between the Labour Party and the SNP. Ideologically, Sillars took as his starting point the popular endorsement of Scottish membership of the European Community in the 1975 referendum, a watershed which Sillars argued both rendered debates about whether an independent Scotland would be 'separatist' less relevant and simultaneously made the need for separate Scottish representation in European decision-making more urgent.[43] Whether the SLP was a party that supported full Scottish independence or an enhanced form of devolution (albeit including significant economic powers) was not initially clear from the public statements of key figures in the party but the SLP's position gradually shaded into outright support for independence following a transitional period in which a maximalist devolutionary settlement would govern Scotland.[44] The party combined support for 'independence in Europe' with a staunch socialism that distinguished it from the more Eurosceptical SNP of the 1970s and displayed some sympathy for models of decentralised popular economic ownership

[41] Bob Tait, 'The Left, the SNP and Oil', in Brown (ed.), *Red Paper on Scotland*, pp. 125–33, quote at p. 133.
[42] Owen Dudley Edwards, 'Socialism or Nationalism?', in Gavin Kennedy (ed.), *The Radical Approach: Papers on an Independent Scotland* (Edinburgh, Palingenesis Press, 1976), p. 99.
[43] Jim Sillars, 'Let's Sit at the Top Table in Europe', *The Highway*, July 1975, p. 6.
[44] Neal Ascherson, 'Sillars Decides to Go It Alone', *Scotsman*, 10 June 1975; Neal Ascherson, 'Sillars Puts New Party on Course', *Scotsman*, 19 January 1976; Neal Ascherson, 'Assembly "Stage to Freedom"', *Scotsman*, 22 October 1976; 'Our Voice in Europe', *Forward Scotland: Journal of the Scottish Labour Party*, no. 1, July 1976, pp. 4–5; Peter Chiene, 'Problems for the SLP', *Question*, no. 14, 22 October 1976, p. 2; 'Scottish Government', draft discussion paper, Scottish Labour Party, n.d. [c.1976], Scottish Labour Party Edinburgh Branch Papers, National Library of Scotland, Acc. 7472/9, pp. 3–6; Alison Livingstone, 'SLP Reconvened Conference Report', *Scottish Worker*, vol. 4, no. 2, February 1977, pp. 10–11.

influenced by the New Left.[45] The SLP was ultimately an ephemeral political organisation, splintering acrimoniously over both policy and personality differences before eventually winding up in 1981. One of the underlying conflicts that destabilised the party's brief life, noted by both Tom Nairn and George Kerevan (two of the many glittering names who were members of the SLP), was between a party leadership steeped in the traditional hierarchical style and workerist worldview of the Labour Party and a middle-class activist base enthused by the new issues and grass-roots democracy broadly associated with the New Left. But the high level of interest in the party among journalists, academics and the radical left was nonetheless an indicator that a significant appetite existed in these groups for a Scottish nationalism garbed in socialist clothes.[46] In this sense, the SLP was an ideological crucible in which important new political arguments were forged. Many influential figures in later Scottish political debate shared some level of involvement in the SLP (Sillars, Nairn, Kerevan, Neal Ascherson, Craig Beveridge, Ronald Turnbull, Lindsay Paterson, Bob Tait as well as the future SNP MSP and Minister Alex Neil (b. 1951) and the future Labour MPs John McAllion [b. 1948], Maria Fyfe [b. 1938] and Sheila Gilmore [b. 1949]).[47] Intriguingly, even Gordon Brown (a staunch Labour loyalist) wrote about Jim Sillars's early moves in the direction of the SLP that while politically inadvisable 'the weight of the policy argument appears to be on his side' insofar as any Scottish parliament should possess significant economic powers and Labour in Scotland should operate more autonomously of London.[48]

Social Democracy and Beyond

Perhaps not coincidentally, it was around the same time as the creation of the SLP that left-wing members of the SNP began to offer a more detailed

[45] Lindsay Paterson, 'What Kind of Scotland?' and Jim Sillars, 'Why I'm Not in the SNP', both in *Crann-Tàra*, no. 1, winter 1977, pp. 3, 4.

[46] Peter Chiene, 'Slimming Session at Stirling', *Question*, no. 15, 5 November 1976, p. 12; Tom Nairn, 'The SLP: Report on the First Year of a New Party', *Planet*, no. 37/38, May 1977, p. 16; George Kerevan, 'The Impending Crisis of the Scottish Left and How to Combat It', *Radical Scotland*, no. 24, December 1986/January 1987, p. 8; Henry Drucker, *Breakaway: The Scottish Labour Party* (Edinburgh, EUSPB, 1978), pp. 60–1, 133–46.

[47] The involvement of many of these figures in the SLP can be traced in the Scottish Labour Party Edinburgh Branch Papers, National Library of Scotland, Acc. 7472. In the case of Ascherson – better known as a commentator than an activist – it is notable how active he was in the Edinburgh branch. See also Neal Ascherson, 'The World of Woad!', *Forward Scotland: Journal of the Scottish Labour Party*, no. 1, July 1976, p. 7; Neal Ascherson, *Stone Voices* (London, Granta, 2002), pp. 90–1.

[48] Gordon Brown, 'Labour – Where the Strength Lies', *Question*, no. 4, January 1976, p. 11.

analysis of the relationship between their goal of independence and socialist ideology. A 1976 volume, *The Radical Approach: Papers on an Independent Scotland,* was critical of the *Red Paper* but drew on the wider socialist debates of the 1970s to make an unvarnished case for independence and support for the SNP.[49] With a foreword by Margo MacDonald, the book's contributors were figures on the left of the SNP such as the economist Gavin Kennedy (1940–2019) and the sociologist Isobel Lindsay (b. 1943). Both sought to connect the traditional decentralising impulses of Scottish nationalism to the participatory and communitarian New Left socialism of the 1960s as a means of moving beyond the 'social democracy' that had been adopted by the party in 1974.[50] In Kennedy's case, this led to an advocacy of an independent Scotland that was neither free market nor straightforwardly social democratic, since in Kennedy's view both economic models required large, bureaucratic corporate units of production – he favoured instead a worker-managed economy.[51]

Isobel Lindsay was an important figure in the campaign for Scottish self-government. As we will see in Chapter 5, her astute (and in retrospect correct) strategic analysis of the importance of gradual coalition-building to advancing independence would eventually put her at odds with the more confrontational form of politics preferred by others in the SNP. She had studied at Glasgow University before taking an academic post in sociology at Strathclyde University, and combined her academic work with activism in the peace movement and the SNP. Lindsay had been a parliamentary candidate for the SNP and held a number of senior roles in the party, including a stint as SNP Vice-Chair for Policy during the 1970s.[52] In *The Radical Approach,* Lindsay suggested that Scottish independence would tackle three problems that had come to the fore in recent radical sociological literature: the damaging impact of the centralised government of the twentieth century on peripheral cultures; the unequal distribution of power (as opposed to a single-minded focus on material inequality); and the loss of a sense of belonging and community membership. To deal with each of these issues, thought Lindsay, would require keeping 'as much decision-making as possible close to those whom it will most effect'. Crucially, though, Lindsay argued that the appropriate units for local political decision-making are best delineated by the extent to which a shared sense of community exists, as bequeathed by history and

[49] Gavin Kennedy, 'Introduction', in Kennedy (ed.), *Radical Approach*, pp. 1–2.
[50] Neal Ascherson, 'The Salad Days Are Over for the SNP', *Scotsman*, 27 May 1976.
[51] Gavin Kennedy, 'Scotland's Economy', in Kennedy (ed.), *Radical Approach*, pp. 54–7.
[52] Tom Freeman, 'Isobel Lindsay's Radical Road to Devolution', *Holyrood*, 1 March 2019, at www.holyrood.com/articles/inside-politics/isobel-lindsays-radical-road-devolution (accessed 2 October 2019).

culture, for example through the persistence of a robust national identity such as Scottishness. On this account, independence represented an essential starting point for a more participatory society in Scotland, though Lindsay hoped that this constitutional change would then lead to wider forms of local and industrial democracy. 'Scottish nationalism is open-ended', said Lindsay, 'it is a beginning not a conclusion'.[53]

The most prescriptive contribution to *The Radical Approach* was by Stephen Maxwell, at that time SNP Press Officer and a local councillor but shortly to become the SNP's Vice-Chair for Publicity. Maxwell, who we have already encountered several times in this book, was born in Scotland but brought up in England. He studied philosophy at Cambridge and international relations at the LSE. He then moved back to Scotland where he became increasingly involved in political work for the SNP.[54] Maxwell's contributions to political debate were always distinguished by an unusual degree of analytical precision and intellectual honesty, which in turn meant that at times he found himself arrayed against party orthodoxy. In *The Radical Approach*, his essay probed more deeply what the SNP might have meant by finally declaring itself to be a 'social democratic' party in 1974. Maxwell drew on New Left ideas to identify the significant social and economic policy shortcomings of the social democratic project that were visible in the 1970s: endemic sectional conflict between corporatist interest groups; the persistence of significant levels of poverty and inequality; and a centralised state that offered insufficient thought to the protection of the rights of individuals and local communities.[55] Given the weakness of the Scottish private sector, and its predominantly non-Scottish ownership, Maxwell believed that a Scottish social democracy would inevitably need to undertake a large programme of state investment and ownership in order to revitalise the Scottish economy and to make the most productive use of Scotland's oil wealth. But this would pose significant dangers:

The combination in an independent Scotland of a potentially overwhelming state power and a conspicuously weak private sector not only makes the social democratic model of a mixed economy dangerously inappropriate; it also challenges the SNP's commitment to the decentralisation of power.[56]

---

[53] Isobel Lindsay, 'Nationalism, Community and Democracy', in Kennedy (ed.), *Radical Approach*, pp. 21–6, quotes at 26.

[54] 'Obituary: Stephen Maxwell', *Scotsman*, 27 April 2012; 'Obituary: Stephen Maxwell', *Herald*, 27 April 2012.

[55] Stephen Maxwell, 'Beyond Social Democracy', in Kennedy (ed.), *Radical Approach*, pp. 9–12.

[56] Maxwell, 'Beyond Social Democracy', p. 14. See also Maxwell's similar remarks in 'The Implications of Prospective Independence: The Problem of State Power', *Nevis Quarterly*, no. 2, January 1979, pp. 14–20.

Maxwell therefore argued that the SNP should seek to move beyond social democracy by supporting a mixed economy that contained conventional nationalised industries, decentralised socially owned enterprises, and employee-owned companies.[57] He also suggested that the welfare state should be reformed with the introduction of a basic income scheme and a wide-ranging programme of constitutional reform undertaken to decentralise and democratise political power within Scotland.[58] In Maxwell's view, nationalism could serve as the popular force capable of initiating such radical change 'by publicising old ideals and proclaiming new standards, by accelerating the rate of social and economic change and by uniting different sectional groups behind a common aim'.[59] Although sceptical of romantic portrayals of Scottish culture as more radical and egalitarian than England's, Maxwell nonetheless thought that Scottish politics had long been anti-metropolitan and anti-establishment and that this impulse could be channelled into creating a participatory and radical Scottish democracy.[60]

Reviewing *The Radical Approach*, Tom Nairn sounded the cautionary note that, on the account of Maxwell, Lindsay et al., a new Scottish state would have to entrench itself against internal opponents and international forces while simultaneously pursuing radical measures of decentralisation and facilitating participatory democracy. Nairn was sympathetic to this agenda but thought that this new Scotland would undoubtedly need a strong state to accomplish it, one that 'will be different from the old English model, and will stand in a substantially different relationship to society'. In other words, Nairn concluded, *The Radical Approach* demonstrated that there was a marked convergence taking place between the ideologies of Scottish socialists and Scottish nationalists.[61] The public profile of the SNP in the late 1970s certainly reflected this more participatory or radical democratic strand of nationalist thinking, with proposals for increased state powers over the economy of an independent Scotland counterbalanced by an emphasis on state support for cooperatives and worker participation in industry. But the political intent behind this positioning was not specifically socialist. Key figures within the party instead hoped to style it as a party of 'radical democracy', empowering citizens against the corporate elites drawn from

---

[57] Maxwell, 'Beyond Social Democracy', pp. 14–15.

[58] Maxwell, 'Beyond Social Democracy', pp. 16–18.

[59] Maxwell, 'Beyond Social Democracy', p. 19.

[60] Maxwell, 'Beyond Social Democracy', p. 19; for a similar view from within the SNP see also Andrew Currie, 'The SNP and Participation', *Question*, no. 7, April 1976, pp. 8–10.

[61] Tom Nairn, 'The Radical Approach', *Question*, no. 10, July 1976, pp. 8–11, quote at p. 11.

politics, business and indeed the trade unions.[62] The status and power of the latter was a subject about which many Scottish nationalists were in fact rather ambivalent if not critical.[63]

The Spirit of '79

These ideas formed the intellectual context in which Maxwell, Kennedy and other like-minded figures (although not Lindsay) sought to give the SNP a clearer and more radical ideological profile as a left-wing party by forming an internal party faction, the '79 Group, after the disappointing referendum and general election results of that year. Writing immediately after the failure to achieve the necessary threshold of support in the 1979 devolution referendum, Neal Ascherson argued that the SNP itself 'lies at the root of the trouble' for failing to adopt a more clearly working-class political profile: 'Great masses of ordinary Scots may one day give their vote to a national party of self-government, but it will have to be a force standing far more boldly for radical democracy and for the interests of the working class to win their trust'.[64] Ascherson reflected a feeling among a number of nationalist intellectuals and activists that the referendum had revealed that Scottish self-government, and ultimately independence, could only be achieved with working-class rather than middle-class support, a point that Tom Nairn had impressed on Ascherson in a phone call the day after the referendum.[65] Nairn himself wrote that this 'new landscape of politics looks very like that hopefully imagined by the founders of the Scottish Labour Party three years ago'.[66]

Senior figures within the SNP were more sceptical. Even William Wolfe, who was probably the most sympathetic, thought that the SNP had lost its way in the late 1970s by failing to project a clear social democratic identity that synthesised the politics of social justice and self-government while appealing *across* social classes.[67] Nonetheless, it was the Ascherson/Nairn analysis of the Scottish electorate that influenced the formation of the '79 Group, which took up their challenge to

---

[62] Neal Ascherson, 'Nationalists Want Economic Prefects', *Scotsman*, 5 March 1976; Neal Ascherson, 'Party in Search of a Strategy', *Scotsman*, 7 June 1978.

[63] Stephen Maxwell, 'The Sacred Bullock', *Question*, no. 21, 4 February 1977, p. 7.

[64] Neal Ascherson, 'Back from the Depths on Black Friday', *Scotsman*, 3 March 1979.

[65] Ascherson, *Stone Voices*, pp. 105–6. But for criticism of this interpretation, see Bayne, 'The Impact of 1979', pp. 57–8.

[66] Tom Nairn, 'After the Referendum', *New Edinburgh Review*, no. 46, summer 1979, p. 9.

[67] William Wolfe, 'Comment on SNP Results and on Matters Affecting Them', memo, 12 May 1979, Robert McIntyre Papers, National Library of Scotland, Acc. 10090/139; William Wolfe, 'Strategy on Self-Government: A Discussion Paper', memo, May 1980, Gordon Wilson Papers, National Library of Scotland, Acc. 13099/35.

the SNP to become a more radical force. Although the story of the '79 Group has often been told,[68] the level of ideological debate that it produced tends to be dismissed as unimpressive – in large part because this was the retrospective verdict of Stephen Maxwell himself.[69] But Maxwell's verdict – rendered in the dog days of high Thatcherism – is too unforgiving, and neglects the extent to which the ideas debated by the '79 Group constituted a first attempt at what would later be hammered into a more precise and politically potent ideological position.

The '79 Group drew together long-standing members of the SNP left such as Maxwell himself, Andrew Currie (1936–2016) and Margo MacDonald, with left-wing members of the party who had joined in the 1970s. This latter group included intellectuals such as the historian and literary scholar Owen Dudley Edwards (b. 1938), the political scientist Jack Brand (1934–2013) and Gavin Kennedy (some of whom had come from the Labour Party and the SLP), and younger activists who were beginning to make a mark in the SNP, or worked in party HQ, such as Roseanna Cunningham (b. 1951), Alex Salmond (b. 1954) and Kenny MacAskill (b. 1958).[70] Jim Sillars also joined the Group when he entered the SNP in 1980. This formidable array of talent was further enhanced by the presence of Tom Nairn at the Group's events, fresh from his involvement in the SLP. The key theme that emerged from the Group's early political discussions was that the SNP had gone astray after its initial 1974 manifesto commitment to social democracy by blurring once again its ideological profile (a consequence in part of conflicting views among the enlarged SNP parliamentary group after 1974). The Group's founders argued that the SNP needed to deepen its left-wing commitments in order to win over working-class and public sector middle-class Labour voters since it was these disaffected groups that were most likely to challenge the status quo, though Group members also believed it would be possible to combine such an appeal with a much less centralised and bureaucratic model of socialism than Labour offered.[71] As

---

[68] Useful accounts of the '79 Group's formation, composition and history can be found in Henry Drucker, 'Crying Wolfe: Recent Divisions in the SNP', *Political Quarterly*, 50 (1979), pp. 503–8; 'Survey: The '79 Group: Where Are They Now?', *Radical Scotland*, no. 5, June/July 1983, pp. 7–9; Stephen Maxwell, 'The '79 Group: A Critical Retrospect', *Cencrastus*, 21 (1985), pp. 11–16; Bayne, 'The Impact of 1979', pp. 56–60; David Torrance, 'The Journey from the '79 Group to the Modern SNP', in Gerry Hassan (ed.), *The Modern SNP* (Edinburgh, Edinburgh University Press, 2009), pp. 162–76.

[69] Maxwell, '"79 Group', pp. 12–13; Torrance, 'Journey', pp. 173–4.

[70] Maxwell, '79 Group', pp. 11, 13.

[71] Stephen Maxwell, 'Radical Strategy for an SNP Revival', *Scotsman*, 15 June 1979; Roseanna Cunningham, 'The SNP '79 Group', *Crann-Tàra*, no. 8, autumn 1979, p. 5.

Nairn put it in a paper to the Group's first meeting on 31 May 1979, the devolution referendum and the 1979 general election marked 'the decisive end of one phase in the growth of Scottish nationalism' and in particular the natural demise of the SNP's 'peculiarly bland, all-purpose nationalist ideology'. Instead, Nairn argued, Scottish nationalism would now have to move left: 'Having failed to break through permanently on the Right of Labourism, it will try to the Left'. The results, Nairn predicted with characteristic confidence, 'will be far more interesting, and more congenial to socialists elsewhere', since 'a less compromising, more republican spirit will emerge from the setbacks'.[72]

Nairn's analysis of Britain and the British left was an important influence on the '79 Group's political thought. Stephen Maxwell posed the choice for the Group as between 'labourism' or 'socialism': Labour's vision, he argued, was unimaginative, defensive, moribund and limited in its emancipatory goals.[73] In a certain sense, he argued, Scottish Labour should be seen as 'Scotland's *first* nationalist party', but one that drew on Scotland's 'sense of grievance' and 'inferiority complex' to use 'the Scottish working class as so much electoral cannon fodder', rewarded only by the right-wing government that must inevitably emerge from Labour's 'compromise with English institutions'.[74] Recapitulating some of the themes of his 'Beyond Social Democracy', Maxwell advocated instead a participatory and decentralised market socialism, although some other voices in the Group were sceptical about how practical moves in this direction would prove to be in the immediate aftermath of independence.[75] A revealing paper by Andrew Currie on the multiple meanings of 'independence' gave a useful summary of the Group's initial ideological orientation. Currie argued that the Group aimed to advance three distinct senses of the term: the first was the straightforward support for Scottish popular sovereignty in a new nation state shared by virtually all Scottish nationalists, coupled with a rejection of both the parliamentary sovereignty

[72] Tom Nairn, 'Scotland after the Elections', in *SNP '79 Group Papers No. 1*, papers discussed at founding meeting on 31 May 1979, Belford Hotel, Edinburgh (no publisher/date), pp. 5–7; see also the similar arguments in Andrew Currie, 'Which Way Forward?' and Robert Crawford, 'In Pursuit of a Consensus', both in the same volume.

[73] Stephen Maxwell, 'Labourism or Socialism', in *SNP '79 Group Papers No. 1*, pp. 10–11.

[74] Stephen Maxwell, 'Scotland and the British Crisis', in *SNP '79 Group Papers No. 3*, report and commentary on conference on 'Scotland and the British Crisis', 23 February 1980 (no publisher/date), p. 11; emphasis in original.

[75] Maxwell, 'Labourism or Socialism', p. 11; see Roger Mullin, 'Socialism: State Control or Community Control?'; Robert Crawford, 'The Scottish Economy after Independence' and Stephen Maxwell, 'Market Socialism', all in *SNP '79 Group Papers No. 5*, report on conference 'Has the Scottish Private Sector a Future?', 17 May 1980, Glasgow (no publisher/date), pp. 16–21.

and hereditary authority embodied in the British constitution.[76] The second was a more instrumental sense of independence, as a means to secure reforms that would not be achievable from Westminster. Currie associated this view with the home rule tradition within the Scottish labour movement and authoritative figures such as Keir Hardie and James Maxton. 'The '79 Group', Currie argued, 'views independence as a means by which an egalitarian and emancipated, democratic society can be achieved within a Scottish state'.[77] A third, and more contested, sense of independence related to the degree of economic sovereignty that a Scottish state could exert while enmeshed in a global trading system. Currie reported that the '79 Group sought a Scottish society that was 'incompatible with the present economic order' in both the capitalist West and the Soviet bloc. This model of an independent Scotland would therefore involve 'the deliberate "distancing" of Scotland from the multi-national economy, the development of specialist manufacture of relatively labour-intensive, low volume products and the achievement of a high level of economic self-sufficiency'.[78]

This strongly sovereigntist, participatory and autarchic model of a socialist Scotland, and the political strategy that underpinned it, was given its clearest and most extended presentation by Maxwell in his pamphlet for the '79 Group, *The Case for Left-Wing Nationalism* (1981). Maxwell's starting point was an unflinching recognition that 'the historic sense of Scottish political and cultural nationality is too weak to serve as the basis for modern political nationalism'.[79] As we saw in Chapter 2, this was not Maxwell's view in the early 1970s, but he had now concluded that Scottish history lacked the grievances necessary to generate a potent form of cultural nationalism. Scotland's political union with the rest of Britain had largely been the result of bargaining between two national elites rather than coercion, while the subsequent economic benefits of, and relatively free cultural assimilation into, the British imperial project provided few clear-cut examples of anti-Scottish oppression. This absence of despotism in the relations between England and Scotland, argued Maxwell, meant that a different sort of nationalism would need to be constructed, one that sought to channel the late twentieth-century social and economic grievances felt by the Scottish

---

[76] Andrew Currie, 'Independence', in *SNP '79 Group Papers No. 1*, p. 8.
[77] Currie, 'Independence', p. 9.   [78] Currie, 'Independence', p. 9.
[79] Stephen Maxwell, 'The Case for Left-Wing Nationalism', *SNP '79 Group Paper No. 6* (Hamilton, Aberdeen People's Press, 1981), p. 24. Maxwell had previously made the same point in a letter to the editor, 'Strategy for an SNP Revival', *Scotsman*, 26 June 1979.

working class into a critique of the British state and a faith in the possibilities opened up by a Scottish state committed to socialism.[80]

In 1972 Maxwell had expressed some scepticism about whether Scottish electoral behaviour could fairly be described as left-wing, on the grounds that Labour in Scotland (unlike in Wales) had never consistently won more than 50 per cent of the Scottish vote. This had led Maxwell to argue that Scottish voters would be 'more likely to support a radical, pragmatic party than a left-wing one'.[81] But by 1981 Maxwell had shifted his position and now argued that Scottish voting patterns were somewhat distinct from those in England insofar as Scottish political culture was broadly anti-establishment, leaving the working classes and a section of the middle class ripe for a left-wing nationalism: 'The SNP should challenge for the Labour vote by presenting itself, inter alia, as a party better equipped than Labour to achieve the goals of full employment and social welfare.'[82] The challenge to Labour would have to be a robust one, and Maxwell offered a scathing analysis of Scottish Labour as a subordinate and ineffective political force, a vehicle for the Scottish middle class to mobilise 'the Scottish working class vote in support of a "dissenting" section of the English middle class which cannot count on the loyalty of its own working class'. The Scottish working class thus serves as 'the poor bloody infantry of the civil war within the English middle class which passes for politics in Britain' and in return gains nothing but 'chronic unemployment, some of the worst housing in Western Europe, record rates of ill health and forced migration. What matter if they fall, the council estates and industrial wastelands of Scotland will furnish abundant replacements.'[83] The emergence of the SDP and Labour's subsequent electoral travails in England served as further confirmation to Maxwell that 'the break-up of the Labour Party' was at hand (he was confident the SDP posed less of a problem for the SNP).[84]

Drawing on the analyses of the Scottish economy to be found in previous '79 Group papers and his own earlier work, Maxwell argued that the decline of Scottish manufacturing industry; the slow growth of any compensating increase in service employment; the increase in foreign

---

[80] Maxwell, 'Case', pp. 2–6.

[81] Stephen Maxwell, letter to the editor, *Scottish International*, vol. 5, no. 1, January 1972, p.18.

[82] Maxwell, 'Case', p. 17.

[83] Maxwell, 'Case', pp. 23–4; see also Maxwell's restatement of this critique of Scottish Labour in his 'Scotland's Cruel Paradox', *Radical Scotland*, no. 1, February/March 1983, pp. 12–14.

[84] Stephen Maxwell, 'SNP '79 Group Political Report Session 1980/81', memo, September 1981, Gavin Kennedy Papers, National Library of Scotland, Acc. 11565/23, pp. 1–2.

(non-Scottish) ownership of the nation's economic assets; and the rise of internationally integrated financial services all pointed to a failed Scottish private sector, incapable of revival except through radical public intervention. The nationalist economic appeal to Labour voters, Maxwell concluded, should therefore be a left-wing one: 'a major extension of the public sector in the form of improved public services, increased public finance for industry conditional on the adoption of cooperative ownership and other forms of industrial democracy, and public control of Scotland's financial institutions'.[85] Scotland's economic condition, and the distinctive voting patterns emergent in Scotland, offered 'an opportunity to create a new, aggressive sense of political nationality to challenge the traditional defensiveness which ties the working class to Labour. The SNP's target should be to establish itself as the radical Scottish alternative to the Labour Party.'[86] As Murray Pittock has observed, this attempt to shift the SNP's focus to 'seats it had never won' was 'an extraordinary political goal for a severely defeated political party to set itself, almost as if Labour had decided to target Tunbridge Wells in preference to Bury'.[87] Nonetheless, the SNP did pursue something like this audacious – and elusive – objective over the next thirty years, yet the way in which it worked out was to be somewhat different from the heady 1970s debates infused with themes from Gramsci and the New Left. In fact some of the great critics of a sclerotic labourism were to find themselves attracted back towards a more conventional interpretation of the Scottish Labour brand.

Labourism without the Labour Party

Stephen Maxwell observed retrospectively – and disapprovingly – that the Labour Party should be seen as a significant intellectual influence on the '79 Group.[88] He recalled suggesting at the Group's launch conference that it should style itself as an advocate of '"radical democracy" rather than socialism – only to be shot down by the accumulation of labourists in [the] SNP's ranks'.[89] In truth, Maxwell's own writings had

---

[85] Maxwell, 'Case', pp. 18–19.   [86] Maxwell, 'Case', p. 24.

[87] Murray Pittock, *The Road to Independence? Scotland in the Balance* (London, Reaktion, 2013), p. 91.

[88] Maxwell, ''79 Group', p. 12.

[89] Stephen Maxwell, 'Social Policy and the Constitutional Debate', *Radical Scotland*, no. 39, June/July 1989, p. 16. The published version of Maxwell's paper omitted the final paragraph included in the earlier draft circulated at the launch conference, which called for 'radical democracy' rather than 'socialism' as an overarching goal: compare Maxwell, 'Labourism or Socialism' with his 'Scotland: Labourism or Socialism', May 1979, Gavin Kennedy Papers, National Library of Scotland, Acc. 11565/23, p. 4.

walked an uneasy line between a supra-social democratic politics and a more straightforward replication of assumptions deeply embedded in Labour's political culture. Not least of these assumptions was a model of class politics that saw the industrial working classes as the key agent of social progress and hence Scottish nationalism's chief task as winning over these working-class Labour voters to independence. One of Maxwell's later criticisms of the '79 Group was its failure to recognise that other social groups – service sector workers, the middle class, women in paid work – were of increasing political significance.[90] The most effective critics of the '79 Group from within the SNP had in fact made a similar point at the time. Jim Fairlie (b. 1940), SNP Vice-Chair for Policy and Deputy Leader from 1981 to 1984, agreed that the SNP should seek to displace Labour but criticised the '79 Group for failing to grasp the diversity of the working classes, with regional differences and a large working-class Conservative vote disturbing any straightforward picture of a united working-class electorate.[91] Isobel Lindsay, a natural ally of many of the members of the '79 Group, offered a similar critique. She later recalled arguing to the members of the Group that 'your notion of the working class hasn't kept up with reality, because they still kind of saw the working class as Clydeside shipbuilders' rather than recognising 'the feminisation of the labour force' and the growing service sector.[92]

This more subtle argument about the possible social bases of nationalism was glossed over at the time by the members of the '79 Group (including Maxwell), who instead presented their internal opponents as cleaving to a fundamentalist appeal on the basis of a shared cultural 'Scottishness' rather than economic or social interests.[93] It was only much later that this point about the changing structure of Scottish society was to become salient to SNP strategy (as it also became central to Labour's rethinking).[94] Instead, after the '79 Group sparked an acrimonious internal conflict within the SNP and was ultimately disbanded in 1982, the approach of independence supporters seeking to yoke nationalism and socialism together was to deepen their appeal to traditional Labour values and traditions. Since the mid 1980s saw Thatcherism at its

---

[90] Maxwell, '79 Group', pp. 12–13.

[91] Jim Fairlie to Gordon Wilson, n.d. [c.1980–1], Gordon Wilson Papers, National Library of Scotland, Acc. 13099/35.

[92] Isobel Lindsay, quoted in Freeman, 'Isobel Lindsay's Radical Road to Devolution'.

[93] Stephen Maxwell, 'SNP '79 Group Political Report, Annual General Meeting August 1980', memo, Gavin Kennedy Papers, National Library of Scotland, Acc. 11565/23, pp. 1–2.

[94] Stephen Maxwell, 'The Scottish Middle Class and the National Debate', in Tom Gallagher (ed.), *Nationalism in the Nineties* (Edinburgh, Polygon, 1991), pp. 126–51.

political peak and the beginning of Labour's journey away from the left, it seemed reasonable to suppose that presenting Scottish nationalism as the custodian of the lost virtues of the Scottish labour movement might indeed yield popular dividends.

The most eloquent exponent of this point of view was Jim Sillars, who had arrived at support for Scottish independence from a working-class Labour background, having worked for the STUC and served as the Labour MP for South Ayrshire from 1970 to 1975 before breaking away to found the SLP.[95] Sillars's memoir and political testament, *Scotland: The Case for Optimism* (1986), drew on the accumulated moral authority of his own political experience to characterise Scottish independence as the logical conclusion for Labour supporters. Kevin Dunion (b. 1955), the founding editor of the pro-home rule magazine *Radical Scotland*, observed in a perceptive review that Sillars articulated a 'minimalist nationalism' grounded on 'economic advantage coupled with a notion of self-respect' rather than cultural distinctiveness, with the aim of 'reducing the entrance fee to nationalism' for Labour voters. Dunion saw much of the book's thinking as an articulate restatement of ideas 'rehearsed in the '79 Group', but this underestimated the degree to which Sillars cast aside the Group's New Left-inflected criticisms of Labour in favour of a more conventional defence of Labour's track record.[96] Sillars in fact reprimanded figures in the SNP for their criticisms of Labour, which he argued were too sweeping and liable to alienate potential converts. He offered a glowing tribute to the labour movement that could rival any sentimental oration ever delivered at Labour Party conference:

The Labour Party is the most important institution in the history of the working people and that part of the intelligentsia which gives itself to progressive causes. Labour was not born in a vacuum but emerged from a movement of struggle for justice which had its roots buried in the formative years of the industrial revolution. The heartbreak, the sense of solidarity, and the stepping-stone victories of that struggle are in its genes. Even although it is a twentieth-century creation, it is in direct descent from the poor, their leaders and their sacrifices of previous times. There is too the history of success to which the Labour Party can lay claim. At the parliamentary and local government level, Labour has been central to the advancement made in housing, education, the welfare services and the creation of an atmosphere in which concern for people can flourish.[97]

[95] Sillars's biography is well told in Arnold Kemp, 'Pushing Water Uphill', in his *Hollow Drum: Scotland since the War* (Glasgow, Neil Wilson, 1993), pp. 154–65; and in Gerry Hassan, 'Jim Sillars', in Hassan and Mitchell (eds.), *Scottish National Party Leaders* (London, Biteback, 2016), pp. 409–34.

[96] Kevin Dunion, 'The Philosopher's Stone', *Radical Scotland*, no. 21, June/July 1986, p. 32.

[97] Jim Sillars, *Scotland: The Case for Optimism* (Edinburgh, Polygon, 1986), p. 25.

In his account of his political views, Sillars declared his commitment to an ethical socialism similar to the beliefs of Keir Hardie and other founders of the ILP and Labour Party, not to mention more recent British Labour figures such as Sillars's own hero, Aneurin Bevan. Sillars argued that democratic socialism required 'converting a significant proportion of society to socialist ethics and ideals', and hence altering 'some of the fundamentals in the character of the people', such as 'greed, the desire to acquire power over others and a propensity to exploit human need for private gain'.[98] This was a hard, gradual road to socialism that would require strenuous efforts at popular persuasion and education.

But Sillars also argued that these ideas, and the political tradition associated with them, had heavily influenced Scottish society in particular: 'Scots still hold firmly to ideas about common care and concern for humanity and the need for a sense of community solidarity.'[99] This was not, he added, because of some intrinsic moral superiority of the Scots, 'but because our history, experience, size and homogeneity makes us more open to its salient features – responsibility and obligations to the community, the sense of solidarity it creates, the unremitting effort to harness economic forces to serve the people and its freedom from hatred'.[100] In particular, Sillars argued that it was the Scottish working class whose material needs and interests could be mobilised behind this vision and persuaded that it was only through Scottish self-government that they would be able to achieve social justice.[101] For example, an extensive programme of public sector investment and state planning was needed to achieve full employment in Scotland – something that Sillars maintained would first require an independent Scottish state.[102] This was because after the 1970s English politics had begun 'an irreversible move to the right' whereas at the same time 'Scots are coming to perceive their national interests as different and better served by a different political philosophy and economic programme'.[103] The argument that Scotland possessed 'different goals and values to that other country south of the border' – which appeared to become more empirically verifiable as the 1980s and 1990s progressed – provided left Scottish nationalists with a rhetorical lever that the '79 Group had ultimately lacked.[104]

Further weight was added to this case by the Scottish struggles against deindustrialisation during the 1970s and 1980s. The epic quality of the

---

[98] Sillars, *Scotland*, p. 135.   [99] Sillars, *Scotland*, p. 140.
[100] Sillars, *Scotland*, pp. 142–3.   [101] Sillars, *Scotland*, pp. 144–61.
[102] Sillars, *Scotland*, pp. 162–80.   [103] Sillars, *Scotland*, pp. 94–5.
[104] Jim Sillars, 'Freedom and Order', *Cencrastus*, no. 34, summer 1989, p. 17; Isobel Lindsay, 'Divergent Trends', *Radical Scotland*, no. 29, October/November 1987, pp. 14–15.

union-led battles for industrial survival in Scottish ship building, coal mining, car manufacturing, and steel making blurred together class and national identities, aiding the injection of the classic themes of Labour politics into Scottish nationalist thinking. The efforts of the workers in these and other industries to maintain their livelihood in the face of decisions meted out from London, or the remote headquarters of multinational corporations, were perceived as national rather than sectional demands, and a strong association developed in this period between working-class politics and efforts to secure home rule for Scotland.[105] This confluence of the politics of national identity and class gave nationalists an opportunity to present industrial closures as an attack on Scottish interests, cementing the link between constitutional change and the industrial working class just as dramatic processes of economic change were reshaping the Scottish economy and social structure.

The most powerful statement of this view was not in fact made by a member of the SNP but by the novelist William McIlvanney in his 1987 Donaldson Lecture to the SNP's annual conference, 'Stands Scotland Where It Did?'.[106] McIlvanney, like Sillars, came from a working-class background in Ayrshire, identified politically as a socialist, and could authentically lay claim to the attractive historical narrative of the Scottish labour movement. McIlvanney channelled his fury at growing social inequality under the Thatcher government into a wider argument that the Conservatives were seeking to destroy the distinctiveness of Scottish identity. It was a government, said McIlvanney, 'determined to unpick the very fabric of Scottish life and make it over into something quite different'.[107] McIlvanney thought that the essence of Scottish identity was not to be found in invocations of a romantic past, rooted in the culture of the Highlands or the medieval trappings of statehood. Rather 'the most nourishing roots of the Scottish identity, the roots that

---

[105] Phillips, *Industrial Politics of Devolution*; Jim Phillips, Valerie Wright and Jim Tomlinson, 'Deindustrialisation, the Linwood Car Plant and Scotland's Political Divergence from England in the 1960s and 1970s', *Twentieth Century British History*, 30 (2019), pp. 399–423. The '79 Group aimed to pursue this issue but the Group was dissolved before it could be fully developed: Alex Salmond et al., 'The Scottish Industrial Resistance', *'79 Group Paper No. 7* (Hamilton, Aberdeen People's Press, 1982).

[106] One metric of McIlvanney's influence is that when interviewing a range of Scottish opinion formers in the 2000s Gerry Hassan found that 'the Willie McIlvanney view of Scotland' as anti-Thatcherite was a standard shorthand reference (both positive and negative) used by a number of interviewees: Gerry Hassan, *Independence of the Scottish Mind* (Basingstoke, Palgrave, 2014), pp. 105–6, 108, 109, 116.

[107] William McIlvanney, 'Stands Scotland Where It Did?', Donaldson Lecture, 1987, in his *Surviving the Shipwreck* (Edinburgh, Mainstream, 1991), p. 245. McIlvanney's lecture was printed at the time in *Radical Scotland*, no. 30, December 1987/January 1988, pp. 19–22.

offer potential for continuing growth, have their soil not in the historically romanticised past but in the more recent industrial history of the nineteenth and twentieth centuries'. It was in 'the characteristic ways we found of responding to the industrialisation of our country' – and by this McIlvanney really meant the struggles of the labour movement – that Scottish identity could be located.[108] Out of this struggle had emerged a humanising ethic founded on social justice and community which, McIlvanney claimed, was entirely opposed to the morality of individualism and material calculation prioritised by the Conservatives.[109] But the problem was that the democratic wishes of the Scottish electorate for a fairer society remained unregistered by the results of British general elections at which the preferences of the South of England necessarily predominated. 'Effectively', said McIlvanney, 'at this moment, we do not have democracy in Scotland'.[110] McIlvanney was elusive in the lecture about whether he ultimately favoured devolution or independence but his argument for 'some kind of power structure separate from Westminster' could certainly be read as favouring a radical break from Britain (in later years McIlvanney was more explicitly a supporter of Scottish independence and voted 'yes' in the 2014 referendum).[111] But he connected his desire to build a Scottish socialism with the radical legacy of the British Labour government of 1945–51. As he put it, 'government changes lives' – Attlee's administration had transformed the life chances of millions just as Thatcher's was ruining the lives of a generation – so 'we had better find a way to change government – and fast'.[112]

All of this was in some ways a paradoxical outcome of the political ideas first elaborated in the 1970s. In effect, the case for Scottish independence had become an argument about how to recapture the authenticity of an earlier, pristine British labour movement, before the compromises and vacillations of the current Labour leadership. What had begun in the 1970s as an attempt to get beyond the paradigm of a defensive 'labourism' had on the contrary by the late 1980s become an attempt to rescue that very same 'labourism' from betrayal by its nominal exponents. Scottish nationalism now rested its appeal on the romance of the British Labour tradition and the need for a strong, fairly conventional social democratic state. But this was not to be the last twist in the case for left-wing nationalism.

---

[108] McIlvanney, 'Stands Scotland', p. 247.
[109] McIlvanney, 'Stands Scotland', pp. 248–9.
[110] McIlvanney, 'Stands Scotland', p. 251.
[111] McIlvanney, 'Stands Scotland', p. 251; William McIlvanney, *Dreaming Scotland* (Edinburgh, Saltire Society, 2014).
[112] McIlvanney, 'Stands Scotland', pp. 252–3, quotes at 253.

A Walk on the Supply Side

By the late 1980s, the economic policy options of an independent Scotland were overdue for another forensic audit by Scottish nationalists. Important studies had been produced in the 1970s that clearly laid out the trade-offs and choices that would face a Scottish state seeking to establish its credibility with trading partners and financial markets. Even at this stage, this more cautious analysis placed greater emphasis than left nationalists on the need to go beyond a purely Keynesian demand-management approach to the Scottish economy. Instead, economists writing on Scottish independence urged nationalists to embrace supply-side reforms designed to foster greater occupational and geographical mobility (through training and skills policy and reforms to social housing tenure); to attract greater inward investment; and to raise real wages through income tax cuts rather than increasing costs to employers (which would in turn also provide a demand-side stimulus to the Scottish economy). The significance of the North Sea oil revenue was therefore that it would create the space for such economic restructuring by allowing the state to compensate and retrain those who lost out from these reforms; invest new resources in industrial development; and cut corporate and income taxes (as well as enabling the creation of a state investment fund). In short, these economists prescribed a significant injection of market forces – as well as more strategic forms of state intervention – into the Scottish economy as a means of ensuring a more dynamic economic performance under independence.[113] In retrospect this work was not taken as seriously as it should have been by a national movement that was more enthused by the radical energies of the 1970s.[114] Reviewing one of these books, Neal Ascherson concluded that it merely showed 'that there is no serious obstacle to running a successful bourgeois mixed economy in an independent Scotland. Can that, in a country where nationalist and revolutionary traditions have always been interlaced (though seldom fused), be the happy end of the story? I suspect not.'[115]

---

[113] Donald MacKay (ed.), *Scotland 1980: The Economics of Self-Government* (Edinburgh, Q Press, 1977); Tony Clarty and Alexander McCall Smith (eds.), *Power and Manoeuvrability: The International Implications of an Independent Scotland* (Edinburgh, Q Press, 1978); see also Clarty's later retrospective on the latter book, 'Independence and the Scottish Political Imagination', *Cencrastus*, no. 11, New Year 1983, pp. 26–8.

[114] Though internally the SNP did convene an economic strategy committee that explored some of these issues: see the papers in the Gavin Kennedy Papers, National Library of Scotland, Acc. 11565/22 and the relatively sober David Simpson, *The Economics of Self-Government* (Edinburgh, SNP Research Office, n.d. [c.1982]).

[115] Neal Ascherson, 'Future Imperfect', *New Edinburgh Review*, no. 44, winter 1978, p. 28. The economic journalist Andrew Hargrave was also critical of this economic analysis on similar grounds: 'Scotland 1980: A Critique', *Question*, no. 32, 8 July 1977, pp. 4–5.

In the 1980s these initial economic analyses were not followed up in any systematic way and instead certain broad economic assumptions characterised nationalist arguments, notably that a Scottish state would enjoy sufficient policy space to pursue a countercyclical fiscal and monetary policy in line with the Scottish rather than the British business cycle; that a Scottish state could promote more Scottish ownership of industry, whether in the private or public sectors; that the dividend of North Sea oil could be channelled into higher social spending and investment; and that state-led investment and planning would revive Scottish manufacturing industry.[116] Core elements of this basically socialist, and somewhat autarchic, view of the relationship between a new Scottish state and the market economy were placed under significant pressure during the 1990s, as economic policy debates focused on the constraints exercised by European and global economic integration on national economic strategies and on the transition of mature capitalist economies from their traditional manufacturing bases to service sector industries. Famously, the Labour Party undertook a significant revision of its economic policy stance in response to these developments, but so too did the SNP.[117] The debate on Scottish self-government, which in the 1970s took as its primary subject whether an elected Scottish assembly would possess sufficient powers to plan and reorganise the Scottish economy, began to focus instead on whether a Scottish parliament had the powers to make the Scottish economy more internationally competitive and to distribute the proceeds of economic growth more equally.[118]

The key figure in recasting the case for left-wing nationalism after the 1980s was the '79 Group alumnus and former Royal Bank of Scotland economist, Alex Salmond, who led the SNP between 1990 and 2000 and then again between 2004 and 2014.[119] Salmond was by some distance the most important politician to advocate independence in modern Scottish history. Among his many political insights was understanding

---

[116] For an early exposition of this case, see Alex Salmond, 'The Economics of Independence', *West Lothian Standard*, spring 1977, pp. 4–5, copy in Robert McIntyre Papers, National Library of Scotland, Acc. 10090/195.

[117] Andrew Glyn (ed.), *Social Democracy in Neo-Liberal Times: The Left and Economic Policy since 1980* (Oxford, Oxford University Press, 2001); Stephanie Mudge, *Leftism Reinvented: Western Parties from Socialism to Neo-Liberalism* (Cambridge MA, Harvard University Press, 2018).

[118] This arc mirrored the trajectory of British economic policy debate more generally: see David Edgerton, *The Rise and Fall of the British Nation: A Twentieth Century History* (London, Allen Lane, 2018).

[119] For excellent biographies of Salmond, see David Torrance, *Salmond: Against the Odds* (Edinburgh, Birlinn, 2011); Murray Ritchie, 'Alex Salmond (Act I)' and James Mitchell, 'Alex Salmond (Act II)', both in James Mitchell and Gerry Hassan (eds.), *Scottish National Party Leaders* (London, Biteback, 2016), pp. 281–99, 325–48.

that the economic credibility of an independent Scotland would be critical to winning majority support for it. During the 1990s he therefore began to argue that it would be possible to combine a vision of Scotland as an internationally competitive economy with support for a strong welfare state – and that it was this combination that constituted social democracy as practised for example in Scandinavia.[120] Salmond welcomed the ratification of the Single European Act in 1987 in part because he recognised that it enormously simplified the economic argument that nationalists would need to prosecute in order to win independence – since Scottish membership of the EEC would ensure continued trading links and freedom of movement across the border with England – but also because he argued it would open up opportunities for Scottish industry to focus on exports and winning new markets. He recognised that participation in the single market would limit the sort of industrial policies that an independent Scotland could pursue but was sanguine about this: 'the desultory rear-guard actions of hanging on to what we have has yielded few long-term results. Better now to take a walk on the supply side in concentrating on how we can project the Scottish company sector into Europe and beyond.'[121] As we will see in Chapter 5, this was one example of a wider rethinking within the SNP at this time about European integration and its interaction with national sovereignty.

The first extended elaboration of Salmond's reading of the new economic terrain of the 1990s came in a series of speeches in 1993, after the 1992 general election had removed Jim Sillars from political prominence. These were notable both for the foregrounding of 'social democratic' rather than 'socialist' as the descriptor of the SNP's ideological position and for explicitly endorsing the private sector rather than state industrial policy as the key driver of economic growth. Instead, Salmond argued, the state should play a role in strategic economic direction by investing in education and training, improving infrastructure, spending on housing, and directing Scottish energy resources toward Scottish industry. A separate Scottish monetary policy would avoid the high interest rates

---

[120] Nordic social democracy had been a long-standing source of inspiration for Scottish nationalists: see for example Clive Archer and Stephen Maxwell (eds.), *The Nordic Model: Studies in Public Policy Innovation* (Farnborough, Gower, 1980); Stephen Maxwell, 'Norway's Economic Lessons for Scotland', *Radical Scotland*, no. 25, February/March 1987, pp. 14–17.

[121] Alex Salmond, 'Scotland in Europe: Living with the Single European Act', *Radical Scotland*, no. 34, August/September 1988, pp. 10–11, quote at p. 11. For criticism of this analysis of the European single market from a nationalist perspective, see Stephen Maxwell, 'Scotland International', *Cencrastus*, no. 35, winter 1989, pp. 15–18. But Maxwell's opposition to the new SNP slogan of 'independence in Europe' was by this point a minority view.

necessary to cool down the overheated South-East at the expense of Scottish economic growth.[122] However, there were already signs at this stage that Salmond and his colleagues were conscious that there were limits to the autonomy of monetary policy for a small country in a globalised economy and were beginning to entertain some form of post-independence currency coordination, either with sterling or with the nascent European Monetary System.[123] The SNP policy document that worked Salmond's ideas into a more formal statement of party doctrine also floated the possibility of an independent Scotland lowering business taxation in order to run 'a more competitive corporate tax regime than that prevailing south of the border'.[124]

Salmond continued to hone this case over the next decade but as he did so there was a perceptible shift in his case for independence towards the political centre. These were the years in which devolution was finally delivered to Scotland but also the years in which the Labour Party's moderate governing programme achieved electoral hegemony in Britain and Scotland. The SNP's tax-raising campaign for the first Scottish Parliament elections in 1999 proved to be a scarring experience for the SNP leadership, analogous to Labour's trauma in the 1992 general election, since it apparently demonstrated that there was limited electoral appetite for increased public spending funded by higher income tax rates.[125] For a time, it seemed an open question as to whether the very goal of Scottish independence had itself become outmoded and rendered less relevant by devolution, as the proponents of devolution in the Labour Party had intended. If the Conservatives were now politically marginal and Scottish democratic autonomy achieved within the Union, what *was* the political case for independence?

In response, Salmond and other leading figures in the SNP imbibed some of the prevailing political wisdom about the new era of globalised capitalism. The leading public outrider for a new form of nationalism that embraced the market economy was George Kerevan, who we last encountered as a Trotskyist member of the SLP. Kerevan had initially

---

[122] Peter Jones, 'SNP Leader Signals Economic Policy Shift', *Scotsman*, 7 August 1993; Ken Smith, 'Salmond Puts the Case for the Economics of Independence', *Herald*, 7 August 1993; Peter Jones, 'Salmond Set for Test of New Policies', *Scotsman*, 18 August 1993; Peter Jones, 'Dedicated Leader of the Band', *Scotsman*, 19 August 1993.

[123] Scottish Centre for Economic and Social Research, *Monetary Policy Options for an Independent Scotland* (Edinburgh, Scottish Centre for Economic and Social Research, n.d. [1989]).

[124] SNP, *For the Good of Scotland: Towards a Better Scotland* (Edinburgh, SNP, November 1995), pp. v, ix.

[125] William Miller, 'Modified Rapture All Round: The First Elections to the Scottish Parliament', *Government and Opposition*, 34 (1999), pp. 299–322.

moved from the far left to the Labour Party, embracing the ascendancy of Tony Benn and the rainbow alliance politics of the new urban left pioneered by Ken Livingstone's Greater London Council. Within Scottish Labour Kerevan had argued that the party should pursue a new broad-based electoral alliance based around an assertion of Scottish popular sovereignty rather than a traditional labourism rooted in the working class. He thought such an alliance could bring together the working class with a radical section of the middle class and other marginalised groups to support economic modernisation via a democratisation of the state, rather than through a more conventional Labour agenda.[126] This was in fact something like the posture that Scottish Labour occupied during the 1990s (as we will see in Chapter 5), but Kerevan himself became dissatisfied with Tony Blair's leadership of the party (in particular Blair's perceived equivocations on devolution when he committed Labour to a referendum on it) and defected to the SNP.[127]

In the wake of the 1999 Scottish Parliament election Kerevan used his weekly column in the pages of the *Scotsman* (of which he became an associate editor in 2000) to advocate a libertarian nationalism that sought to win the support of a rising generation that was in his view more apolitical and less inclined to support large bureaucratic projects of social reform than the baby boomers who currently dominated Scottish public life. Instead of making the SNP 'a John Smith-type moderate Labour Party', Kerevan argued that the SNP should cultivate an anti-paternalist politics that sought to enhance 'personal and community choice' through lower taxes, a less expansive state, and a more dynamic market economy. Kerevan framed the strategic choice for the SNP as moving beyond a romantic left-wing view of Scottish independence to appeal to 'the bankers, entrepreneurs and software writers who have to take the SNP into the twenty-first century'. This should be done, he said, by redefining independence as 'independence from the bureaucratic Whitehall state. Independence from the nanny quango state here in Scotland itself. And independence from the increasingly self-absorbed Brussels bureaucracy.'[128] Philosophically, Kerevan identified this position as a classical

---

[126] George Kerevan, 'Labourism Revisited', *Chapman*, 35/36, July 1983, pp. 25–31; Kerevan, 'Impending Crisis', pp. 7–9.
[127] 'Kerevan Says More Members Will Quit Labour', *Herald*, 15 July 1996.
[128] George Kerevan, 'Back to the Drawing Board for Nationalists', *Scotsman*, 10 May 1999; George Kerevan, 'Tax System That Can Unite Scotland', *Scotsman*, 16 August 1999; George Kerevan, 'Remember, There Is No Such Thing as Inevitability in Politics', *Scotsman*, 20 September 1999; George Kerevan, 'The Way Forward for SNP Success', *Scotsman*, 17 January 2000.

liberal one that drew on Adam Smith's combination of economic individualism and 'communitarian morality' to claim that voluntary action rather than state coercion would be for the most part sufficient to create 'the friendly and compassionate society we all wish to live in'. Kerevan argued that Scottish independence should therefore be portrayed electorally as about decreasing the importance of the state and politicians so that the market, a liberal personal morality, and voluntary collective action could be combined in a Scotland 'free of bureaucracy and taxes'.[129]

Kerevan deliberately pitched his ideas as controversially as possible but he had undoubtedly tapped into a growing interest among Scottish nationalists in how the apparently hegemonic language of market economics might be pressed into service for the independence cause. One indicator of this was that Alex Salmond himself increasingly looked to Ireland as much as to Scandinavia as a model of the kind of successful small trading economy Scotland could become once independent.[130] There was an obvious logic to this – it would have been political malpractice to neglect the economic boom enjoyed by the one nation to have seceded from the United Kingdom and which had strong social and cultural links with Scotland. A further electoral bonus was that this parallel also underlined the seriousness with which Salmond and his colleagues were now addressing the historic weakness of the SNP among Scottish Catholics, the vast majority of whom were of Irish descent. On the other hand, the economic and social policy record of the Irish Republic was at odds with the achievements of Nordic social democracy that Salmond had previously admired. One theme which Salmond thought united the economic strategies of both the Nordic social democracies and Ireland was the use of government policy tools to give their respective national economies a 'competitive edge' that would attract business investment. In particular, Salmond argued that significantly lower corporation tax would both entice businesses to relocate to Scotland and increase corporation tax revenue overall. He argued that the Laffer curve – which purported to show that reducing taxes could nonetheless increase the overall tax take and was a key plank of New Right supply-side economics – applied to business taxation but

---

[129] George Kerevan, 'This Way Forward for the SNP, Mr Swinney', *Scotsman*, 22 September 2000; George Kerevan, 'The Utopian Guff of Tommy Sheridan', *Scotsman*, 17 November 2000.

[130] Alex Salmond, 'Unleash the Power to Create Our Own Tiger Economy', *Herald*, 20 March 1996; Alex Salmond, 'Irish Show Scots Road to Success', *Irish Times*, 1 May 1997; Torrance, *Alex Salmond*, pp. 219–21, 241–2, 297–8.

not to income taxes.[131] In Salmond's view, both Ireland and Nordic economies such as Finland exemplified the wisdom of an economic strategy based on investment in education and training, participation in European economic integration, fiscal discipline and a reduction in corporate taxation.[132]

This economic analysis was supported by another former member of the '79 Group turned MSP, Kenny MacAskill, in his book, *Building a Nation* (2004). MacAskill started from the now familiar premise that it was essential for Scottish nationalism to have a clear political identity as a social democratic movement, but his definition of that political identity was one that accepted the strongest – and crudest – version of the globalisation argument. MacAskill noted the attractions of Swedish social democracy but flatly concluded that 'whilst the Swedish social welfare model may have been possible in the past it is not an option now'.[133] The rigours of global economic competition (not least from Ireland itself) were such that it would not be possible for Scotland to pursue a high tax social model – instead it must seek a 'competitive edge' (MacAskill adopted Salmond's use of this phrase) by reducing business taxation.[134] In the past, the SNP had campaigned against industrial closures, he recalled (having led some of them himself), but 'when more recently closure came at Motorola no such action occurred. Neither because the closure was less catastrophic nor because the Party was less supportive of those afflicted but simply because nothing could be done.'[135] MacAskill offered instead a vision of an independent Scotland competing in a modern knowledge economy, with the state investing in public goods such as education and health, reducing business taxes to boost overall revenues, and constructing a welfare state with many universal elements but also recognising that 'universality of each and every benefit is unsustainable'.[136]

A more extravagant, and no longer social democratic, version of this case was subsequently made by the SNP MSP Michael Russell (b. 1953) and the Scottish-Canadian businessman Dennis MacLeod in their book, *Grasping the Thistle* (2006). They straightforwardly adopted the rhetoric of

[131] Alex Salmond, *The Economics of Independence* (Glasgow, Strathclyde University Economics Department, 2003), pp. 40–3. For the origins of the Laffer curve and its ideological pedigree on the right, see Jude Wanniski, 'Taxes, Revenues, and the "Laffer Curve"', *Public Interest*, winter 1978, pp. 3–16. The phrase 'competitive edge' had earlier been used in the same context in the SNP's *For the Good of Scotland*, pp. 6, 9.
[132] Salmond, *Economics*, pp. 51–5.
[133] Kenny MacAskill, *Building a Nation: Post-Devolution Nationalism in Scotland* (Edinburgh, Luath Press, 2004), p. 52.
[134] MacAskill, *Building*, pp. 52–3.   [135] MacAskill, *Building*, p. 53.
[136] MacAskill, *Building*, pp. 54–60, quote at p. 58.

the neoliberal right by arguing that an independent Scotland should offer 'economic freedom' to its citizens, claiming that to do so 'we need to reduce the size of government in our country'.[137] Written at the height of Labour's programme of increased public spending, Russell and MacLeod even made the historically unprecedented nationalist argument that the UK government was probably spending too much on Scotland and hence depressing Scotland's economic growth.[138] Their prescriptions were a remarkable list: extensive spending cuts, the marketization of public services (including the NHS), and significant tax reductions, including the complete abolition of inheritance and corporation taxes and a 25 per cent cut in every band of income tax.[139] As they put it with some understatement: 'we are no longer great fans of a wide application of the principle of universality', although they did favour some form of guaranteed minimum income for all citizens.[140] As practical proposals, these ideas had little purchase and were intentionally presented as noisily as possible. Although Russell had been a close ally of Salmond's, Salmond himself was privately perturbed by its political implications when he read a draft of it before publication.[141] Nonetheless, there was a sense in which Russell (like Kerevan) was also an important outrider for Scottish nationalism at a time when future political progress seemed to require some dilution of its left-wing character.

In 2008 Alex Salmond – by then First Minister in the first SNP government – gave a speech at Harvard University that summarised the new SNP view of Scotland's economic prospects. He lauded Scotland as an example of the kind of 'small, open and dynamic economy' for which 'the winds of globalisation are blowing strongly in our favour'.[142] In making this case he drew on Tom Nairn's 2008 Edinburgh Lecture, which had suggested that the rise of global economic integration offered a 'new deal' for small nations because it was now no longer necessary for reasons of security or market access to be part of a large, autonomous state if a nation aspired to lead the world economically.[143] In this new

---

[137] Dennis MacLeod and Michael Russell, *Grasping the Thistle* (Glendaruel, Argyll Publishing, 2006), p. 95.

[138] MacLeod and Russell, *Grasping*, p. 116.

[139] MacLeod and Russell, *Grasping*, pp. 132–9, 154–8.

[140] MacLeod and Russell, *Grasping*, pp. 161, 165.

[141] Paul Hutcheon, 'Salmond Causes Rival to Change "Dangerous" Book', *Sunday Herald*, 1 October 2006.

[142] Alex Salmond, 'Free to Prosper: Creating the Celtic Lion Economy', speech at Harvard University, 31 March 2008, at www.gov.scot/News/Speeches/Speeches/First-Minister/harvard-university (accessed 2 October 2019).

[143] Tom Nairn, 'Globalisation and Nationalism: The New Deal', Edinburgh Lecture, 4 March 2008, reprinted in Tom Nairn, *Old Nations, Auld Enemies, New Times: Selected*

context, Salmond argued, the right economic strategy could see Scotland achieve growth rates comparable to 'those small independent nations around us – Ireland, Iceland, Norway, Finland and Denmark'. Such a strategy would involve state support for economic growth by investment in 'human capital'; inducing greater inward investment from places such as the United States; and learning from the competitive strategies undertaken by those other small European economies, including the tax cutting strategy of Ireland.[144] By this time the SNP had also abandoned its support for a separate Scottish monetary policy. After 1997 this had been expressed as a desire to join the eurozone for both economic and political reasons, since it avoided the need for an independent Scotland to create a new currency or remain dependent on sterling. As MacAskill candidly put it: 'For the SNP, like Scotland, membership of the euro is best.'[145] But after the financial crisis, this option became less appealing and by the 2014 referendum it was proposed that an independent Scotland would retain sterling and remain subject to the monetary policy of the Bank of England.[146]

The form of social democracy that had been placed at the heart of Scottish nationalism by the time the SNP took office in Edinburgh in 2007 was therefore one that sought to yoke together economic efficiency and social justice by stressing the importance of public investment in raising economic performance and the need for lower levels of poverty and inequality to build a productive and cohesive society. It was also a form of social democracy that emphasised the crucial role of wealth creation by the private sector. Scottish nationalists therefore adopted an ideological position that was quite similar to the leading politicians in the Labour Party at that time, although there were also differences insofar as Scottish nationalist leaders offered a more rhetorically forthright defence of their social democratic philosophy and differentiated themselves from Labour on a few key symbolic policy areas.[147] Nonetheless, as Stephen

Essays, edited by Jamie Maxwell and Pete Ramand (Edinburgh, Luath Press, 2014), pp. 396–405.

[144] Salmond, 'Free to Prosper'.

[145] MacAskill, *Building*, p. 67; for the initial economic case made by the SNP, see Alex Salmond, 'Learning to Love the Euro', *Herald*, 7 November 1997.

[146] Coree Brown Swan and Bettina Petersohn, 'The Currency Issue', in Michael Keating (ed.), *Debating Scotland: Issues of Independence and Union in the 2014 Referendum* (Oxford, Oxford University Press, 2017), pp. 65–83.

[147] A quantitative content analysis of SNP manifestos shows broadly the same pattern: from 1970s centrism to 1980s leftism back to a 1990s/2000s centrism that mirrors Labour's ideological trajectory. See Murray Stewart Leith and Daniel Soule, *Political Discourse and National Identity in Scotland* (Edinburgh, Edinburgh University Press, 2011), pp. 46–51.

Maxwell pointed out, this nationalist social democracy ultimately contained an unacknowledged and unresolved political choice between two different social models: Nordic social democracy on the one hand – which requires high levels of direct and indirect taxes and social spending as well as active labour market policies – and the low tax and low social spending of Ireland. As Maxwell observed in 2009, 'over the last decade, as the SNP's social heart has become more attached to social democracy, its economic head has inclined to neo-liberalism', leaving it with 'a persisting ambivalence about the social democratic model itself'.[148]

Radical Independence?

Although left-wing nationalism in the twenty-first century was a less radical creed than its sponsors had initially envisaged in the 1970s and 1980s, it remained a powerful line of argument for Scottish independence in the run-up to the 2014 referendum. From the 1990s onwards, the SNP was skilful at positioning itself rhetorically and substantively slightly to the left of the Labour Party, aided by Labour's own strategy of presenting itself as offering something distinctive from earlier Labour governments – something less radical. There was therefore an opening for Scottish nationalists to dismiss the Blair and Brown governments as in essence the continuation of the Thatcherite project. The claim that the two major parties of the British state were ideologically homogeneous became a commonplace of the nationalist movement. Meanwhile, the tension between liberal economics and Scandinavian social democracy in nationalist thinking in fact proved to be an artful combination for the purposes of building a diverse coalition of political support for independence, particularly after 2010 when the slogan of being 'anti-austerity' could unify nationalists against the Conservative-led government at Westminster and the perceived equivocations of the Labour leadership on fiscal retrenchment.

However, this delicate arrangement was shaken by the emergence of a new and energetic left campaign for independence in the run-up to the 2014 referendum. The advocates of 'radical independence' sought to go beyond the delicately wrought compromises of the official SNP and Yes campaigns by making an unashamed argument for independence as a

[148] Stephen Maxwell, 'Social Justice and the SNP', in Gerry Hassan (ed.), *The Modern SNP: From Protest to Power* (Edinburgh, Edinburgh University Press, 2009), pp. 128–133, quote at p. 131. See also Stephen Maxwell, 'Tackling Scottish Poverty – Principles and Absences: A Critique of the Scottish Government's Approach to Combating Scotland's Problem of Poverty and Inequality', *Scottish Affairs*, no. 67 (2009), pp. 57–69.

blow to British imperialism and capitalism.[149] This return to the concerns that had motivated Gramscian Scottish socialists of the 1970s was one of the liveliest political features of the referendum campaign and provided a marked contrast with the more restrained character of official SNP discourse. Yet it remained a difficult argument for Scottish nationalists to prosecute because the political context of the twenty-first century was quite different from the situation faced by socialist supporters of independence in the 1970s. The message of continuing and deepening Scotland's place in the international economic order had been carefully crafted by Alex Salmond and his colleagues to make Scottish independence into a goal that would not seek to disrupt the profits, jobs and property of large corporations and the Scottish middle class, since they believed that unified opposition from these powerful groups would doom independence in a referendum. As Stephen Maxwell acknowledged in his 2012 summation of the arguments for Scottish independence, the measures necessary even to approach a Nordic-style social democracy in Scotland would include substantial additional income and wealth redistribution; a significant expansion of, and democratisation of, public services; and a more activist economic policy. The politics of carrying through such a programme, Maxwell argued, 'would be distinctly problematic'. As he candidly observed: 'there is nothing in Scotland's recent political record to suggest a pent-up demand for radical social and economic change waiting to be released by independence'.[150]

Maxwell himself therefore thought that arguments for independence based on making Scottish government more democratically responsive and improving Scotland's economic performance carried greater weight in the early twenty-first century than the socialist case he had once made.[151] Maxwell was certainly correct that a radical independence prospectus that foregrounded measures such as the nationalisation of North Sea oil and other key industries; the creation of a new Scottish currency; and significant new taxes on income and wealth would require a much more challenging popular appeal, one that placed on the ballot paper the economic interests that dominate Scottish society.[152] Although

[149] James Foley and Pete Ramand, *Yes: The Radical Case for Independence* (London, Pluto, 2014); Neil Davidson, 'Yes: A Non-Nationalist Argument for Independence', *Radical Philosophy*, no. 185, May/June 2014, pp. 2–7. Jim Sillars also made a welcome return to the independence fray in a similar vein with his *In Place of Fear II* (Glasgow, Vagabond Voices, 2014).

[150] Stephen Maxwell, *Arguing for Independence: Evidence, Risk and the Wicked Issues* (Edinburgh, Luath Press, 2012), pp. 106–13, quote at p. 108.

[151] Maxwell, *Arguing*, pp. 33–50, 55–94, 99–112.

[152] These policies are taken from the immediate programme outlined by Foley and Ramand, *Yes*, pp. 110–17.

a vibrant grass-roots view within the independence movement, the leaders of the SNP judged this to be too risky a proposition in 2014. They argued instead for a vaguer form of left-wing nationalism that was ultimately about making Scotland more like a variety of other successful European countries than about systematically adopting the Nordic model of economic and social policy, let alone pursuing a more fundamental battle against capitalism.

5   Sovereignty and Post-Sovereignty

> I have come to the paradoxical conclusion that it is in the process of
> merging its sovereignty with other member states in the [European]
> Community that Ireland has found the clearest *ex post facto* justification
> for its long struggle to achieve sovereign independence of the United
> Kingdom.   Garret Fitzgerald, 1989[1]

Sovereignty – the question of who exercises ultimate authority in a state
and of the recognition of that state's independence by the rest of the
international system – was of intense interest to Scottish nationalists in
the late twentieth century. Aside from the obvious general importance of
sovereignty to the project of founding a new state (and hence Scottish
popular control over Scotland's affairs), there was a more specific reason
for this. As we saw in Chapter 1, from the 1940s a new and influential
account of the idea of sovereignty in Scottish history took shape, which
proclaimed that Scottish constitutional tradition construed the concept
quite differently from its English counterpart. Whereas the English
tradition of parliamentary sovereignty emerged from the transfer of the
absolute power of the monarch to Parliament, culminating in the Glorious Revolution settlement of 1688, the Scottish tradition (nationalists
argued) located sovereignty in the hands of the people. While this proved
to be an alluring characterisation of what was taken to be a fundamental
constitutional difference between Scotland and England – especially in
the context of the confrontation between the Thatcher government and
Scottish public opinion – during the 1980s and 1990s this account was
complemented by a more detailed anatomy of the specific powers that an
independent Scotland should or could ultimately exercise. The conclusion of leading Scottish nationalists was that it would in fact be desirable
for a Scottish state to pool some of its sovereignty at a British and
European level, thus endorsing a model of national independence
that worked with the grain of the growing political and economic

---

[1] Garret Fitzgerald, 'Better Relationships in Europe than at Home', *Scots Independent*,
no. 223, October 1989, p. 4.

interdependencies between states in the late twentieth and early twenty-first centuries. From this perspective, nationalists came to regard the European integration of the late twentieth century as a trend that was highly favourable to their cause, since the European single market would enable Scotland to achieve independence without disrupting any of the nation's trading relationships with the rest of the United Kingdom. Of course, such an analysis assumed that British membership of the EU constituted an immovable fixed point in the geopolitical landscape – an assumption that looked reasonable in 2014, if not afterwards.

We Are the People

As we saw in Chapter 1, the claim that there is a distinctively Scottish tradition of popular sovereignty was a theme that first gained widespread attention as a result of the efforts of an earlier generation of Scottish nationalists. This aspect of the case for Scottish independence in the late twentieth century therefore stood in ideological continuity with, rather than breaking from, the nationalist pioneers of the mid-twentieth century. Douglas Young and then John MacCormick had publicised this historical narrative about sovereignty in their court cases of the 1940s and 1950s, during which they had drawn on the nationalist histories of Scotland written in the 1930s and 1940s by authors such as Agnes Mure MacKenzie and Duncan MacNeill.[2] MacNeill and MacKenzie related a narrative of Scottish political development that stressed an abiding distinction between the nascently democratic Celtic model of society found in unconquered Scotland and the more hierarchical and feudal Teutonic social vision of England. Where the English constitution originated with the power of monarchs to assert their control over society, they argued, in Scotland kings and queens had themselves been subject to the law and a greater degree of popular participation in government had developed (as it had in church governance with the rise of Presbyterianism).[3]

---

[2] For MacCormick's friendship with MacNeill, see John MacCormick, *The Flag in the Wind* (London, Victor Gollancz, 1955), p. 45.

[3] Agnes Mure MacKenzie, *Scotland in Modern Times 1720–1939* (London, W & R Chambers, 1941), pp. 52–3; Agnes Mure MacKenzie, *Scottish Principles of Statecraft and Government* (Glasgow, Scottish Convention, 1942), pp. 7–13; Duncan H. MacNeill, *The Scottish Constitution* (Glasgow, SNP, 1943), inter alia, pp. 10–11, 23–5, 28–9; Duncan H. MacNeill, *The Scottish Realm: An Approach to the Political and Constitutional History of Scotland* (Glasgow, A. and J. Donaldson, 1947). For examples of the dissemination of this view, see Robert McIntyre, 'The Challenge of Today', *Scots Independent*, no. 299, July 1951, p. 1; Richard Finlay, 'Robert McIntyre', in Gerry Hassan and James Mitchell (eds.), *Scottish National Party Leaders* (London, Biteback, 2016), pp. 191–3.

Unsurprisingly, Douglas Young's legal debut of this argument – in the cases he fought in 1942 and 1944 to evade conscription into the British war effort – was not acknowledged as such by subsequent Scottish nationalists.[4] Instead, a more politically acceptable origin myth developed around the celebrated 1953 court case *MacCormick* v. *Lord Advocate*. John MacCormick, as we have seen one of the founders of the SNP and a long-standing advocate of home rule for Scotland, argued that the British government was acting *ultra vires* by styling the new British monarch Elizabeth II in Scotland, since Elizabeth I had of course only reigned over England, Wales and Ireland.[5] MacCormick's case was in key respects the same as Young's, namely that the Treaty of Union between England and Scotland functioned as a kind of basic law or written constitution that constrained Parliament from acting in a way that would undermine those provisions of the Treaty that it stipulated to be unalterable. The classical English concept of parliamentary sovereignty, MacCormick continued, therefore no longer applied to the new British Parliament after 1707. Indeed, MacCormick suggested (echoing Young) that Scottish constitutional tradition was quite distinct from England's on this point: 'Scotland and England had taken different views of sovereignty. In England sovereignty had been regarded as coming from above, while in Scotland the sovereign body was the community of Scotland.'[6] As MacCormick later elaborated on this point in his autobiography, published two years after the case: 'In England the law was the law of conquest. The king, having imposed himself upon the people, could do no wrong. He was above all law and could never be challenged in the Courts.' In contrast, Scotland 'had never been conquered' and so 'the "community of Scotland"' rather than the monarch had come to represent the Scottish nation, with the king or queen understood to have a quasi-contractual relationship with the Scottish people. The Scottish Parliament had thus 'always been subject to the ultimate sanction of community assent, had no sovereign powers itself and could not, therefore, by the Act of Union convey sovereign powers to its successor the Parliament of the United Kingdom'.[7] This latter claim

---

[4] See Chapter 1 for further discussion of Young's legal actions in the 1940s.

[5] Gavin Little, 'A Flag in the Wind: *MacCormick v Lord Advocate*', in John Grant and Elaine Sutherland (eds.), *Scots Law Tales* (Dundee, Dundee University Press, 2010), pp. 23–44. A helpful analysis is Neil MacCormick, 'Does the United Kingdom Have a Constitution? Reflections on *MacCormick v Lord Advocate*', *Northern Ireland Legal Quarterly*, 29 (1978), pp. 1–6. A later, more critical account is Adam Tomkins, 'The Constitutional Law in *MacCormick v Lord Advocate*', *Juridical Review*, 2004, pt 3, pp. 213–24.

[6] *MacCormick* v. *HM Advocate*, 1953 SC 396, p. 406.

[7] MacCormick, *Flag in the Wind*, pp. 189–90.

about a Scottish constitutional tradition of popular sovereignty was to acquire great political importance in the late twentieth century.[8]

MacCormick was fortunate that, after the case was initially dismissed, the presiding judge when he appealed the verdict was Lord Cooper of Culross, who combined a staunch political unionism with a pioneering legal nationalism (though Cooper had in fact earlier denied Young's case without in any way acknowledging its force).[9] Like the lower court, Lord Cooper and his colleagues dismissed MacCormick's case but in his judgment Cooper nonetheless took the opportunity to offer his own startling summary of the nature of the Union settlement:

> The principle of the unlimited sovereignty of Parliament is a distinctively English principle which has no counterpart in Scottish constitutional law. It derives its origin from Coke and Blackstone, and was widely popularised during the nineteenth century by Bagehot and Dicey, the latter having stated the doctrine in its classic form in his *Law of the Constitution*. Considering that the Union legislation extinguished the Parliaments of Scotland and England and replaced them by a new Parliament, I have difficulty in seeing why it should have been supposed that the new Parliament of Great Britain must inherit all the peculiar characteristics of the English Parliament but none of the Scottish Parliament, as if all that happened in 1707 was that Scottish representatives were admitted to the Parliament of England. That is not what was done.[10]

The main thrust of Lord Cooper's remarks was that he was sympathetic to MacCormick's argument that the Treaty of Union should indeed be treated as a fundamental constitutional law that constrained parliamentary sovereignty (though he had doubts about whether the Treaty was in practice justiciable in relation to what the Treaty of Union referred to as 'public right' since it was unclear which court had the jurisdiction to adjudicate on an infringement of the Treaty).[11] However, Lord Cooper was silent in his judgment on what precisely the distinctively Scottish

---

[8] Although in Neil MacCormick's view this aspect of John MacCormick's argument was actually legally less persuasive than the claim that the Treaty of Union functions as a form of fundamental law for Britain: 'Doubts about the "Supreme Court" and Reflections on *MacCormick v Lord Advocate*', *Juridical Review*, 2004, pt 3, pp. 241–2.

[9] Hector MacQueen, 'Legal Nationalism: Lord Cooper, Legal History and Comparative Law', *Edinburgh Law Review*, 9 (2005), pp. 395–406; Hector MacQueen, 'Two Toms and an Ideology for Scots Law: T. B. Smith and Lord Cooper of Culross', in Elspeth Reid and David Carey Miller (eds.), *A Mixed Legal System in Transition: T. B. Smith and the Progress of Scots Law* (Edinburgh, Edinburgh University Press, 2005), pp. 44–72; Hector MacQueen, 'Public Law, Private Law, and National Identity', in Cormac Mac Amhlaigh, Claudio Michelon and Neil Walker (eds.), *After Public Law* (Oxford, Oxford University Press, 2013), pp. 188–93. For Cooper on Young, see Douglas Young, *An Appeal to Scots Honour: A Vindication of the Right of the Scottish People to Freedom from Industrial Conscription and Bureaucratic Despotism under the Treaty of Union with England* (Glasgow, Scottish Secretariat, 1944), pp. 4–5.

[10] *MacCormick v. HM Advocate*, p. 411.   [11] *MacCormick v. HM Advocate*, pp. 412–13.

principle of sovereignty actually *was* in contrast with the English parliamentary notion (a point that was sometimes neglected in subsequent nationalist references to the case). But one intriguing hint is that Cooper was also a scholar of Scottish medieval history and law, for example writing authoritatively on the 1320 Declaration of Arbroath, which he described as 'one of the masterpieces of political rhetoric of all time'.[12]

The Declaration of Arbroath is the document usually – although controversially – invoked as the point of origin for the Scottish tradition of resting sovereignty with the people.[13] This document, an official letter sent to Pope John XXII in defence of King Robert I ('Robert the Bruce') and the independence of Scotland from English conquest, has been interpreted as exhibiting a precocious quasi-contractarian view of the relationship between the Scottish king and the wider Scottish community. In a key, frequently quoted, passage, the authors of the Declaration stated that Robert was their rightful king thanks to 'divine providence, the succession to his right according to our laws and customs which we shall maintain to the death, and the due consent and assent of us'.[14] The Declaration continues:

Yet if he should give up what he has begun, seeking to make us or our kingdom subject to the King of England or to the English, we would strive at once to drive him out as our enemy and a subverter of his own right and ours, and we would make some other man who was well able to defend us our King; for, as long as a hundred of us remain alive, we will never on any conditions be subjected to the lordship of the English. For we fight not for glory, nor riches, nor honours, but for freedom alone, which no good man gives up except with his life.[15]

How far this statement can reasonably be taken to represent a medieval form of popular (or at least, non-monarchical) sovereignty is a complex question. It has been debated in some detail by historians, who are for the most part critical of the strongest interpretations of the Declaration as embodying proto-democratic sentiments.[16] For our purposes, however,

---

[12] T. M. Cooper [Lord Cooper of Culross], 'The Declaration of Arbroath Revisited' [1949], in his *Selected Papers 1922–54* (Edinburgh and London, Oliver and Boyd, 1957), p. 332.

[13] For example MacNeill, *Scottish Constitution*, pp. 15–16; Roland Muirhead, Robert McIntyre and Mary Dott, 'The Scottish Nation's Claim of Right to UNO', *Scots Independent*, no. 254, October 1947, p. 1; Agnes Mure MacKenzie, *On the Declaration of Arbroath* (Edinburgh, Saltire Society, 1951); 'The National Party in Conference', *Scots Independent*, no. 321, May 1953, p. 5.

[14] A. A. Duncan, *The Nation of Scots and the Declaration of Arbroath (1320)* (London, Historical Association, 1970), p. 35.

[15] Duncan, *Nation of Scots*, p. 36.

[16] See for example Terry Brotherstone and David Ditchburn, '1320 and a' that: The Declaration of Arbroath and the Remaking of Scottish History', in Terry Brotherstone and David Ditchburn (eds.), *Freedom and Authority: Scotland c. 1050–c. 1650* (East

the more important point is that in a loose sense this document has been appropriated by later generations of Scottish writers and activists – by no means all explicitly nationalist and chiefly in the late twentieth century – to argue that a contractualist notion of sovereignty represents the authentically Scottish approach to the fundamental questions of political rule and legitimacy.

A resonant example was Geoffrey Barrow's (1924–2013) landmark work of Scottish history, *Robert the Bruce and the Community of the Realm of Scotland* (1965). Barrow located Bruce's kingship and the Declaration within a broader sense of Scottish collective identity – 'the community of the realm' – given institutional expression in the collaboration of the nobility, the clergy and possibly other social groups – 'the totality of the King's free subjects' – in maintaining the integrity of an independent Scotland during the succession crises that afflicted the kingdom after Alexander III's death in 1286. This community, according to Barrow, underpinned Robert's rule, representing the wider Scottish society that the Bruce had to win over to reign. It was, on Barrow's account, a rudimentary form of the later idea of the nation, or as near to such an idea as it was possible to get in the medieval period. This 'precocious Scottish democracy' was in Barrow's view distinct from the English concept of the community of the realm, which was initially specifically aristocratic in its connotation and then shifted in the early fourteenth century to denote the non-aristocratic 'commons'. In contrast, in the Scottish case the community of the realm had less distinct, and therefore more inclusive, boundaries.[17] From this perspective, the Declaration of Arbroath should be seen as expressing 'the essence of the theory underlying the community of the realm'.[18] Barrow's book was widely read and discussed (going through four editions and numerous reprints), but one tangible indicator of his impact is that one of his greatest admirers in Scottish public life was Alex Salmond, who as a student in medieval history at the University of St Andrews had taken Barrow's special subject on the Scottish Wars of Independence.[19] Salmond often used

---

Linton, Tuckwell Press, 2000), pp. 10–31; Grant Simpson, 'The Declaration of Arbroath Revitalised', *Scottish Historical Review*, 56 (1977), pp. 11–33; E. J. Cowan, 'Identity, Freedom, and the Declaration of Arbroath', in Dauvit Broun, Richard Finlay and Michael Lynch (eds.), *Image and Identity: The Making and Re-making of Scotland through the Ages* (Edinburgh, John Donald, 1998), pp. 38–68.

[17] Geoffrey Barrow, *Robert the Bruce and the Community of the Realm of Scotland* (London, Eyre and Spottiswoode, 1965), pp. xiii–xv, 23–5.

[18] Barrow, *Robert the Bruce*, p. 426.

[19] David Torrance, *Alex Salmond: Against the Odds* (Edinburgh, Birlinn, 2011), p. 60; Robert Crawford, *Bannockburns: Scottish Independence and Literary Imagination, 1314–2014* (Edinburgh, Edinburgh University Press, 2014), p. 179.

the idea of the 'community of the realm of Scotland' in his public statements as a term connoting both Scottish society and public opinion. Strikingly, in the opening lines of his victory speech had the 'Yes' campaign won the 2014 Scottish independence referendum, Salmond would have said 'the community of this realm has spoken. Scotland shall be independent again'.[20]

In addition to the Declaration of Arbroath, a further strand of the history of Scottish political thought is usually pressed into service to substantiate the notion that Scotland played host to an early proto-democratic concept of sovereignty. This is the radical theory of popular sovereignty espoused by George Buchanan, the celebrated sixteenth-century Scottish humanist, political theorist and historian, who argued that the people retained a right of resistance against monarchs who act as tyrants. In his 1579 work of political theory, *De Iure Regni apud Scotos Dialogus* ['Dialogue on the Law of Kingship among the Scots'], and his 1582 history, *Rerum Scoticarum Historia* ['History of Scotland'], Buchanan depicted an ancient Scottish monarchy that had been allowed to rule by the people only as long as the monarch remained subject to the law. According to Buchanan, monarchs who act *ultra vires*, and thus in their own self-interest rather than for the common good, can then legitimately be resisted and even, in the most startling twist of the theory, assassinated. Buchanan did not refer to the Declaration of Arbroath in making this case – the Declaration itself was largely forgotten until about 1680 – and relied instead on a mixture of natural law political theorising and his own historical scholarship.[21] Nonetheless, Buchanan and the Declaration were yoked together in seventeenth-century debates in the radical Presbyterianism of the Covenanters, as they contested the state's right to interfere in the affairs of the Church of Scotland, and ultimately in the 1689 Claim of Right – a more radical document than the equivalent

---

[20] 'In Full: Alex Salmond's Independence Speech', *Scotsman*, 16 September 2015, at www.scotsman.com/news/politics/in-full-alex-salmond-s-independence-speech-1-3888006 (accessed 2 October 2019). For earlier examples, see Alex Salmond, 'Scotland's Place in the World', Hugo Young Lecture, 24 January 2012, at www.theguardian.com/politics/2012/jan/25/alex-salmond-hugo-young-lecture (accessed 2 October 2019); Severin Carrell, 'Alex Salmond Predicts Million-Strong Movement for Independence', *Guardian*, 25 May 2012.

[21] Roger Mason, 'Introduction' to George Buchanan, *A Dialogue on the Law of Kingship among the Scots* [1579], translated and edited by Martin Smith and Roger Mason (Edinburgh, Saltire Society, 2006), pp. 9–18; Roger Mason, 'Beyond the Declaration of Arbroath: Kingship, Counsel and Consent in Late Medieval and Early Modern Scotland', in Steve Boardman and Julian Goodare (eds.), *Kings, Lords and Men in Scotland and Britain, 1300–1625* (Edinburgh, Edinburgh University Press, 2014), pp. 265–8. Duncan MacNeill also edited an edition of Buchanan: *The Art and Science of Government among the Scots* (Glasgow, MacLellan, 1964).

English Declaration of Rights. The Claim of Right endorsed the notion of a legally limited monarchy as formal Scottish state policy, ejecting James VII from the throne on the grounds that he had 'forefaulted the right to the Croune'. The first publication of an English text of the Declaration of Arbroath was also in 1689, while the works of Buchanan were reprinted in 1689 and 1690.[22]

Sovereignty Retrieved

It is doubtful that a coherent theory of popular sovereignty based on these ideas played a major role in Scottish political argument before 1707. As John Robertson and Colin Kidd have shown, such early modern debates contained a bewildering variety of different perspectives on sovereignty, the most prominent of which were decidedly feudal in character and focused for example on the historic credentials of Scotland's independent monarchy as signifying Scotland's sovereignty.[23] It might nonetheless be possible to salvage a more modest form of this historical claim. As Neal Ascherson has argued, the relative weakness of the central Scottish state (and monarch) did mean that a looser, more decentralised notion of political authority evolved in Scotland in comparison to England, with the monarch and nobility effectively forced into sharing power rather than fighting over it.[24] In any case, though evident in some earlier Scottish discourse, the notion that a long-standing constitutional tradition of popular sovereignty could be distilled from Scottish history was not particularly prominent until it was retrieved by Scottish nationalists in the mid-twentieth century, just as democratic ideas of self-determination acquired a new legitimacy amid the global clash between democratic states and totalitarian fascism and communism.

After the pioneering elaboration of this narrative in the 1940s and 1950s, the Declaration of Arbroath and George Buchanan began to

---

[22] Claim of Right Act 1689, at www.legislation.gov.uk/aosp/1689/28 (accessed 2 October 2019); Colin Kidd, *Subverting Scotland's Past* (Cambridge, Cambridge University Press, 1993), pp. 20–1, 28; Caroline Erskine, 'George Buchanan, English Whigs and Royalists and the Canon of Political Theory', in Caroline Erskine and Roger Mason (eds.), *George Buchanan: Political Thought in Early Modern Britain and Europe* (Aldershot, Ashgate, 2012), pp. 235–6.

[23] John Robertson, 'An Elusive Sovereignty: The Course of the Union Debate in Scotland 1698–1707', in John Robertson (ed.), *A Union for Empire* (Cambridge, Cambridge University Press, 1995), p. 218; Colin Kidd, 'Sovereignty and the Scottish Constitution Before 1707', *Juridical Review*, 2004, Part 3, pp. 225–36.

[24] Neal Ascherson, *Stone Voices: The Search for Scotland* (London, Granta, 2002), pp. 262–74. For a detailed historical argument along similar lines, see Alice Taylor, *The Shape of the State in Medieval Scotland, 1124–1290* (Oxford, Oxford University Press, 2016).

make sporadic appearances in the 1960s and 1970s as a lineage of Scottish democratic constitutionalism that fitted Scotland for a new era of popular self-determination.[25] During the parliamentary debates on devolution in the late 1970s, for example, Winnie Ewing remarked that if Scotland hadn't entered the Union in 1707 it 'would have had a written constitution' since Scotland was at that time part of the mainstream European legal tradition. Instead, she argued, Scotland had been absorbed into an English system which was 'thirled to the theory of parliamentary sovereignty as some sort of holy cow'. In Ewing's view, *MacCormick* v. *Lord Advocate* had 'established that there was a separate constitutional concept in Scots law about the sovereignty of the people, and not the sovereignty of Parliament' (as demonstrated, she added, by the Declaration of Arbroath's injunctions about making the monarch legally accountable).[26] As we have seen, this was not precisely what Lord Cooper had concluded in *MacCormick* v. *Lord Advocate*. But Ewing's slippage from Cooper's rejection of parliamentary sovereignty to a full-throated endorsement of popular sovereignty as the Scottish tradition was a common move in nationalist political rhetoric in the late twentieth century.

Such rhetoric became politically important during the debates about devolution between 1974 and 1979, since it enabled many nationalists to support Labour's devolution proposals as a staging post towards independence (the so-called gradualist position within the SNP – as opposed to the 'fundamentalist' argument that independence could be achieved without this intermediate stage). The gradualists, such as George Reid and the legal theorist and later SNP MEP Neil MacCormick, defended devolution on the grounds that it would create a political institution that for the first time authentically embodied Scottish popular sovereignty and would therefore offer the opportunity to advance towards independence via a Scottish parliament, should the Scottish popular will support such a course.[27] Reid told the House of Commons in 1974 that we 'must not think of devolution as being a static, once-for-all, fixed, immutable

---

[25] For example H. J. Paton, *The Claim of Scotland* (London, George Allen & Unwin, 1968), pp. 48–9, 64–5; William Wolfe, *Scotland Lives* (Edinburgh, Reprographia, 1973), p. 147; Neal Ascherson, 'SNP Road to Success', *Scotsman*, 21 November 1978; Finlay, 'Robert McIntyre', pp. 191–3. Stephen Maxwell offered a slightly more sceptical treatment of this tradition in his 'Can Scotland's Political Myths Be Broken?', *Question*, no. 16, 19 November 1976, p. 5 and his 'Beyond Social Democracy', in Gavin Kennedy (ed.), *The Radical Approach* (Edinburgh, Palingenesis Press, 1976), p. 19.

[26] Winifred Ewing, Hansard, HC Debates, fifth series, vol. 943, cols. 551–3 (1 February 1978).

[27] Roger Levy, *Scottish Nationalism at the Crossroads* (Edinburgh, Scottish Academic Press, 1990), pp. 70, 123; George Reid, 'A State of Flux', *Question*, no. 5, February 1976,

change. Devolution is a continuing process, and when the Scottish people say "enough" that will be enough for me.'[28] The notion that devolution should be seen as 'a process not an event' – later associated with the Labour architects of Welsh and Scottish devolution, Ron Davies (b. 1946) and Donald Dewar (1937–2000) – was therefore first elaborated by the gradualist wing of the SNP (and when Dewar made remarks along these lines in 1998 they were duly welcomed by the then constitutional affairs spokesman for the SNP, one George Reid).[29]

As we saw in Chapter 3, the concept of popular sovereignty subsequently took on a wider significance in the debate over Scotland's constitutional status during the 1980s and 1990s as it became increasingly central to the nationalist critique of the British state.[30] Amid the widely discussed crisis of British governance in the 1970s, nationalists had begun to argue that Britain's failure to develop a modern democratic constitution was at the heart of the dysfunction that was consuming British politics. As Neal Ascherson put it in one early formulation of this case: 'The absolutism of Parliament has become as much a Leviathan as the absolute right of kings, because it has prevented the emergence in Britain of the doctrine of popular sovereignty as the true source of power.' By contrast, Ascherson thought, 'Scotland residually and legally had conserved such a doctrine'.[31] Ascherson later summed up this historical analysis as demonstrating that Britain – and British progressive politics in particular – had been fundamentally hobbled by its failure to embrace a Jacobin politics rooted in popular sovereignty, individual rights and a written constitution.[32]

---

pp. 4–5; Neil MacCormick, 'Westminster Must Beware of Pushing the SNP into an All-Out Battle', *The Times*, 17 May 1977.

[28] George Reid, Hansard, HC Debates, fifth series, vol. 880, col. 968 (5 November 1974).

[29] Ron Davies, *Devolution: A Process Not an Event* (Cardiff, Institute of Welsh Affairs, 1999); Stephen Goodwin, 'Dewar Accepts Scotland's "Evolutionary Nationalism"', *Independent*, 1 December 1998.

[30] Lindsay Paterson, 'Ane End of Ane Auld Sang: Sovereignty and the Re-Negotiation of the Union', *The Scottish Government Yearbook*, 1991, p. 104; Lindsay Paterson, *The Autonomy of Modern Scotland* (Edinburgh, Edinburgh University Press, 1994), pp. 167–73; Antonia Kearton, 'Imagining the "Mongrel Nation": Political Uses of History in the Recent Scottish Nationalist Movement', *National Identities*, 7 (2005), pp. 35–9. See Chapter 3 for a detailed discussion of this point in relation to the political thought of Tom Nairn.

[31] Neal Ascherson, 'Divine Right of Parliaments', *Scotsman*, 18 February 1977; Neal Ascherson, 'Devolution Diary', entry for 13 February 1977, printed in *Cencrastus*, no. 22, winter 1986, pp. 6–7.

[32] Neal Ascherson, 'Ancient Britons and the Republican Dream', John Mackintosh Memorial Lecture, Edinburgh University, 16 November 1985, published in *Radical Scotland*, no. 18, December/January 1986 and reprinted in Ascherson's *Games with Shadows* (London, Radius, 1988), pp. 146–58.

Advocates of the creation of a new Scottish parliament – whether through devolution or outright independence – subsequently deployed the language of popular sovereignty with ever greater conviction as the notion that British parliamentary rule over Scotland was 'undemocratic' gained purchase on Scottish public debate. The uncompromising character of the Thatcher government, and the rapid decrease in the number of Scottish parliamentary seats it held at each successive general election after 1983, made arguments that the government possessed 'no mandate' to rule Scotland irresistible. Equally, as Lindsay Paterson pointed out at the time, the ferocity of the Thatcherite assault on long-standing Scottish institutions forced Scottish elites to seek new legitimacy for them by reference to a strengthening popular sense of Scottish identity. No longer in alliance with the state, Scottish civil society and its middle class were forced to turn to the people.[33] More prosaically, the marked divergence between Scottish and English voting patterns in the 1980s inaugurated the powerful argument for independence that only in a separate Scottish polity would the government of Scotland necessarily be one that had been chosen by the Scottish people. The force of this point was much weaker when Scottish and English voting patterns were basically similar, but after 1974 the discrepancy between the expressed will of the Scottish electorate and the outcome of every British general election until 1997 made the issue inescapable in Scottish public life. This was a point that the '79 Group in the SNP had highlighted shortly after the election of the Thatcher government. As Stephen Maxwell observed as early as 1981, 'the slogan "no Scottish mandate"' could widen the campaign against the Thatcher government by offering a national rather than a traditionally left-wing response – 'attacking the Tories' minority position in Scotland' – an approach that Maxwell urged on the Scottish labour movement, no doubt conscious that the rise of such rhetoric was also likely to benefit the SNP.[34]

In these circumstances, it seemed that a persuasive line of argument was that parliamentary sovereignty should be regarded as secondary to the sovereign popular will of the Scottish people. As Neil MacCormick summarised this view, this could be seen as perfectly in keeping with Scottish constitutional tradition:

---

[33] Paterson, 'Ane End of Ane Auld Sang', pp. 113–16.
[34] Stephen Maxwell, 'Lothian Region: Showdown or Copout?', '79 Group News, September 1981, p. 4; 'SNP '79 Group – Political Report, Annual General Meeting, August 1980', memo, Gavin Kennedy Papers, National Library of Scotland, Acc. 11565/23, p. 2.

The old Scottish constitution, as Scots authorities like George Buchanan were very insistent, was never a constitution based on conquest. Hence the *Ius Regni*, the law of the kingdom, could never be interpreted as constituting an absolute monarchy whether in or out of Parliament, but only as authorising a limited one dependent on popular assent. From this, and from such other iconic texts as the Declaration of Arbroath, has derived the thesis that in Scottish constitutional tradition, sovereignty belonged to the people, to the community of the realm, rather than to Parliament, or, strictly, King or Queen in Parliament.[35]

Scottishness, on this account, had become a national identity that was distinguished by its long adherence to democratic values.[36]

The most potent expression of this historical narrative was not by an exponent of Scottish independence but by a cross-party initiative aimed at building support for a new Scottish assembly within the context of the United Kingdom. The Campaign for a Scottish Assembly, established in 1980 to keep the goal of home rule alive as a political option after the 1979 referendum defeat, formed a Constitutional Steering Committee after the 1987 general election with the aim of setting out the case for a full-blown Scottish Constitutional Convention to draw up plans for a new Scottish parliament. The Steering Committee was deliberately made up of leading figures from Scottish civil society rather than party representatives, drawing on the churches, business, trade unions, academia and the voluntary sector. The committee was chaired by Sir Robert Grieve (1910–95), a retired chief planner at the Scottish Office, with the secretarial work of the Committee undertaken by Jim Ross, who had been the Scottish Office civil servant in charge of the devolution legislation in the late 1970s. As Scott Hames has observed, Ross's pivotal role in drafting the Committee's public output meant that he 'is by some distance the most wily and consequential Scottish writer of the period'.[37] Among the other members of the Steering Committee were leading figures in the articulation of a left-leaning nationalist vision of Scottish home rule, particularly Isobel Lindsay; the former diplomat and author,

---

[35] Neil MacCormick, *Questioning Sovereignty: Law, State and Nation in the European Commonwealth* (Oxford, Oxford University Press, 1999), p. 55. MacCormick had espoused this reading of Scottish constitutional history since the 1970s: see his 'Constitution', in Colin MacLean (ed.), *The Crown and the Thistle: The Nature of Nationhood* (Edinburgh, Scottish Academic Press, 1979), pp. 149–51.

[36] Anthony Cohen, 'Personal Nationalism: A Scottish View of Some Rites, Rights, and Wrongs', *American Ethnologist*, 23 (1996), pp. 807–8. This democratic discourse therefore converged with the account of Scottish distinctiveness given by George Davie (see Chapter 2).

[37] Scott Hames, *The Literary Politics of Scottish Devolution* (Edinburgh, Edinburgh University Press, 2019), p. 304.

Paul Henderson Scott (1920–2019); and Neil MacCormick.[38] The document that the Steering Committee produced in July 1988 was entitled *A Claim of Right for Scotland*, inviting a parallel with its counterpart in 1689 and the 1842 document issued by the Church of Scotland against state interference in the ability of congregations to select their ministers.[39]

This third Claim of Right was a powerful document because it crystallised the emerging sovereigntist discourse of the home rule movement and embedded the demand for what would ultimately end up as the devolutionary proposals of the Scottish Constitutional Convention in a more radical political theory.[40] The *Claim of Right* opened with a reprise of some of the themes voiced (in a different context) by Lord Cooper, noting that in the 'British' Parliament 'it is impossible to trace in the history or procedures of that Parliament any constitutional influence other than an English one'.[41] The *Claim of Right* therefore set out to expose the flaws of this 'English constitution' for the governance of Scotland.[42] This opening salvo was then followed by a coruscating critique of the impact of the Union on the distinctive character of Scottish culture. While Scottish culture had waxed and waned since 1707, the *Claim* argued, 'there is no ground for any claim that, overall or even at any particular time, it has benefited from the Union. On the contrary the Union has always been, and remains, a threat to the survival of a distinctive culture in Scotland.'[43] This was a remarkable departure from the traditional Scottish view that the value of the Union was precisely that it had protected Scotland's cultural distinctiveness from assimilation into English norms.

The radical Thatcherite restructuring programme in social and economic policy hovered in the background, and at times the foreground, of this argument. 'Scotland faces a crisis of identity and survival', the *Claim of Right* concluded. 'It is now being governed without consent and

[38] David Stewart, *The Path to Devolution and Change: A Political History of Scotland under Margaret Thatcher* (London, IB Tauris, 2009), pp. 197, 210–12; Andrew Marr, *The Battle for Scotland* (London, Penguin, 1995), pp. 195–9; Paul Henderson Scott, *Scotland Resurgent* (Edinburgh, the Saltire Society, 2003), pp. 331–5; Owen Dudley-Edwards (ed.), *A Claim of Right for Scotland* (Edinburgh, Polygon, 1989), pp. 1–2; Bob McLean, *Getting It Together: The History of the Campaign for a Scottish Assembly/Parliament 1980–99* (Edinburgh, Luath Press, 2005), pp. 45–122.

[39] Paul Henderson Scott recollected that he suggested the use of this title: *Scotland Resurgent*, p. 332.

[40] A similar point about the *Claim of Right* has been made in the perceptive close reading of it by Hames, *Literary Politics of Scottish Devolution*, pp. 176–83.

[41] Campaign for a Scottish Assembly, *A Claim of Right for Scotland*, July 1988, reprinted in Owen Dudley-Edwards (ed.), *Claim of Right for Scotland*, p. 13.

[42] For example *Claim of Right for Scotland*, pp. 18–19, 27, 52.

[43] *Claim of Right for Scotland*, p. 14.

subject to the declared intention of having imposed upon it a radical change of outlook and behaviour pattern which it shows no sign of wanting.'[44] Articulating a similar critique of the British constitution to that offered by Charter 88 around the same time, the *Claim* argued that no solution to this democratic crisis would be possible until 'the concentration of power that masquerades as "the Crown-in-Parliament" has been broken up'.[45] 'Scotland, if it is to remain Scotland, can no longer live with such a constitution and has nothing to hope for from it.'[46] The *Claim*'s positive proposal was the formation of a Scottish Constitutional Convention to draw up proposals for a new Scottish assembly and to act as 'a focus of resistance and political negotiation, which rejects comprehensively the authority of existing government on matters peculiar to Scotland'.[47] This was a much more radical, and audacious, suggestion than is often remembered. The authors of the *Claim* were proclaiming that a non-parliamentary, but more authentic, representation of Scottish popular sovereignty should be convened in order to 'negotiate with the government' over a Scottish assembly.[48]

Nonetheless, this approach to the debate over Scottish government proved to be highly successful. The Scottish Constitutional Convention was duly convened on 30 March 1989 with the support of the Labour Party, the Liberal Democrats, the Green Party, the trade unions, the churches, business representatives, local government, women's groups and other elements drawn from Scottish civil society (but not – as we will discuss shortly – the SNP). The members of the Convention included fifty-eight of the seventy-two Scottish MPs – all of the Scottish Liberal Democrat and Labour MPs, except for the veteran anti-devolutionist, Tam Dalyell (1932–2017). They all signed another document that was, confusingly, also entitled *A Claim of Right for Scotland*. This 1989 *Claim of Right* offered an unequivocal endorsement of Scottish popular sovereignty:

We, gathered as the Scottish Constitutional Convention, do hereby acknowledge the sovereign right of the Scottish people to determine the form of government best suited to their needs, and do hereby declare and pledge that in all our actions and deliberations their interests shall be paramount.[49]

---

[44] *Claim of Right for Scotland*, p. 51.   [45] *Claim of Right for Scotland*, p. 51.
[46] *Claim of Right for Scotland*, p. 52.   [47] *Claim of Right for Scotland*, p. 33.
[48] *Claim of Right for Scotland*, p. 46; see also p. 52 and the observations of Jim Ross, 'Towards a New Scotland: A Choice of Weapons', *Cencrastus*, no. 35, winter 1989, p. 28.
[49] Scottish Constitutional Convention, *Towards Scotland's Parliament* (Edinburgh, Scottish Constitutional Convention, 1990), p. 1.

The ideological context of this statement can be gleaned from the recollections of the Executive Chairman of the Convention, Canon Kenyon Wright (1932–2017), who remembered that when this (second) *Claim of Right* was signed

I felt the guardian presence of those Scots who in the 1320 Declaration, so far in advance of its time, told the King at Arbroath that he ruled 'subject to the consent of the realm' and who pledged their lives 'not for honour, glory or riches but for freedom alone'. I felt the presence of those who in the Claim of Right of 1689 had deposed the King for abusing his power and those who in 1842 had walked out of the General Assembly of the Church of Scotland in defiance of Westminster's right to impose patronage on Scotland.[50]

As Wright recognised, the signing officially marked a significant turn in Scottish political argument that had many ramifications. One important consequence was that the Convention enabled Scottish feminists to exert some influence over the constitutional debate for the first time. Feminists drew on the newly legitimised language of popular sovereignty to develop the framing of a 'woman's claim of right', which placed on the Convention's agenda the pressing need for a new Scottish parliament to increase significantly female political representation and to make gender equality a political priority.[51] The constitutional debates of the 1990s featured a much stronger commitment to women's rights and representation than in the equivalent discussions of the 1970s or 1980s, a result of many years of feminist activism but also of the way in which the revitalised democratic rhetoric of the Convention could be used to imagine claims for gender equality as a national cause that would set a new Scottish Parliament apart from Westminster.[52]

At the time, little attention was given to how far towards a nationalist position the rhetoric of Scottish popular sovereignty took the principal architects of Scottish devolution (in part no doubt because the SNP refused to endorse the 1989 *Claim of Right* and participate in the Constitutional Convention). But by invoking what was said to be a distinctively Scottish constitutional tradition in opposition to the

---

[50] Kenyon Wright, *The People Say Yes* (Glendaruel, Argyll, 1997), p. 14, quoted in Kearton, 'Imagining the "Mongrel Nation"', pp. 37–8. See also Jonathan Hearn, *Claiming Scotland* (Edinburgh, Polygon, 2000), pp. 155–91 on the wider cultural and ideological resonances of the Convention and the *Claim of Right*.

[51] Liz Collie, 'A Woman's Claim of Right', *Radical Scotland*, no. 39, June/July 1989, pp. 12–13; Woman's Claim of Right Group (ed.), *A Woman's Claim of Right in Scotland* (Edinburgh, Polygon, 1991).

[52] Tom Nairn, 'Gender Goes Top of the Agenda' [1994] and Alice Brown, 'Deepening Democracy: Women and the Scottish Parliament' [1998], both reprinted in Fiona MacKay and Esther Breitenbach (eds.), *Women and Contemporary Scottish Politics: An Anthology* (Edinburgh, Polygon, 2001), pp. 195–6, 213–29.

dominant English/British one, and by focusing on the sovereign rights of the Scottish rather than British people, this rhetoric had the potential to unleash a more fundamental critique of the existence of the Union itself. Isobel Lindsay – one of the sponsors of the 1988 *Claim* – had explicitly described this line of argument as a subtle but extremely powerful victory for Scottish nationalists since it shifted the terms of political debate in their favour:

The 'no mandate' argument is not about constitutional law; it is an argument to encourage people to reject the democratic legitimacy of the British system in ruling Scotland. As soon as you begin to question the right of a government for which Scotland did not vote to impose policies on Scotland, you have started to accept the case for Scottish independence.[53]

According to Robert McCreadie, the Liberal Democrats' chief negotiator in the Constitutional Convention, the language about Scottish popular sovereignty had been included at the insistence of the Liberal Democrats precisely to persuade the SNP to rejoin the Convention.[54] Kenyon Wright himself had stressed this very point to the then leader of the SNP, Gordon Wilson (1938–2017), presenting the Convention as in effect an embodiment of the 'gradualist' logic earlier espoused by figures within the national movement. The *Claim of Right*, argued Wright, recognised 'something rooted deeply in the Scottish understanding of sovereignty and power, ie that it is limited and rests ultimately not with the "Crown in Parliament" but with the people'.[55] But in spite of the eloquent, and impeccably gradualist, counterarguments that Isobel Lindsay marshalled to persuade the SNP to join the Constitutional Convention, an SNP leadership that was still scarred by the toxic legacy of the 1970s devolution debates, and buoyed by Jim Sillars's victory in the Glasgow Govan by-election in November 1988, decided that the Convention would not give serious enough consideration to the option of independence, for example by offering a multi-option referendum that would include independence alongside devolution.[56]

[53] Isobel Lindsay, 'Divergent Trends', *Radical Scotland*, no. 29, October/November 1987, p. 15.
[54] Robert McCreadie, 'Scottish Identity and the Constitution', in Bernard Crick (ed.), *National Identities* (Oxford, Blackwell/Political Quarterly, 1990), p. 51. McCreadie later backed the 'Lawyers for Yes' group during the 2014 referendum: Andrew Whitaker, 'Scottish Independence: Lawyers for Yes Launched', *Scotsman*, 23 June 2014.
[55] Canon Kenyon Wright to Gordon Wilson, 9 February 1989, Gordon Wilson Papers, National Library of Scotland, Acc. 13099/57, p. 2.
[56] Isobel Lindsay, 'Why We Should Participate in the Convention', paper for discussion at SNP National Executive Committee, 29 January 1989, Gordon Wilson Papers, National Library of Scotland, Acc. 13099/57; Stewart, *Path to Devolution and Change*, pp. 213–14; McLean, *Getting It Together*, pp. 113–17. For an incisive critique of the SNP's

All of this meant that it was underestimated how significant an ideological move it was for the Labour Party to accept that a separate Scottish popular mandate was essential to rule Scotland legitimately. One of the few to make this point at the time, Roger Levy, observed: 'The *Claim of Right* represents a substantial political coup for the nationalists which can be cashed in at some future date.'[57] Or, to give a slightly different interpretation of this development, the *Claim of Right* showed that Labour could successfully match the SNP on the politics of national identity. But once committed to such a course Labour would have to maintain over time a clearly distinct Scottish profile if it was not then to lose that ground back to the SNP. Labour ultimately failed to do this, so the promissory note of the *Claim of Right* was indeed duly cashed by the SNP during the 2014 independence referendum, to the intense discomfort of a Scottish Labour Party that had allowed its skilful 1990s positioning on Scottish autonomy to decay. The Scottish government's draft constitution for an independent Scotland was based on an affirmation of popular sovereignty, in conscious distinction from UK parliamentary sovereignty. Citing the famous remarks of Lord Cooper to buttress this case, the explanatory notes for the constitution stated of popular sovereignty that

It is a principle charged with historical resonance, affirming the ancient Scots constitutional tradition that monarchs and parliaments are the servants of the people. Sovereignty of the people was clearly set out as early as the Declaration of Arbroath in 1320, refined in the writings of George Buchanan in the late sixteenth century, declared in Scotland's first Claim of Right in 1689 and proclaimed again for modern Scotland by the Constitutional Convention in 1989.[58]

By 2014, it was possible to incorporate the pioneering devolutionists of the 1980s and 1990s into this national sovereigntist tradition. The Scottish Labour Party's use of the Constitutional Convention in 1989 to outmanoeuvre the SNP over devolution had, in the end, proved to be a double-edged sword.

---

positioning at the time, see Tom Nairn, 'The Timeless Girn', in Owen Dudley-Edwards (ed.), *Claim of Right for Scotland*, pp. 163–78.

[57] Levy, *Scottish Nationalism at the Crossroads*, pp. 123–30, 138–9, quote at p. 138. For Labour's journey to this point, see Jack Geekie and Roger Levy, 'Devolution and the Tartanisation of the Labour Party', *Parliamentary Affairs*, 42 (1989), pp. 399–411; Gerry Hassan and Eric Shaw, *The Strange Death of Labour Scotland* (Edinburgh, Edinburgh University Press, 2013), pp. 21–62.

[58] Scottish Government, *The Scottish Independence Bill: A Consultation on an Interim Constitution for Scotland* (Edinburgh, Scottish Government, 2014), p. 27. Though for a critical reading of this interim constitution that suggests it was in fact less democratic than earlier nationalist thinking on this issue, see W. Elliot Bulmer, *Constituting Scotland: The Scottish National Movement and the Westminster Model* (Edinburgh, Edinburgh University Press, 2016), pp. 196–9.

A Diffusionist Tendency

The discussion of sovereignty so far might suggest that Scottish nationalism is an ideology that demands only democratic control for Scotland. But this would be misleading (as we already saw in relation to economic policy in Chapter 4). Scottish nationalists have in fact developed a sophisticated account of how an independent Scotland would simultaneously enjoy self-determination in certain respects but in others share institutions, laws and society with foreign nations. This aspect of the political thought of Scottish nationalism gave the independence case greater credibility from the 1980s onwards, because it acknowledged the realistic limits to Scottish autonomy, and situated the quest for Scottish statehood in a more general reinterpretation of ideas about national sovereignty in the wake of European integration and growing global economic interdependence.[59]

In this sense, Scottish nationalists have at times even suggested that they are not nationalists at all but rather support a revisionist form of unionism. Alex Salmond, for example, has on occasion described himself as a 'post-nationalist'.[60] One of Salmond's most persuasive arguments during the long campaigning preamble to the 2014 independence referendum was his shrewd insistence that Scotland was actually a member of six unions, five of which could be retained after independence. Salmond invoked the great opponent of the 1707 Union of Parliaments, Andrew Fletcher of Saltoun, who had observed that 'all nations are dependent, the one on the many, this we know' but warned that if 'the greater must always swallow the lesser, we are all diminished'. In this light, Salmond argued, even after independence Scotland would remain part of a web of intricate institutional and social interconnections:

We will remain members of the European Union – but with a seat of our own at the top table, and without the endless and desultory London-centric debate about withdrawal. We will still be members of NATO – co-operating with our neighbours and friends in collective security. But we can still decide not to be a nuclear power – like 25 out of 28 current NATO members. We will be part of a currency union with the rest of the UK – but we will now have the full taxation powers we need to promote jobs and investment, social justice and prosperity. And we will retain the monarchy – making the Queen the Head of State of 17 independent countries, rather than 16. However we will adopt a new

---

[59] For this international context, see Michael Keating, *Plurinational Democracy: Stateless Nations in a Post-Sovereignty Era* (Oxford, Oxford University Press, 2001); Eve Hepburn, *Using Europe: Territorial Party Strategies in a Multi-Level System* (Manchester, Manchester University Press, 2010).

[60] Alex Salmond, quoted in Torrance, *Alex Salmond*, p. 244.

constitution, written and endorsed by the people, asserting rights as well as promoting liberties and enshrining the ancient Scottish principle that ultimate sovereignty rests with the people. Those unions – the European Union, the defence union, the currency union and the union of the crowns – are ones which the SNP would propose to maintain because they make sense for both Scotland and the rest of the UK . . . There is a final union which does not rely on the choices made by politicians and parliaments. The social union unites all the peoples of these islands. After independence we will still watch the X-Factor or EastEnders. People in England will still cheer Andy Murray, and people in Scotland will still support the Lions at rugby . . . Under independence, we will continue to share ties of language, culture, trade, family and friendship. The idea that these ties are dependent on a Parliament in London is and has always been totally nonsensical.[61]

Although this pluralist stance on sovereignty has come to the fore only in the most recent iteration of Scottish nationalist thought, as we saw in Chapter 1 it does have precedents in earlier nationalist ideology. In part, this is because the quest for Scottish statehood is fundamentally grounded on an anti-centralising impulse: a biting critique of the government of Scotland from Westminster and the doctrine of parliamentary sovereignty that ideologically animates it. But it is also because of the realpolitik of an independent Scotland: as a small country, Scotland would need to find a place within international relations that combined its new-found autonomy with the constraints inevitably imposed on national self-determination by global power structures and economic integration. There has therefore always been a pluralist dimension to Scottish nationalism. Neil MacCormick, the most important nationalist theorist of this pluralism, observed that his own 'diffusionist' theories pointed back towards earlier ideas about associational autonomy associated with nineteenth and early twentieth-century figures such as the German jurist and historian, Otto von Gierke, and the French jurist and sociologist, Maurice Hauriou, who had rejected the 'undue pretensions of the state to total mastery of a territory' and were concerned about 'the independence and vitality of the manifold communities, guilds, associations, and corporations to be found in civil society'.[62]

Such pluralist currents – although not perhaps the specific theories of Gierke and Hauriou – were also influential at certain junctures in the early formation of Scottish nationalist discourse. As we have seen, what MacCormick called this 'diffusionist tendency' in early Scottish

---

[61] Alex Salmond, 'The Six Unions', speech at Nigg Fabrication Yard, 12 July 2013, at http://news.scotland.gov.uk/Speeches-Briefings/The-six-unions-introduction-51e.aspx (accessed 2 October 2019).

[62] MacCormick, *Questioning Sovereignty*, p. 77.

nationalism was initially expressed in the lively debate among nationalists during the interwar period about how an autonomous Scotland
should relate to England (and the rest of the United Kingdom) and to
the wider British Empire.[63] As Richard Finlay has shown, this was the
source of considerable ideological disagreement in the run-up to the
formation of the SNP and in the rocky early years of the party's existence. An uneasy division existed within the NPS between a more
radical separatist or sovereigntist analysis that sought a Scottish state
that had complete control over domestic and foreign policy and was
firmly anti-imperialist, and a rival view that supported a Scottish parliament as a part of the British Empire, with control over domestic
Scottish matters but wider 'imperial' policy remaining the province
of the Parliament at Westminster. The Scottish Party, the second,
and more establishment, nationalist party that merged with the NPS
to form the SNP in 1934, had many members who saw Scottish self-
government as primarily about enabling Scotland to play a more active
role as a distinct mother nation of the British Empire. After its foundation, SNP policy reflected these tributaries and arrived at the delicate,
and purposefully vague, compromise that a new Scottish parliament
should be created to tend to Scottish affairs, while foreign, defence, and
imperial policy would be determined by new joint committees shared
between England and Scotland. In the course of the 1930s, this compromise frayed under pressure from more radical currents in the SNP,
as the party developed a more staunchly anti-imperialist profile and key
figures in the SNP ended up opposing the British war effort during the
Second World War.[64] In this phase of Scottish nationalism, therefore,
the idea of sharing Scottish sovereignty with both the rest of the United
Kingdom and the British Empire was widely canvassed and endorsed by
leading figures in the movement.

These diffusionist strands of nationalist thought were largely focused on
the relationship between Scotland, the increasingly centralised British state
and economy, and the British Empire. But in the late twentieth century the
development of European integration, and Britain's membership of the
EEC, posed new questions for Scottish nationalism about the nature of
sovereignty and how an independent Scotland might relate to the wider
world. The SNP had been supportive of initial efforts at European integration in the 1940s and 1950s, but grew more sceptical over the course of

[63] MacCormick, *Questioning Sovereignty*, p. 70.
[64] Richard Finlay, '"For or Against?" Scottish Nationalists and the British Empire,
1919–39', *Scottish Historical Review*, 71 (1992), pp. 184–206; Colin Kidd, *Union and
Unionisms*, pp. 259–97.

the 1960s and 1970s.[65] Forthright criticism of Britain's accession to the EEC was mounted by William Wolfe, Winnie Ewing and Gordon Wilson, then the deputy leader of the SNP parliamentary group (1974–9), and they led the SNP in campaigning for a 'no' vote in the 1975 referendum on Britain's membership.[66] In their view, the EEC constituted a further layer of undemocratic and centralised government that would merely exacerbate the problems faced by nations on its periphery such as Scotland. 'It is the aim of the Common Market', argued Wolfe, 'to establish political domination of the whole of Western Europe and to tolerate no deviations from this line. The Common Marketeers of today are as much doctrinaire centralists as their opposite numbers in the Kremlin in Moscow.' Continued membership of the EEC would result, he said, in 'a political dark age of remote control and undemocratic government'.[67]

It was telling, however, that the language the SNP used against European integration was a pluralist, decentralising rhetoric rather than a more straightforwardly nationalist one. As Winnie Ewing argued, 'decision-makers must be where the people live, or a valuable part of the enjoyment of life to the full is lost', whereas the EEC offered 'an undemocratic community' that was 'controlled by bureaucrats'.[68] Scottish nationalist sceptics of the EEC perceptively noted that the pro-European case in Britain was itself one that at times relied on a rather conventional notion of British exceptionalism. Ewing observed that the pro-European argument seemed to be 'that Britain must be great again' by leading in Europe: 'if we want to play at influencing events, we are told, it has to be from within a superpower'. But in Scotland, she said, 'we are not particularly worried that we lost the Empire'.[69] The belief

---

[65] As we saw in Chapter 3, this was not true of other, non-SNP intellectual sympathisers with independence, such as Tom Nairn: see his pioneering *The Left against Nationalism?* (Harmondsworth, Penguin, 1973); and 'Old and New Scottish Nationalism', in G. Brown (ed.), *The Red Paper on Scotland* (Edinburgh, EUSPB, 1975), pp. 49–54, the latter of which clearly articulated an early version of the 'independence in Europe' approach that the SNP would subsequently adopt in the 1980s.

[66] Paolo Dardanelli, *Between Two Unions: Europeanisation and Scottish Devolution* (Manchester, Manchester University Press, 2006), pp. 29–30; Peter Lynch, *Minority Nationalism and European Integration* (Cardiff, University of Wales Press, 1996), pp. 29–36; Robert Saunders, *Yes to Europe! The 1975 Referendum and Seventies Britain* (Cambridge, Cambridge University Press, 2018), pp. 351–6.

[67] Wolfe, *Scotland Lives*, p. 139; William Wolfe, *Scotsman*, 22 May 1975, quoted in Robert Saunders, '"An Auction of Fear?" The Scotland in Europe Referendum, 1975', *Renewal*, 22 (2014), p. 89; 'Overwhelming "No" to EEC from Nationalists', *Scotsman*, 2 June 1975.

[68] Winifred Ewing, Hansard, HC Debates, fifth series, vol. 796, cols. 1086, 1088 (24 February 1970).

[69] Winifred Ewing, Hansard, HC Debates, fifth series, vol. 883, col. 1956 (19 December 1974).

among the English elite that Europe was 'a substitute for their lost Empire', claimed an SNP leaflet, had little force north of the border: 'Must these absurd dreams of renewed English imperial greatness and domination lead to Scotland being dragged into the Common Market, with all its economic and political dangers'?[70] Even Robert McIntyre, who had supported the early steps towards European integration in the 1940s and 1950s, accepted the party line on the EEC when he stood for Parliament. As the SNP candidate in the 1971 Stirling and Falkirk by-election, his campaign literature baldly stated: 'I am opposed to going into the Common Market', since it would put up prices, damage farming and (more idiosyncratically) extend the influence of trade unionism across Europe, allowing 'even more remote control than at present'.[71]

Independence in Europe

Yet this Euroscepticism eventually gave way to a more sympathetic engagement with European integration. The EEC itself evolved in a more regionalist and welfarist direction in the 1980s, to Scotland's tangible benefit, while the British state had of course done the opposite. In this context, senior figures in the SNP began to rethink their initial opposition to the EEC and instead to see a putative Scottish member-ship of the organisation as offering a context within which independ-ence seemed a less radical and economically fraught step. Both Gordon Wilson, who became party leader after 1979, and Winnie Ewing shifted their positions on the EEC as these advantages became clear (Ewing herself served as an MEP 1975–99), and the SNP officially changed its position on the EEC at its 1983 conference, recommending Scottish membership, though only after a post-independence referendum on the subject.[72]

But the most powerful advocate of this change of policy – because of his unimpeachable socialist credentials – was Jim Sillars, who when a Labour MP had been an advocate of a 'no' vote in the 1975 referendum. While still a Labour MP, however, Sillars had made clear that he thought that there was a qualitative difference between Scottish devolution in the context of the United Kingdom and in the context of the EEC. If Britain remained in the EEC as it was currently constituted, he argued in 1974,

---

[70] 'Common Market: Stop the Sell-Out', SNP leaflet, n.d. [c. 1970–2], SNP Papers, National Library of Scotland, Acc. 7295/24.

[71] Robert McIntyre, election leaflet, Stirling by-election, 16 September 1971, SNP Papers, National Library of Scotland, Acc. 7295/23.

[72] Lynch, *Minority Nationalism*, pp. 36–44; Atsuko Ichijo, *Scottish Nationalism and the Idea of Europe* (London, Routledge, 2004).

then 'part of the price of entry may be an end to the Union as we know it'. Sillars thought that in this scenario Scotland's interests would likely require separate representation in Brussels for Scotland's voice to be heard on an equal basis: 'we might need to go to Brussels as a separate entity, like the Danes, the Belgians and the Southern Irish'.[73] Sillars decisively shifted his position in favour of this view when he formed the ill-fated breakaway SLP in 1976, which as we saw in Chapter 4 aimed to synthesise left-wing and nationalist politics in response to the rise of the SNP. 'Scotland in Europe' became a cornerstone of the SLP's ideological positioning as a means of distinguishing it from the SNP's Euroscepticism, but it also reflected Sillars's conviction that, since membership of the EEC was now resolved, separate Scottish representation in European institutions was essential to securing Scottish interests.[74] The SLP's argument – later to become a very familiar one in Scottish politics – was that European integration had now constrained the sovereignty of all member states and that 'separate' statehood no longer existed as a viable option for either Scotland or Britain. Instead, Europe could provide a framework in which some policy autonomy could be exercised by a Scottish state without disrupting any of the existing trading relationships between Scotland and the rest of the United Kingdom.[75] Sillars carried these views with him into the SNP in 1980 and continued to develop them in response to the changing character of the EEC in the 1980s.

Sillars argued that global economic changes, including the rise of Pacific economies such as Japan and China, were bringing about a new era of large economic blocs in which European nations would need to work together to form a coherent counterweight.[76] Sillars also observed that the pace of European integration in the late 1980s was bringing about 'a process of change in the nature of national sovereignty that cannot be averted or reversed'. The arrival of a single European market in 1992, he predicted, would in due course create further pressure to

---

[73] Jim Sillars, Hansard, HC Debates, fifth series, vol. 880, cols. 135–6 (29 October 1974).

[74] Jim Sillars, 'Let's Sit at the Top Table in Europe', *The Highway*, July 1975, p. 6; 'Our Voice in Europe', *Forward Scotland: Journal of the Scottish Labour Party*, no. 1, July 1976, pp. 4–5; Henry Drucker, *Breakaway: The Scottish Labour Party* (Edinburgh, EUSPB, 1978), pp. 59, 107; Jim Sillars, *Independence in Europe* (Glasgow, SNP, June 1989), p. 2.

[75] 'Scottish Government', draft discussion paper, Scottish Labour Party, n.d. [c. 1976], Scottish Labour Party Edinburgh Branch Papers, National Library of Scotland, Acc. 7472/9, pp. 1–3.

[76] Jim Sillars, *Scotland: Moving on and up in Europe* (no publisher/place of publication, June 1985), p. 9; Jim Sillars, *No Turning Back: The Case for Scottish Independence within the European Community and How We Face the Challenge of 1992* (no publisher/place of publication, August 1988), pp. 7–8; Sillars, *Independence*, pp. 7–8.

integrate 'currencies, monetary policies, fiscal policies, and social policies'. Although Sillars thought it was as yet unclear precisely how this integration would proceed, the nationalist concern was that Scottish interests could not be adequately represented in the ensuing discussions via the British state. Scotland could only have a serious role in these debates if it took its place as a full member with veto power rather than being restricted to lobbying the British government.[77] The great value of an independent Scotland as a member of the EEC for Sillars was that it would magnify Scottish influence: as an equal member of the community, Scotland would have full voting rights and bargaining power in European negotiations and in the Council of Ministers; would periodically hold the European presidency; would nominate a commissioner and member of the European Court of Justice; and would gain additional MEPs.[78] In Sillars's view, participation in European integration even had the potential to bring about a cultural change within Scotland by making Scottish politics less provincial and more outward looking.[79] Indeed, Sillars maintained that the goal of independence should itself be reframed as part of a 'world-wide movement of people who, caught in an increasingly internationalised world, know that their sovereign power cannot be exercised any longer in the style of the old "sovereign state"'. As a result, he claimed, 'all over the world there is a search for a balance between the international need to group and pool sovereignty, and the human desire to feel in control of certain essential elements of social and economic life'.[80] Independence within the EEC would provide the solution to this dilemma for Scotland.

Although Sillars's analysis accepted that European integration was changing the parameters of national sovereignty, it was nonetheless unclear whether he personally favoured further European integration on monetary, social and fiscal policies. His main point was the procedural one that Scotland would only be in a position to influence, and if necessary veto, such policies if it was an independent member of the EEC.[81] Sillars was broadly supportive of the signing of the Single European Act in 1986, though he warned that the single market would only work fairly for Scotland if combined with a stronger European regional policy, an independent Scottish state focused on developing a more dynamic Scottish economy, and ultimately greater democratisation of

[77] Sillars, *Independence*, pp. 5–7, quotes at p. 5; Jim Sillars, *Scotland: The Case for Optimism* (Edinburgh, Polygon, 1986), pp. 188–91.

[78] Sillars, *Scotland: Moving on and up*, pp. 5–8; Sillars, *No Turning Back*, pp. 9–11; Sillars, *Independence*, pp. 15–20.

[79] Sillars, *No Turning Back*, pp. 3–4; Sillars, *Independence*, pp. 21–3.

[80] Sillars, *Independence*, p. 44.   [81] Sillars, *Independence*, pp. 16–18.

European institutions.[82] But he did stress – and this was of great political importance – that one consequence of European integration, and the single market in particular, was that Scottish independence would no longer be vulnerable to the charge of 'separatism' from unionists. This was a point he had already made while in the SLP: Scottish independence in the EEC, Sillars said in 1977, would mean 'a change in Scotland's political status and standing, but no fundamental change in our trading relations with the rest of the UK, or alteration to our right of access to a home market of 250 million people in Europe'.[83] Sillars continued to hammer home this message in the SNP in the 1980s. An independent Scotland in Europe could simply retain all of its existing international links: 'continued membership means continuity in traditional trading patterns, access to markets, maintenance of the economic framework within which companies have planned their investment' and also 'continuity for the free movement of people with no barriers to the family and social relationships that exist between the peoples in the British Isles'.[84] Membership of the EEC would therefore also preserve what Sillars termed the 'social union' between Scotland and England:

That is the easy familiarity with each other's ways, the network of families and friendships, the ease of travel to see each other, the business contacts, and the close working relationship between trade unionists north and south of the border who frequently share a common employer in Britain and, increasingly, with other workers in Europe. Already developing is a new social union with the European Community as a whole.[85]

In 1988 the SNP formalised its policy as 'Independence in Europe', which was also very successful as a pithy slogan that captured the essence of this strand of nationalism – or, as some commentators (and, as we have seen, Alex Salmond himself) called it, 'post-nationalism'.[86]

---

[82] Sillars, *No Turning Back*, pp. 13–17; Sillars, *Independence*, pp. 8–15.

[83] Jim Sillars, Hansard, HC Debates, fifth series, vol. 939, cols. 137–8 (14 November 1977).

[84] Sillars, *Scotland: Moving on and Moving up*, pp. 4–6, quote at p. 5; Sillars, *No Turning Back*, pp. 6–7; Sillars, *Independence*, pp. 37–8; see also Alex Salmond, 'Scotland in Europe: Living with the Single European Act', *Radical Scotland*, no. 34, August/September 1988, p. 10.

[85] Sillars, *Independence*, p. 38; see also Sillars, *Scotland: The Case for Optimism*, pp. 183–6. The notion of a persisting 'social union' after the end of the political union dates back to SNP debates in the 1970s: James Mitchell, 'Varieties of Independence', in Gerry Hassan and James Mitchell (eds.), *After Independence* (Edinburgh, Luath Press, 2013), p. 48.

[86] David McCrone, 'Post-Nationalism and the Decline of the Nation State', *Radical Scotland*, no. 49, February/March 1991, pp. 6–8; Richard Kearney, 'Towards a Post-Nationalist Archipelago', *Edinburgh Review*, no. 103, 2000, pp. 21–35; Alex Salmond, quoted in Torrance, *Alex Salmond*, p. 244.

Yet it was also possible to argue that this embrace of Europe was rather instrumental in character. As Stephen Maxwell put it, the SNP's new-found zest for Europe 'assesses the European Community almost entirely in terms of its usefulness to the cause of Scotland's independence', rather than representing a serious engagement with the reasons for European integration.[87] Both Maxwell and Isobel Lindsay, who had been long-standing critics of the EEC, maintained that a clear-eyed analysis of European integration in fact revealed a basic tension between the SNP's sovereigntist nationalism and the project of European federalism. They saw the direction of travel within the EEC – towards the single market and monetary union – as depriving national parliaments of key policy powers, including some that an independent Scotland would need to use to revive the Scottish economy, such as state aid, preferential public procurement policies, preventing foreign takeovers of Scottish companies, and limiting the rights of non-Scottish citizens to own Scottish land. Maxwell and Lindsay argued that the mere fact of growing economic interdependence did not in itself narrow national sovereignty: a nation's sovereignty, said Maxwell, was best understood as 'the right to shape its own future' and in the context of a more integrated global economy 'that claim is to the right by a community to decide its own priorities between the options deter-mined by the realities of interdependence, with all the costs and benefits involved'.[88] From this perspective, Maxwell and Lindsay judged that the EEC was pursuing a model of integration that would foreclose rather than facilitate this right of decision for Scotland.

As we have seen, there was also some ambiguity in this respect in Jim Sillars's presentation of his case *for* European integration insofar as he reserved judgement on issues such as monetary or fiscal union. Sillars explicitly stated that the new position he had set out for the SNP was not a federalist one, but rather embraced a 'confederal system, where ultim-ate political and legal supremacy rests with the constituent members'. The central institutions of the EEC, Sillars argued, were subordinate to the 'sovereign, independent states' that had agreed 'through inter-national treaties to pool a certain amount of their sovereignty' but only to a specific and delimited extent.[89] Sillars was therefore an advocate of an intergovernmental rather than federal model of Europe in the 1980s and 1990s. His subsequent advocacy of a 'leave' vote in the 2016 Europe

---

[87] Stephen Maxwell, 'Scotland International', *Cencrastus*, no. 35, winter 1989, p. 17.

[88] Stephen Maxwell, 'Scotland in a Wider Europe', *Radical Scotland*, no. 40, August/September 1989, pp. 24–6, quote at p. 25; Maxwell, 'Scotland International', pp. 17–18; Isobel Lindsay, 'The SNP and the Lure of Europe', in Tom Gallagher (ed.), *Nationalism in the Nineties* (Edinburgh, Polygon, 1991), pp. 84–101.

[89] Jim Sillars, Hansard, HC Debates, sixth series, vol. 199, col. 364 (20 November 1991).

referendum – on the grounds that the national veto had lost its decisive power in EU affairs and the unaccountable Commission had now become too powerful in its own right – suggests that he had long had underlying doubts about how far European integration should go.[90] However, during the 1990s a more fleshed-out, principled case for Scottish independence in Europe was in fact constructed that, among other things, aimed to address the concerns about sovereignty raised by figures such as Lindsay and Maxwell. This case was more sympathetic than Sillars to the trend of European integration at the end of the twentieth century and was given its most powerful theoretical expression in the writings of Neil MacCormick.

MacCormick v. the Sovereign State

Neil MacCormick was a long-standing SNP member who combined his activism for the party (and a stint as an MEP) with a distinguished career as a legal philosopher, serving as the Regius Professor of Public Law and the Law of Nature and Nations at Edinburgh University from 1972 until 2008.[91] Although a staunch supporter of the SNP, MacCormick adopted a cautious and gradualist stance towards the ultimate goal of Scottish independence.[92] His earliest writings on Scottish government confessed some ambivalence about whether he ultimately supported advanced devolution rather than independence. He was also certain that establishing a devolved Scottish parliament would in any case represent a necessary first step on the road to independence, since the complexities of establishing a new Scottish state from scratch were in his view prohibitive.[93] MacCormick's explicit commitment to Scottish independence became stronger over time (although he remained a gradualist with respect to devolution as a necessary first step towards full Scottish statehood).[94]

---

[90] Jim Sillars, 'Why Scottish Nationalists Should Back Brexit', *CommonSpace*, 9 May 2016, at www.commonspace.scot/articles/3976/jim-sillars-why-scottish-nationalists-should-back-brexit (accessed 2 October 2019). Sillars did favour an independent Scotland joining EFTA.

[91] Drew Scott, 'Neil MacCormick: Public Intellectual', in Neil Walker (ed.), *MacCormick's Scotland* (Edinburgh, Edinburgh University Press, 2012), pp. 205–19.

[92] An early criticism of MacCormick as too conservative philosophically and legally to offer a serious challenge to the British state is Tony Clarty, 'Scottish Legal Culture and the Withering Away of the State: A Study in MacCormick's Nationalism', *Cencrastus*, no. 14, autumn 1983, pp. 5–9.

[93] Neil MacCormick, 'Introduction' and 'Independence and Constitutional Change', in Neil MacCormick (ed.), *The Scottish Debate: Essays on Scottish Nationalism* (Oxford, Oxford University Press, 1970), pp. 2, 58–64.

[94] Neil MacCormick, 'Unrepentant Gradualism', in Owen Dudley-Edwards (ed.), *Claim of Right for Scotland*, pp. 99–109.

By the electoral peak of the SNP in the 1970s MacCormick was involved
with the party both as an unsuccessful parliamentary candidate and as
one of the authors (along with for example Isobel Lindsay and Robert
McIntyre) of the SNP's draft constitution for an independent Scotland
in 1976–7, the text that formed the basis of later revised versions
(under MacCormick's guidance) until 2002.[95] As we have seen, he
was closely involved in the home rule campaigns of the 1980s and the
1988 *Claim of Right*.

Nonetheless, MacCormick had understandable reservations about the
historical record of the nation state as a purely sovereigntist assertion of
national identity and, as early as 1979, noted that the 'hesitant moves' in
the direction of 'the supranational confederation towards which the
European Community is groping' offered welcome new opportunities
to develop 'a diffusion of governmental power among various levels of
government'.[96] At this stage, MacCormick noted that it seemed appropriate that future constitutional reform should recognise that the nations
that made up the United Kingdom had sufficient common interests to
retain shared political institutions, 'whether through common membership of the European Community, or through specifically British institutions such as a common crown, or both'. MacCormick also suggested
that he was willing to see a scheme for British federalism 'given a full and
fair trial', though he doubted that in the absence of nationalist pressure
from Scotland and Wales there was any chance of such a scheme
emerging as a practical possibility.[97] This was an early sketch of what
was later to become a crucial theme in MacCormick's legal and political
philosophy. In parallel with the debates about 'independence in Europe'
that preoccupied the SNP in the late 1980s and early 1990s, MacCormick began to engage theoretically with the implications of European
integration for the concept of sovereignty more generally and for Scotland's constitutional future in particular.

As the ratification of the Maastricht Treaty consumed the energies of
the British (and indeed European) political class, MacCormick gave a
path-breaking Chorley lecture at the LSE on 3 June 1992 entitled
'Beyond the Sovereign State'. MacCormick's work in legal philosophy

---

[95] Neil MacCormick, 'An Idea for a Scottish Constitution', in Wilson Finnie, Chris
Himsworth and Neil Walker (eds.), *Edinburgh Essays in Public Law* (Edinburgh,
Edinburgh University Press, 1991), pp. 159–84; W. Elliot Bulmer, 'An Analysis of the
Scottish National Party's Draft Constitution for Scotland', *Parliamentary Affairs*, 64
(2011), pp. 687–8; Bulmer, *Constituting Scotland*, pp. 103–4.

[96] Neil MacCormick, 'Nation and Nationalism' [1979], in his *Legal Right and Social
Democracy* (Oxford, Oxford University Press, 1982), pp. 261–2.

[97] MacCormick, 'Nation and Nationalism', in his *Legal Right and Social Democracy*, p. 264.

had led him to develop a theory of law as an institutional normative order, by which he meant that law is present not only through the state but in a variety of contexts in which individual judgement is superseded by general rules underpinned by institutions with responsibility for formulating and enforcing those rules.[98] It was therefore possible for multiple legal systems to coexist, and 'overlap and interact', with one another, as opposed to the idea that 'all law must originate in a single power source, like a sovereign'.[99] MacCormick drew on this pluralistic vision of a multiplicity of legal orders to detect within the emerging structures of the newly renamed European Community (EC), and the wider growth of global international cooperation, a 'post-sovereign' political order. For members of the EC, MacCormick argued, state sovereignty no longer existed in its traditional sense, but this did not mean that instead the EC as an institution itself exercised this sovereignty. Instead, there was 'a pooling or a fusion' of member states' legal powers with respect 'to a wide but restricted range of subjects', which left some issues in the hands of 'one normative system or normative order' while others were the province of a different one.[100] As MacCormick observed, the implication of this analysis of sovereignty was not only that existing states could transfer appropriate powers to supranational bodies, but also that power might be diffused downwards from the state level. MacCormick argued that the European doctrine of subsidiarity, that decisions should be taken at the lowest level possible, should be central to this emerging new constitutional order. In the case of the United Kingdom, such a 'diffusion of political power centres as well as of legal authorities' would lead to the abandonment of parliamentary sovereignty and place on the agenda 'diffusing legal authority inside the UK to the constituent nations or other subdivisions where subsidiarity makes this seem sound'.[101]

This analysis left tantalisingly indeterminate how far it would indeed be desirable on these grounds for Scotland to secure independence rather than some form of advanced devolution, although MacCormick was also a leading advocate of the political theory of 'liberal nationalism', which depicted national identities as crucial (historically given) contexts in which individuals can 'acquire character and self-consciousness' and therefore regarded the preservation of civic national identities as a

---

[98] Neil MacCormick, 'Institutional Normative Order: A Conception of Law', *Cornell Law Review*, 82 (1997), pp. 1051–70; and in a later form in his *Questioning Sovereignty*, pp. 1–26.

[99] Neil MacCormick, 'Beyond the Sovereign State', *Modern Law Review*, 56 (1993), p. 8.

[100] MacCormick, 'Beyond the Sovereign State', p. 16.

[101] MacCormick, 'Beyond the Sovereign State', pp. 17–18.

legitimate goal of progressive politics.[102] MacCormick further developed his analysis over the course of the 1990s, culminating in his response to the arrival of Scottish devolution as government policy after 1997. Mac-Cormick predicted that the new Scottish Parliament would turn the anomaly of Scotland's constitutional position from an inconspicuous one to a highly visible one, in which Scottish MPs would continue to play a role in many aspects of governing England but without themselves having any say over the equivalent policy decisions in Scotland. He believed that the foundations of the devolution settlement were therefore unstable, and that Scotland's constitutional status would eventually require further attention.

In MacCormick's view, the seemingly 'logical' solution of constructing a fully federal British constitution was unlikely to work, since the size of England was too large to achieve the necessary balance between the different members of the federation (given the small number of members of any putative British federation structured along national lines). Even were England to be divided into regional assemblies, he noted, this would not tackle the central difficulty of the legislative powers held by the Scottish Parliament. It seemed highly unlikely that English lawmaking powers of the kind exercised in Edinburgh would or could be split between different English regions (with, for example, regional diver-gences in health provision). MacCormick therefore argued that the most promising solution to this impasse was an independent Scotland as a member of the EU, complemented by an intergovernmental Council of the Isles to deal with issues specific to the British archipelago. With these arrangements in place, Scotland would secure a relationship of equality with the rest of the United Kingdom, and other European states, as fellow members of the European Union.[103] The 'process of division and com-bination' of national sovereignty offered by European integration thus opened the way to a model of Scottish independence in which a Scottish state would take over important powers held at Westminster while in other domains sharing powers at a European and even British level.[104] In a framing that probably influenced Alex Salmond's later remarks about the five unions of which an independent Scotland would remain a

---

[102] Neil MacCormick, 'Liberalism, Nationalism and the Post-Sovereign State', *Political Studies*, 44 (1996), pp. 562–6, quote at p. 564. MacCormick drew here on Yael Tamir, *Liberal Nationalism* (Princeton, NJ, Princeton University Press, 1993), although he had made similar observations in his own earlier work: for example 'Nation and Nationalism', in Colin MacLean (ed.), *The Crown and the Thistle: The Nature of Nationhood* (Edinburgh, Scottish Academic Press, 1979), pp. 101–3, 109.

[103] MacCormick, *Questioning Sovereignty*, pp. 61–2, 193–9.

[104] MacCormick, *Questioning Sovereignty*, p. 133.

member, MacCormick described independence as Scotland simply exchanging 'new unions for old' rather than striking out on its own.[105]

Oh, to Be in Britain?

MacCormick's theoretical vision of a pluralist pooling of sovereignty at the national and supranational level percolated quite deeply into the practical case that nationalists articulated for Scottish independence in the early twenty-first century. Their enthusiastic embrace of post-sovereignty was also encouraged by a growing interest among nationalists in Ireland's successful transformation into a vibrant European economy. Ireland was thought to show that participation in Europe could enhance the power of small states and, most importantly, enable England's neighbours to stand in a relationship of equality with it for the first time in their history.[106] This was a point that was made with particular force by the former Irish Taoiseach, Garret Fitzgerald (1926–2011), in a 1989 lecture at Stirling University and then in the 1990 John Mackintosh lecture at Edinburgh University, which were widely discussed by Scottish nationalists.[107]

George Reid, as we have seen a leading figure in the SNP of the 1970s, returned from a long exile from active politics to deliver an influential Donaldson lecture to the 1995 SNP conference which made a compelling case for the importance of 'post-sovereignty' to the cause of independence. Drawing on MacCormick's work, as well as Fitzgerald's lectures and like-minded writers such as Neal Ascherson and Tom Nairn, Reid argued that a historical 'pincer movement' was undermining the British state – on the one hand, the need for supranational structures for economic cooperation and on the other a desire for greater local control: 'the state today is too big to address the needs of minorities like the Catalans and Scots. It is too small, in an age of global macroeconomics, to operate the old economic particularism.' As a result, argued Reid, Scottish nationalists should abandon 'the language of the nineteenth-century nation state' (and the absolutist British notion of

---

[105] MacCormick, *Questioning Sovereignty*, pp. 193–204; Neil MacCormick, 'New Unions for Old', in William Miller (ed.), *Anglo-Scottish Relations from 1900 to Devolution and Beyond* (Oxford, Oxford University Press/British Academy, 2005), pp. 249–55.

[106] *The Power of Small Nations in the New Europe* (Edinburgh, Scottish Centre for Economic and Social Research, 1994), pp. 2–8.

[107] Garret Fitzgerald, 'Anglo-Irish Relations After 1921', *Scots Independent*, no. 221, August 1989, pp. 4–5; Garret Fitzgerald, 'Evolving Relationships After 1973', *Scots Independent*, no. 222, September 1989, pp. 4–5; Fitzgerald, 'Better Relationships', pp. 4, 9; Garret Fitzgerald, 'The British and Irish in the Context of Europe', John Mackintosh Memorial Lecture, October 1990, Edinburgh University, reprinted in Crick (ed.), *National Identities*, pp. 7–24.

parliamentary sovereignty) and instead enthusiastically embrace the sharing of power with other European nations.[108] As the remarks by Alex Salmond quoted earlier illustrate, this was not just a matter of pooling resources and sharing sovereignty with the EU. Scottish nationalists were for example content with a new Scottish state retaining the 1603 union of the crowns and thus with Elizabeth I (of Scotland) remaining as its head of state. Membership of NATO would embed the new state in the transatlantic military alliance. Some nationalists even suggested that a number of state institutions and services might be shared by a Scottish state and the rest of the United Kingdom: the Ordinance Survey, say, or the DVLA, or the Civil Aviation Authority, or even some aspects of national defence.[109] Andrew Wilson (b. 1970), a newly elected SNP MSP close to Alex Salmond, provoked controversy in the national movement by arguing in 1999 that it would be possible for citizens of an independent Scotland to remain culturally British after the Anglo-Scottish political union was dissolved.[110] These examples could also be extended to embrace the realm of macroeconomic policy, as in the run-up to the 2014 referendum the Scottish government proposed that an independent Scotland would continue to use sterling as its currency and the Bank of England as its central bank.[111]

Yet, as MacCormick himself noted, there was no definitive logical relationship between the advent of 'post-sovereignty' and an independent Scotland. Rather, this analysis established independence as 'one among a range of reasonable choices, not that it is a required or obligatory outcome'.[112] In this sense, it was certainly possible – at least before 2014 – to envisage an advanced devolutionary settlement that pooled

---

[108] George Reid, 'Oh, to Be in Britain?', Donaldson Lecture (Edinburgh, SNP, September 1995); Eddie Barnes, 'What the New Form of Independence Is All About', *Scotsman*, 14 May 2011. Reid cited here Neal Ascherson, 'Local Government and the Myth of Sovereignty', Fifth Sovereignty Lecture, 25 February 1994, Royal Museum of Scotland (London, Charter 88 Trust, 1994).

[109] Kenny MacAskill, *Building a Nation: Post-Devolution Nationalism in Scotland* (Edinburgh, Luath Press, 2004), pp. 29–30; George Kerevan, 'SNP on Thin Ice Until It Finds a Real Vision', *Scotsman*, 19 April 2004; Dennis MacLeod and Michael Russell, *Grasping the Thistle* (Glendaruel, Argyll Publishing, 2006), pp. 12–13, 150; Angus Robertson, quoted in Barnes, 'New Form of Independence'.

[110] 'Scottish Nationalism Second Thoughts', *Economist*, 23 September 1999.

[111] James Stafford, 'The Revenge of Sovereignty: The SNP, the Financial Crisis and UK Constitutional Reform', *SPERI Paper no. 20* (Sheffield, SPERI, March 2015); Coree Brown Swan and Bettina Petersohn, 'The Currency Issue', in Michael Keating (ed.), *Debating Scotland: Issues of Independence and Union in the 2014 Referendum* (Oxford, Oxford University Press, 2017), pp. 65–83.

[112] MacCormick, *Questioning Sovereignty*, p. 204. For a helpful analysis of the issues here, see Neil Walker, 'Scottish Nationalism For and Against the Union State', in Walker (ed.), *MacCormick's Scotland*, pp. 163–90.

sovereignty between Edinburgh, London and Brussels in a sufficiently flexible and pluralistic fashion to satisfy MacCormick's theoretical desiderata. Before the referendum of 2014, this was the major ideological victory of the 'gradualist' position within the SNP: Scottish autonomy had become conceptualised as an open-ended process whereby ever greater powers could accrue to the Scottish Parliament, when Scottish public opinion demanded it, with the ultimate goal of independence representing a distant objective that would only be reached (if desired by the voters) across a long time horizon. The opportunity to hold a referendum on Scottish independence, when it unexpectedly arose because the SNP won a majority in the 2011 Scottish Parliament election, placed pressure on this strategic outlook, since the referendum had the effect of popularising independence as a rupture from the status quo, something that stood in tension with the SNP's previous efforts to make the enhancement of Scottish autonomy appear to be a slower and less risky proposition. The 2016 referendum on Britain's membership of the EU added a further dilemma for the advocates of 'post-sovereignty', since it confronted supporters of independence with the very forced choice that they sought to escape from by embracing European integration back in the 1980s: between an independent Scotland with unhindered economic relations with the rest of the United Kingdom out of the EU, or a Scotland separated from the United Kingdom's single market as a full member of the EU. The delicate balance between sovereignty and post-sovereignty in the case for Scottish independence therefore remains a pressing issue that will require careful rethinking in the future.

Conclusion
'The Dream Shall Never Die'

> I am a nationalist only in the sense that the sane Heptarchian was a Wessexman or a Mercian or what not: temporarily, opportunistically. I think the Braid Scots may yet give lovely lights and shadows not only to English but to the perfected speech of Cosmopolitan Man: so I cultivate it, for lack of that perfect speech that is yet to be. I think there's a chance that Scotland, especially in its Glasgow, in its bitter straightening of the economic struggle, may win to a freedom preparatory to, and in alignment with, that cosmopolitan freedom, long before England: so, a cosmopolitan opportunist, I am some kind of Nationalist. Lewis Grassic Gibbon, 1934[1]

The 2014 referendum on Scottish independence was a political drama unlike any other in modern Scottish history. The level of popular engagement was extraordinarily high – reflecting the political stakes – and generated an impassioned and forthright public discussion. Although for some in the 'no' camp the referendum was an unpleasant experience, the debate was in fact a relatively sophisticated one. The case for independence that was voiced in the run-up to September 2014 was kaleidoscopic, or even rather chaotic, as some Unionists argued. But while many different arguments were produced by supporters of the 'Yes' campaign, the overall structure of the case marshalled by the SNP and their allies was greatly indebted to the authors and texts examined in this book. The ideas of a whole generation of nationalist writers, activists and politicians – born between the 1930s and the early 1950s and formed politically by the hopes and disappointments of the 1970s rise of Scottish nationalism – at last came to fruition. These '79ers – figures such as Neal Ascherson, Winnie Ewing, George Kerevan, Isobel Lindsay, Neil MacCormick, Margo MacDonald, William McIlvanney, Stephen Maxwell, Tom Nairn, George Reid, Alex Salmond and Jim Sillars – had steadily constructed a powerful and influential ideology of Scottish nationalism

---

[1] Lewis Grassic Gibbon, 'Glasgow', in Lewis Grassic Gibbon and Hugh MacDiarmid, *Scottish Scene or the Intelligent Man's Guide to Albyn* (London, Jarrolds, 1934), p. 146.

over the course of the preceding fifty years. Yet as we have seen through-out this book, the balance of their arguments had also changed by the time the 2014 referendum came into view.

The Political Thought of 2014

Stephen Maxwell authored a powerful final intellectual statement in his book, *Arguing for Independence*, published posthumously in 2012. It was a particularly informative document about the way in which Scottish nationalist thinking had evolved since the 1960s. Maxwell sought to establish, as parsimoniously as possible, the advantages that would be enjoyed by a new Scottish state. Although he set out a number of distinct arguments for independence, the core of Maxwell's case was democratic and economic. In democratic terms, Maxwell argued, Scottish independ-ence would ensure that the Scottish people would be ruled by a govern-ment that had the support of a plurality or majority of the Scottish electorate, and that the Scottish state was a fully liberal democratic one, organised around a written constitution, a proportional electoral system, the full panoply of modern rights protections, and a public culture that would hold executive power to account.[2] Maxwell was joined by George Kerevan in articulating this democratic argument. Kerevan's own extended 'Case for Yes' presented Scottish independence as motivated by the need to break from, and help to reform, the 'over-centralised, elitist political superstructure' of the British state, which had never shaken off its historical roots as a 'political compromise between aristocratic landowners and early mercantile capitalists'. For Kerevan, independence was desirable because it would make Scotland more democratically governed, a result that would enable a more coherent modernisation of Scotland than had been possible under British rule.[3] William McIlvanney also penned a characteristically eloquent version of this argument in 2014, depicting England as constitutionally frozen after 1688 into a precedent-bound traditionalism, which impeded political progress and had been best expressed by the political theory of Edmund Burke. As McIlvanney summarised this quintessentially 'English' philosophy: 'what this leads to is a kind of intellectual *mortmain*: the dead hand of the collective past clenched around the possibility of serious change'.[4]

---

[2] Stephen Maxwell, *Arguing for Independence: Evidence, Risk and the Wicked Issues* (Edinburgh, Luath Press, 2012), pp. 33–50.

[3] George Kerevan, 'The Case for Yes', in George Kerevan and Alan Cochrane, *Scottish Independence: Yes or No* (Stroud, History Press, 2014), pp. 9–28, quotes at pp. 17–18.

[4] William McIlvanney, *Dreaming Scotland* (Edinburgh, Saltire Society, 2014), pp. 10–12, quote at p. 11.

Neal Ascherson, meanwhile, argued that with independence for Scotland 'the people would become sovereign in the normal European way' rather than continuing to endure 'England's weird doctrine of parliamentary absolutism'.[5]

Although Maxwell, Kerevan, McIlvanney and Ascherson wore the theoretical depth of these arguments lightly in what were intended to be accessible short works, they clearly drew on the intellectual sources analysed in this book (and in some cases on their own earlier work). The claim that a Scottish tradition of popular sovereignty had been frustrated by the Union, and in particular by the Thatcher government, animated them, while their critique of the archaic quality of British democracy, sure to be improved upon in an independent Scotland, put forward the Anderson–Nairn and later Charter 88 reading of the arrested consti-tutional development of the United Kingdom. As Maxwell put it: 'The explicit replacement in a Scottish constitution of the English doctrine of parliamentary sovereignty by the Scottish doctrine of popular sovereignty as the source of political authority would open the door to more radical versions of popular democracy than Westminster politics are ever likely to accommodate.'[6] Attempts were also made by independence support-ers to link this democratic case for independence to women's rights, with a new Scottish state presented as an arena in which gender inequality would be decisively addressed and narrowed, although Meryl Kenny has argued that this was not done as consistently or as successfully as in the 1990s debates about a devolved Scottish parliament.[7] Meanwhile, it was quite common in the popular language of the 'Yes' campaign to hear the critique of the Union pitched as a broader anti-imperialist argument, with the echoes of Tom Nairn audible in each fierce rhetorical blow against that 'imperialist, class-based state' that continued to perpetuate the mentality of 'the British Empire'.[8]

Economically, Maxwell and Kerevan maintained that Scottish inde-pendence would ensure that the new state's economic policies reflected Scottish interests, as mediated through a Scottish democratic system, rather than the interests of Britain as a whole. Both argued that the recent

---

[5] Neal Ascherson, 'Why I'm Voting Yes', *Prospect*, 17 July 2014.

[6] Maxwell, *Arguing*, p. 46.

[7] Meryl Kenny, 'Engendering the Independence Debate', *Scottish Affairs*, 23 (2014), pp. 323–31.

[8] Irvine Welsh, 'Scottish Independence and British Unity', *Bella Caledonia*, 10 January 2013, at https://bellacaledonia.org.uk/2013/01/10/irvine-welsh-on-scottish-independence-and-british-unity (accessed 2 October 2019); Robin McAlpine, 'The Butterfly Rebellion', *Bella Caledonia*, 14 September 2014, at https://bellacaledonia.org.uk/2014/09/14/the-butterfly-rebellion (accessed 2 October 2019).

economic record showed that the existing framework of economic decision-making from a distant metropolis had not worked for Scotland. An investigation of the record of other comparably sized countries demonstrated that stronger economic performances were possible by relatively small nations. Maxwell drew on evidence from political science and comparative political economy to conclude that 'shorter lines of internal communication make it easier for small countries to develop a political consensus between key social and economic interests on how to respond to new challenges and opportunities' and that a readiness to invest in human capital characterised such nations in order to make up for their size.[9] Kerevan provided a narrative of recent Scottish economic history to demonstrate that Scotland's economic growth had been driven lower by Westminster's decision-making, notably because of the loss of indigenous Scottish business ownership thanks to the nationalisation of industry post-1945 and then because of deindustrialisation under Thatcher (and the slower population growth through the emigration it caused). An independent Scotland, said Kerevan, would flourish thanks to the ability to introduce a more efficient tax structure; to increase social mobility and entrepreneurship; to welcome higher levels of immigration; and to boost capital investment.[10] Tom Nairn even reprised his case that independence was the right option for a new era of global capitalism in which small states were the optimal political model both economically and democratically (at least as long as they could also collaborate as part of broader international structures).[11] These points echoed the political economy of Scottish independence that, as we have seen, had been carefully developed by Alex Salmond and his colleagues in the course of the 1990s.

The most notable aspect of the democratic and economic framing of the nationalist case, however, was that many of the '79ers had become more reserved about what Maxwell had once called 'the case for left-wing nationalism'. In Maxwell's view there was good reason to think that an independent Scotland would pursue a moderately social democratic course, construed primarily in terms of the defence of a large public sector, but he no longer argued that a Nordic social democracy or even a more radical socialist option was the likely outcome of a new Scottish state. Maxwell himself had little doubt that a Nordic course would still be

---

[9] Maxwell, *Arguing*, pp. 55–94, quote at p. 74.

[10] Kerevan, 'Case for Yes', pp. 29–41; George Kerevan, 'Scotland in the Wider World: Does Size and Sovereignty Matter?', in Gerry Hassan and James Mitchell (eds.), *After Independence* (Edinburgh, Luath, 2013), pp. 151–61.

[11] Tom Nairn, 'Old Nation, New Age', April 2014, reprinted in Tom Nairn, *Old Nations, Auld Enemies, New Times: Selected Essays*, edited by Jamie Maxwell and Pete Ramand (Edinburgh, Luath Press, 2014), pp. 416–19.

a desirable one, but he was sceptical that the radical reforms necessary to achieve such low levels of poverty and inequality would be feasible in Scotland because of resistance from business and the middle class, groups whose support were in all likelihood essential to obtaining independence in the first place.[12] Kerevan, as we saw in Chapter 4, had switched away from this socialist argument for independence altogether during the 2000s and instead portrayed independence as a cause aimed at promoting individual freedom from state paternalism and dependency, which he saw as inextricably linked to the Union and to the politics of the Labour Party.[13] The radical case for independence, as a blow against neoliberalism, was instead articulated by a younger generation of activists loosely organised around the Radical Independence Campaign, with the support of Jim Sillars, who unlike other '79ers remained undaunted about postulating a close connection between Scottish popular sovereignty and a radical new socialist economic model.[14] But perhaps the most rhetorically effective version of the left-wing argument was the recognisably conservative move of portraying the independence cause as less about institutional novelty and more about returning to an earlier British way of life – to the post-1945 years – and to retrieve, as Neal Ascherson put it, the 'post-war British settlement' displaced by the 'barbaric neo-liberalism' of the 1980s and 1990s.[15]

Maxwell was also sceptical of cultural arguments for independence, including attempts to revive the ideal of the democratic intellect, since he thought (as he had argued since the 1980s) that 'interpretations or reinventions of distinctive cultural traditions – whatever their strengths – are too narrow to carry the complex identity of modern Scotland'.[16] In a weaker sense, Maxwell believed that Scottish public culture would be strengthened by independence precisely because it would be less influenced by metropolitan norms and also because a Scottish state was likelier to support Scottish national cultural institutions. Indeed, Maxwell argued that independence would be valuable culturally chiefly because it would at last test the moralistic quality of Scottish public

[12] Maxwell, *Arguing*, pp. 99–112.   [13] Kerevan, 'Case for Yes', pp. 57–69.
[14] Gregor Gall (ed.), *Scotland's Road to Socialism: Time to Choose* (Glasgow, Scottish Left Press, 2013); James Foley and Pete Ramand, *Yes: The Radical Case for Independence* (London, Pluto, 2014); Cat Boyd and Jenny Morrison, *Scottish Independence: A Feminist Response* (Edinburgh, Word Power Books, 2014); Jim Sillars, *In Place of Fear II: A Socialist Programme for an Independent Scotland* (Glasgow, Vagabond Voices, 2014). A similar, although more elusive, case along these lines was made by Alasdair Gray, *Independence: An Argument for Home Rule* (Edinburgh, Canongate, 2014).
[15] Ascherson, 'Why I'll Vote Yes'; Neal Ascherson, 'The "Glorious" Anglo-Scottish Union Belongs to a Past Era', *Financial Times*, 15 July 2014.
[16] Maxwell, *Arguing*, pp. 139–52; George Davie is discussed at pp. 139–40.

debate by forcing Scotland as a community to take responsibility for acting on such rhetoric:

How much would we be prepared to pay in higher taxes for our opposition to spending cuts? How many more asylum seekers or economic migrants would we be ready to welcome to Scotland when the UK Border Agency is no longer there to do the dirty work of control and deportation? How much redistribution of income and wealth are the better off prepared to accept in the name of a fairer and more compassionate Scotland? How many jobs are we prepared to jeopardise in the short term as the price of terminating our role in the UK's delusional defence strategy? The answers might be unsettling, but our public culture would be the better for being able to subject politicians' rhetoric to the test of practical responsibility.[17]

McIlvanney likewise wryly noted his own role in propagating 'the popular myth' that Scotland 'has a desire for a just society more radical than it has the parliamentary power to express'. McIlvanney still hoped that this was true but acknowledged 'at the moment it can only be a theory but I think it's time we tested it'. Scotland now faced a moment where it could 'grow up and take full responsibility for ourselves'.[18] As we have seen, Kerevan was much less enamoured of this left-wing construction of Scottishness but he also stressed the importance of independence for 'the recovery of Scotland's traditional moral universe' in which Scots would at last 'stand on their own two feet'.[19]

The Scottish government helpfully summarised the 'case for independence' in the white paper it issued in the run-up to the 2014 referendum, *Scotland's Future*. The 'heart of the case' it presented was similar to the foregoing arguments and comprised three main contentions about independence: first, 'the people of Scotland will always get governments we vote for'; second, 'we will control our own resources and make our own decisions about our economy'; and third, 'we can decide how we use our wealth to benefit all the people in our society'.[20] In these claims – and in the wider literature of the 2014 referendum – we can observe the trajectory of nationalist political thought since the 1960s. The currents of nationalist thinking that this book has examined initially emerged with the aims of protecting the distinctiveness of Scottish institutional and cultural life; opposing an undemocratic imperial British state; and advancing an egalitarian socialist society. But these arguments were considerably modified and augmented over the fifty years or so prior to the

---

[17] Maxwell, *Arguing*, p. 148.   [18] McIlvanney, *Dreaming Scotland*, pp. 17–18.
[19] Kerevan, 'Case for Yes', pp. 57–9, quotes at pp. 57, 59.
[20] Scottish Government, *Scotland's Future: Your Guide to an Independent Scotland* (Edinburgh, Scottish Government, November 2013), p. 3.

2014 referendum on Scottish independence. In particular, a revived language of sovereignty and democratisation proved to have greater political vitality than a socialist language of economic transformation or a concern with the defence of Scottish culture (however expansively defined). Meanwhile, the improvement of Scotland's economic performance in more conventionally capitalist terms emerged as a distinctive line of argument in its own right, separate from its initial conjunction in the 1970s with the socialist case for the expansion of state intervention in the economy to rescue an anaemic private sector.[21] What had prompted these shifts over time in the political thought of Scottish nationalism?

The Road to 2014

The intellectual origins of modern Scottish nationalism lie in the new political openings of the 1960s and 1970s, though nationalists built on an earlier tradition of anti-bureaucratic, decentralist thinking that had pre-occupied the supporters of independence from the interwar period onwards. Scottish nationalism is a child of the upheavals of 'the long 1960s', albeit in a more minor key than the famous examples of radical movements elsewhere, whether in the Northern Irish civil rights struggle or the French and German 1968.[22] Some of the central themes of the politics of this period – an erosion of traditional forms of authority and social deference; a desire for new, more localised forms of political participation; the disappointment of expanded post-war material expectations – can be mapped fairly straightforwardly on to the rise of Scottish nationalism and the home rule movement more generally.[23] The existence of a coherent Scottish national identity that nonetheless lacked separate political representation allowed the characteristic post-1960s desire for greater autonomy to take a nationalist form in Scotland. The initial expression of electoral support for the SNP in the years around the

---

[21] Stuart Whigham's discourse analysis of the SNP's main policy documents and manifestos in the run-up to the 2014 referendum comes to a similar conclusion: the most common arguments given by the SNP for independence are 'the achievement of political sovereignty for Scotland' and 'using these newly gained levers of Scottish independence to achieve economic growth for Scotland': 'Nationalism, Party Political Discourse and Scottish Independence: Comparing Discursive Visions of Scotland's Constitutional Status', *Nations and Nationalism*, 25 (2019), p. 1225.

[22] Gerd-Rainer Horn, *The Spirit of '68: Rebellion in Western Europe and North America, 1956–76* (Oxford, Oxford University Press, 2007); Richard Vinen, *The Long '68: Radical Protest and Its Enemies* (London, Allen Lane, 2018).

[23] For the social history of these themes in Britain, see Emily Robinson, Camilla Schofield, Florence Sutcliffe-Braithwaite and Natalie Thomlinson, 'Telling Stories about Post-War Britain: Popular Individualism and the "Crisis" of the 1970s', *Twentieth Century British History*, 28 (2017), pp. 268–304.

1967 Hamilton by-election should be understood in this context: a loss of confidence in the post-imperial British state's capacity to deliver sufficient economic prosperity via a Labour government triggering youthful and socially mobile support for greater Scottish self-government.[24] But the radical political thought of the 1960s and 1970s was also notably socialist, much more so than the established figures in the SNP leadership of the time would ever have countenanced, in spite of their initial tack towards 'social democracy' under the leadership of William Wolfe. As Ewan Gibbs and Rory Scothorne have argued, the trajectory of nationalist political thought to the left after the 1960s should therefore be set in the context of the broader rise of the New Left as a political formation aimed at forging a separate path between Soviet-style communism on the one hand and orthodox social democracy on the other.[25]

The first important contribution of the New Left as it evolved across the 1960s was that it raised criticism of the British state to a more rigorous level by scrutinising in greater depth its apparent failure to modernise and progress beyond its roots in an ossified imperialism. The caustic polemics of theorists such as Tom Nairn charted a course for a left-wing nationalist rhetoric that depicted Britain as a ramshackle feudal construct, a deviant case from the path of democratic modernity, and a declining asset to which the Scots should bid farewell. The New Left's second contribution was to legitimise a left-wing politics that drew on, or more accurately constructed, a distinctive Scottish radical tradition. The irony is that the advanced wing of the New Left, led by Nairn and Perry Anderson, had initially set out to subvert earlier New Left efforts to appropriate English or British national traditions for the left. But the work of Antonio Gramsci, who Nairn and Anderson had drawn on, directed the New Left back towards the importance of ideology and culture in the entrenchment of capitalist domination and, in the Scottish case, to an attempt to demonstrate how Scottish national traditions might offer resources for a socialist politics. One implication of this

---

[24] This has been well brought out by Jimmi Østergaard Neilsen and Stuart Ward, '"Cramped and Restricted at Home?" Scottish Separatism at Empire's End', *Transactions of the Royal Historical Society*, 25 (2015), pp. 159–85; James Mitchell, *Hamilton 1967: The By-Election That Transformed Scotland* (Edinburgh, Luath Press, 2017), especially pp. 129–42. On the SNP vote in this period as youthful and socially mobile, see William Miller, *The End of British Politics?* (Oxford, Oxford University Press, 1981), pp. 147, 122–3, 217–28; David McCrone, *Understanding Scotland: The Sociology of a Nation* (2nd ed., London, Routledge, 2001), pp. 118–21.

[25] Ewan Gibbs and Rory Scothorne, '"Origins of the Present Crisis?": The Emergence of "Left-Wing" Scottish Nationalism, 1956–79', in Evan Smith and Matthew Worley (eds.), *Waiting for the Revolution: The British Far Left from 1956* (Manchester, Manchester University Press, 2017), pp. 163–81.

analysis was that Scotland offered a 'natural' small unit – that is, one to which history had delivered a sufficiently coherent sense of community identity – in which to explore more decentralised and participatory forms of government. Put in these terms, the case for a left-wing Scottish nationalism looked inviting for those Scots who felt disaffected from metropolitan British political culture and a British socialism that tended to yoke together economic egalitarianism with the social hierarchies of the Westminster system. The difficulty was that, even at the mid-1970s peak of Scottish nationalist mobilisation, such New Left visions were arrayed against a formidable rival in the form of the British Labour Party.

The initial iterations of left-wing nationalism therefore ran aground in the 1970s on Labour's enduring electoral and ideological power. In spite of the disappointments of Labour in government in the 1960s and 1970s, and what the New Left regarded as the party's overly cautious and unreflective political thought, Labour remained a force to be reckoned with ideologically as well as electorally. The history of the British labour movement remained a resonant one, marked by notable strategic successes, and its language of reformist socialism and class representation offered an idealism that was still capable, in the right hands, of conjuring up a more persuasive radical alternative than Scottish independence. Labour socialism also contained within it a home rule tradition that was reactivated under SNP pressure to offer devolution as a way to express Scottish communitarian sentiment within a British context.[26] The persistent appeal of Labour ultimately led Scottish nationalists in the 1980s to define their politics in more labourist terms, as the continuation of Keir Hardie's historic mission which had been abandoned by a rightward-trending Labour Party.

Yet the greater traction later gained by this left nationalist rhetorical strategy was ultimately the result of the startling economic changes that the Thatcher government presided over, including the substantial weakening of the traditional social base of the Labour Party. Any study of the development of Scottish nationalist ideology must eventually reckon with the intellectual consequences of Thatcherism. In one sense, it is an all too familiar idea that the Thatcher government's lack of popular legitimacy played a formative role in driving Scottish politics in a nationalist direction, whether in terms of support for devolution or independence. But it is less widely recognised that Thatcherism solved a serious intellectual problem that had bedevilled Scottish nationalism

---

[26] Michael Keating and David Bleiman, *Labour and Scottish Nationalism* (London, Macmillan, 1979); Gerry Hassan and Eric Shaw, *The Strange Death of Labour Scotland* (Edinburgh, Edinburgh University Press, 2012), pp. 21–78.

until the 1980s: how to construct a distinctive Scottish identity with sufficient cultural weight to legitimise independence as a viable political option? While recognising that 'the icon of national identity is not complete without the scar left by a foreign sword', Neal Ascherson has nonetheless argued that Scottish identity is unusual in that it is not formed in response to such a historical grievance: 'remarkably, the Scots are not obsessed by the evil which others have done to them. Instead, the iconic wounds are the self-inflicted ones'.[27] It is an elegant formulation, but Ascherson underestimated the importance of Thatcherism – understood as an undemocratic imposition on Scotland – in the construction of nationalist ideology.

As we have seen in earlier chapters, at the outset of the 1980s both Tom Nairn and Stephen Maxwell had observed that Scottish history could not be straightforwardly recruited to support nationalist ideology: the great cultural achievements of the Scottish Enlightenment and the economic modernisation of the industrial revolution had been accomplished as part of Britain. It was therefore hard – although not impossible – to make the case that Scottish cultural and economic development had been historically blocked by the Union. The writings of George Davie and his successors offered one way of making this case, which stressed the indigenous Scottish roots of the Enlightenment tradition and – for good measure – the extent to which the Union was ripping them out. But taken in the round Nairn and Maxwell were surely correct to think that Scottish history did not present an easy set of materials for nationalist purposes. As Colin Kidd later pointed out, in Scottish history 'the core values of democracy, liberalism and nationalism seem to have taken their rise, respectively, from different sources, each in its own way contaminated': democracy in Scotland emerged from the seventeenth-century Presbyterian Covenanters, notable for their militancy and intolerance; Scottish liberalism originated amid Scottish Enlightenment thinkers keen on Anglicisation; and Scottish nationalism first took concrete form in the Jacobite rebellion against the British state in defence of an authoritarian Catholic monarchy, later lapsing in the hands of figures such as Walter Scott into a sentimental tartanised romanticism.[28] The historical resources available for Scottish nationalists were therefore problematic – except perhaps for a vaguer popular history of the exploitation and suffering of the Highlands that commanded a wide audience in

---

[27] Neal Ascherson, *Stone Voices: The Search for Scotland* (London, Granta, 2002), pp. 174–6, quote at p. 174.
[28] Colin Kidd, 'Lord Dacre and the Politics of the Scottish Enlightenment', *Scottish Historical Review*, 84 (2005), pp. 219–20.

the latter decades of the twentieth century, notably in the widely read history books of John Prebble (1915–2001) and in John McGrath's play, *The Cheviot, the Stag and the Black, Black Oil*.[29] Even here, though, significant ambiguities remained about how far the Highlands could straightforwardly act as a synonym for a highly industrialised nation such as Scotland and how far the dispossessions of, say, the Highland Clearances were national rather than class injustices.

The pressures on the political economy of Scotland in the 1970s began to germinate an alternative line of analysis that focused on the consistent underperformance of the Scottish economy under the Union in the twentieth century. But it was still hard to generate a specifically national popular grievance from a diagnosis of economic failure because the experience of frustrated economic expectations was not consistently attributable to policy decisions by the British state. On the contrary, the British state remained ideologically an activist one that sought to address Scottish economic problems (even if it did not always succeed in doing so). While the discovery of North Sea oil in the 1970s elevated the case for Scottish independence to a new level of economic credibility, the ideological uses of the oil were more complicated. At one level the many pertinent questions about who would benefit from the oil's extraction did have the potential to animate a nationalism grounded on hostility to both American multinational companies and a declining British state as the agents of Scottish economic exploitation. But the awkward counterpoint to this was that the fundamental argument behind the SNP's famous slogan 'It's Scotland's Oil' was that Scotland had the potential to become much richer at the expense of the rest of the United Kingdom at a time when the idea of a Union based on risk-sharing and resource-pooling still looked like a widely convincing one.[30]

The Thatcher government and its self-consciously tough-minded approach to Britain's industrial economy therefore offered a significant opportunity for Scottish nationalists to construct a case for independence that could escape from these dilemmas. The rise in Scottish unemployment, poverty and income inequality under Margaret Thatcher's premiership was more easily attributable to the actions of the British state, in large part because of the engaging willingness of leading Thatcherites (and Thatcher herself) to claim that these significant shifts in the

[29] Tom Devine, *Independence or Union: Scotland's Past and Scotland's Present* (London, Penguin, 2016), pp. 188–9.

[30] Geoffrey Lee, 'North Sea Oil and Scottish Nationalism', *Political Quarterly*, 47 (1976), pp. 313–15; Roger Levy, *Scottish Nationalism at the Crossroads* (Edinburgh, Scottish Academic Press, 1990), pp. 52–5; Christopher Harvie, *Fool's Gold: The Story of North Sea Oil* (London, Penguin, 1995), pp. 248–54.

structure of the British economy represented a material improvement for which their implacable decision-making was ultimately responsible.[31] A more complicated story can undoubtedly be told about Britain's transition from an industrial to a service-sector economy, and its implications for Scotland, but amid the hurly-burly of political debate the Thatcher government's unabashed rhetorical enthusiasm for economic change made it all too easy for Scottish economic grievances to be squarely focused on the actions of Westminster.[32]

This growing national sense of economic unfairness had several important further consequences. The clear divergence in voting patterns between Scotland and England during the 1980s and 1990s heightened the salience of the language of popular sovereignty, since it was evident that Scotland as a democratic community had not voted for the policies that were being imposed on it. Equally, the otherness of England could now be more convincingly construed in political rather than cultural terms, as a nation dominated by a right-wing English nationalist voting bloc bent on dissolving the welfare state and the labour movement. Most startlingly, the progress of Thatcherism, and the eventual emergence of a more right-wing Labour Party in response, made far-reaching historical questions about Scottish identity much less salient to Scottish political argument. The deep historical issues that had seemed pressing to intellectuals in the 1970s – about why Scotland was historically anomalous in lacking a coherent nationalism of its own and about how the Union had positively influenced Scottish development – could now simply be put to one side. Instead, a new kind of Scottish nationalism could be articulated that pragmatically conceded that the Union had historically not necessarily been an impediment to the rise of Scotland's industrial economy or to the achievements of the Enlightenment, but nonetheless insisted that the Union in the late twentieth century *had* now become a block on Scottish potential and should therefore be dispensed with. The problem

---

[31] Richard Finlay, 'Thatcherism, Unionism and Nationalism: A Comparative Study of Scotland and Wales', in Ben Jackson and Robert Saunders (eds.), *Making Thatcher's Britain* (Cambridge, Cambridge University Press, 2012), pp. 172–4.

[32] For the complexities, see Jim Phillips, 'Deindustrialisation and the Moral Economy of the Scottish Coalfields, 1947–91', *International Labor and Working Class History*, 84 (2013), pp. 99–115; Jim Phillips, 'The Closure of Michael Colliery in 1967 and the Politics of Deindustrialisation in Scotland', *Twentieth Century British History*, 26 (2015), pp. 551–72; Gerry Hassan, *Caledonia Dreaming: The Quest for a Different Scotland* (Edinburgh, Luath Press, 2014), pp. 129–41; Jim Tomlinson, 'Deindustrialisation Not Decline: A New Meta-Narrative for Post-War British History', *Twentieth Century British History*, 27 (2016), pp. 76–99; Andrew Cumbers, 'The Scottish Independence Referendum and the Dysfunctional Economic Geography of the UK', *Political Geography*, 41 (2014), pp. 33–6; Ewan Gibbs, 'The Moral Economy of the Scottish Coalfields: Managing Deindustrialisation, *c.* 1947–83', *Enterprise and Society*, 19 (2018), pp. 124–52.

for defenders of the Anglo-Scottish Union was that the nationalist construction of the 1980s lived on as a vital force in Scottish politics, sustained not just by social memory but by the actions of the Conservative Party in government at Westminster after 2010. A Conservative agenda of public sector austerity and tax cuts for the better off was not a promising backdrop to the 2014 independence referendum and enabled a potent revival of the classic anti-Thatcherite nationalist stance first honed in the 1980s.

The 1980s and 1990s were a critical period in the development of Scottish nationalism for a further reason. It was amid the growing debates about European integration, globalisation and devolution of that time that the goal of Scottish independence acquired much greater precision. While earlier models of Scottish independence, such as those mooted in the early meetings of the SNP's '79 Group, proposed an autarchic, sovereigntist vision of Scottish economic policy, precisely because there was little prospect of Scottish independence occurring in the near future significant questions about how a small resource-rich economy could maintain its policymaking autonomy amid an integrated world economy were left unresolved. How to reconcile a Scottish state with the constraints of global financial markets and international trade flows became a more pressing issue for the advocates of independence as the declining power of the nation state became a staple topic of elite political discussion in Britain and elsewhere around the world at the end of the twentieth century. When decolonisation remained a live issue in the 1960s and 1970s, the foundation of new states hardly seemed an outlandish development. But this mood changed markedly as the 1980s progressed and, even amid the upheavals of the collapse of the Soviet Union and Yugoslavia, a new elite conventional wisdom cohered in which the limited capacity of nations to set their own economic course was the dominant note. What looked on the face of it to be a serious objection to the project of Scottish independence in fact proved to be the making of it as a practicable policy proposal. Scottish nationalists embraced the new argot of global political economy and European integration with aplomb, making the case that there were numerous nations of a similar size to Scotland who had flourished in this environment by positioning themselves as highly competitive members of European and global economic structures.

There was also a democratic strand to this globalist argument, insofar as nationalists argued that Scottish interests could only be adequately represented in the decision-making of EU or global institutions by a specifically Scottish government rather than by a British state that would inevitably place less weight on Scottish economic fortunes when representing the United Kingdom. But alongside this point nationalists also deployed a more exuberant enthusiasm for the project of pooling sovereignty in principle, as the most effective way to meet the challenge of international economic integration. As a result, what was fundamentally a rather cold-hearted concession to the reality of an unchained global capitalism (and a Scottish economy inextricably linked with the rest of the United Kingdom) could be flavoured with a more principled support for international cooperation. This embrace of 'post-sovereignty' was therefore both idealistic and strategic: it looked outward to a European order of peace and prosperity (at a time when English politics was wracked by dissension on this very subject), but it also demonstrated that 'independence' need not be economically frightening or even radical, since established trading and social relationships within the United Kingdom would remain intact within the European Union. The advent of a new devolved Scottish Parliament in 1999 amplified the power of this argument because independence could then be seen as a natural progression from a system in which power was shared between Edinburgh, London and Brussels. Scottish nationalists now assumed the guise of hard-headed advocates of a redistribution of powers between these three decision-making centres. The most audacious aspect of this transformation was a growing emphasis on the preservation of a British dimension to Scottish policy after independence.

While this vision of an independent but 'post-sovereign' Scotland delivered a prospectus for Scottish nationalism that was politically viable, it also tied the nationalist cause to a specific analysis of the global economy that proved to be more contestable than prominent nationalists, beguiled by the boosterish rhetoric of the 1990s, had come to believe. The financial crisis of 2007–8 and its aftermath therefore had a paradoxical impact on Scottish nationalism: it simultaneously resuscitated a populist anti-austerity discourse that was highly beneficial to the independence cause while also undermining certain elements of the economic model that Alex Salmond and his colleagues had created to make independence a more plausible objective. One highly visible example was a retreat from the euro as the currency of choice for an independent Scotland, leaving nationalists defending the continued use of the pound, though it seemed likely that many of the issues that had deflated nationalist enthusiasm for the euro – the lack of fiscal policy space permitted by the European Central Bank; the formulation of a monetary policy that would not adequately represent Scottish interests – would have been replicated in any arrangement reached with the Bank of England.

But a broader challenge posed by the financial crisis was to the complacency of policymakers during the era of the 'great moderation', when it was assumed that the essential questions of running a successful market economy had been settled. Leading Scottish nationalists, in common with many other figures in the political establishment of the time, had accommodated themselves to the power of the market. They sought to build a more nimble Scotland that could take advantage of the new global economic opportunities by investing in education and in creating a 'competitive edge' for the Scottish economy by reducing business taxation. The limits of this thinking were exposed by the financial crisis, which placed back on the political agenda larger questions of macroeconomic management and distributive justice that had retreated to the margins of political debate in the preceding decades. The crisis also exposed the extent to which the role of the state had in fact *grown* since the 1960s as a provider of direct employment and wage subsidies.[33] It would be too strong to say that the financial crisis therefore undercut the case for independence, because it is clear that much of the power of the 'Yes' campaign in 2014 was that it offered independence as an alternative to a British state discredited by its close connections with the City of London and by its highly unequal distribution of the burdens of post-crisis fiscal retrenchment. But the 'Yes' campaign was placed in the uneasy position of maintaining this caustic approach to the politics of the British financial sector while stipulating that the Bank of England would make a suitable guardian of Scottish monetary policy.

Means and Ends

When Alex Salmond announced his resignation as First Minister the day after the 2014 independence referendum his memorable parting line was: 'For me as leader my time is nearly over, but for Scotland the campaign continues and the dream shall never die.'[34] Put in those terms, the aspiration for Scottish independence might have sounded like a goal that had preoccupied idealistic campaigners for centuries all the way back to 1707. As this book has shown, in fact the dream of a Scottish state is of more recent provenance and its character has been a contingent one, its rationale shifting in response to wider intellectual and social trends. Critics of Scottish nationalism often claim that the sheer variety of justifications that have been offered for independence reveals a movement opportunistically determined to recruit every issue, no matter how

---

[33] Jim Tomlinson, 'Imagining the Economic Nation: The Scottish Case', *Political Quarterly*, 85 (2014), pp. 170–7.

[34] Tom Peterkin, 'Alex Salmond to Stand Down as First Minister', *Scotsman*, 19 September 2014.

remotely connected, to the existential cause of founding a new Scottish state. This line of criticism overlooks that many other political movements have also made significant changes to their ideological profiles over the last fifty years and prioritise their ideological goals precisely to impose some coherence on the vast range of issues that will necessarily confront any political party or movement. Meanwhile, the proponents of independence have developed hard ideological parameters around their nationalism that tend to be glossed over too quickly in this critique, not least a definition of Scottish national identity firmly based on residency rather than ethnicity; an openness to immigration and multiculturalism; and support for European integration. These were clear ideological choices made by an independence movement that earlier in its history had been more conflicted on each of these questions.

A more accurate diagnosis of the intellectual history of Scottish nationalism is that, although lively debates have taken place outside of the SNP, the party itself has been less hospitable to self-conscious ideological conflict when compared to other parties. While the Labour Party has never risen to the theoretical heights that intellectuals fondly imagine to be the necessary foundation of any truly socialist party, it has nonetheless hosted several well-publicised and clarifying debates about how to revise social democratic ideology in the face of changing political circumstances. The SNP has never undertaken any similar exercise, in part because until the foundation of the Scottish Parliament it is doubtful that the party possessed sufficient organisational resources to be able to cope with such bouts of dissent, but also because a degree of ideological obfuscation has been an asset to it. A broad commitment to enhancing Scottish self-government and representing Scottish identity usually stood the party in good stead in electoral terms, with the need for greater specificity only really becoming pressing after 1999, when Scottish political debate resolved into a starker polarity between the advocates of independence and the proponents of devolution.[35] Yet even in the devolutionary era, Scottish nationalists remained reluctant to engage each other in spirited public debate about their political objectives. As nationalists saw it, they were a reforming movement surrounded by opponents in the media, in business, and in the unionist political parties; internal ideological controversy would only weaken their already embattled position.

---

[35] James Mitchell, 'The Meaning of Independence', in Gerry Hassan and Simon Barrow (eds.), *A Nation Changed? The SNP and Scotland Ten Years on* (Edinburgh, Luath Press, 2017), pp. 299–304.

In revisionist debates about social democracy, a classic distinction has often been made between the persisting 'ends' sought by social democrats and the varying 'means' by which these ends might be achieved. From this perspective, revisionist socialists argued that public ownership should not be seen as synonymous with socialism but rather as one means among many towards achieving the end of a more egalitarian society.[36] If we apply the distinction between means and ends to Scottish nationalism, it might seem obvious that the 'end' goal for the movement is independence. But this is not how important figures in the history of Scottish nationalism have presented the matter. Neil MacCormick, for example, in an early essay famously expressed support for a 'utilitarian nationalism', which sought independence insofar as it was 'the best means to the well-being of the Scottish people'; independence was thus 'a means to an end'.[37] MacCormick's point was later appropriated by Nicola Sturgeon, then Deputy First Minister of Scotland, in an influential speech of 2012. Somewhat embellishing MacCormick, Sturgeon attributed to him a distinction between an 'existentialist' and a 'utilitarian' Scottish nationalism:[38] 'The former described those who thought Scotland was entitled to be independent simply because we are a nation, the latter that independence was a tool to deliver a better society.' Sturgeon noted that most members of the SNP would ultimately see themselves as endorsing both types of nationalism, but her main message to the public was that 'independence is essential for Scotland – not as an end in itself but as a means to achieve the Scotland we seek'. The better society that independence could deliver, Sturgeon argued, was chiefly characterised by 'democracy and social justice', with the latter objective glossed as creating a Scotland 'that sees enterprise and fairness as two sides of the same coin'. In fact, argued Sturgeon, democracy and social

---

[36] Ben Jackson, 'Social Democracy', in Michael Freeden, Lyman Tower Sargeant and Marc Stears (eds.), *Oxford Handbook of Political Ideologies* (Oxford, Oxford University Press, 2013), pp. 349–51, 355–7.

[37] Neil MacCormick, 'Independence and Constitutional Change' in Neil MacCormick (ed.), *The Scottish Debate* (Oxford, Oxford University Press, 1970), pp. 52–5, quote at p. 52.

[38] MacCormick himself didn't explicitly contrast his 'utilitarian' nationalism with any other type. But he did say that to argue that Scotland should be independent simply because it is a nation required accepting 'a variety of metaphysical beliefs about the nature of nations, beliefs about which rational discussion can scarcely be conducted; one takes pure nationalism, or one leaves it. For my part I leave it' ('Independence and Constitutional Change', p. 52). In a later speech, Sturgeon substituted 'existential' for 'existentialist': 'The Constitutional Future of an Independent Scotland', speech at Edinburgh Centre for Constitutional Law, 16 June 2014, at https://news.gov.scot/speeches-and-briefings/the-constitutional-future-of-an-independent-scotland (accessed 2 October 2019).

justice were intertwined because 'you cannot guarantee social justice unless you are in control of the delivery'.[39] This 'utilitarian' – or as it is sometimes called 'instrumental' – case for independence was one that was widely used by the SNP in their official publications and discourse from the 1980s onwards.[40] But if independence was indeed a means to an end rather than an end in itself, then there is a sense in which the evolution of the political thought of Scottish nationalism has been the reverse of the classic social democratic revisionist dichotomy: while the means have remained the same over several decades, it is the ends that have been more mutable in the face of changing historical circumstances.

While this might appear to return us to the interpretation of Scottish nationalism as opportunistic, mentioned a few paragraphs ago, a fairer observation is that the lack of explicit ideological controversy within the SNP has meant that the question of whether independence is a means or an end is actually less clear than Nicola Sturgeon suggested: at times a largely 'utilitarian' nationalist approach has been foregrounded by advocates of independence, at others a more 'existential' one. The 2014 independence referendum revealed that Scottish nationalism could still make very considerable political progress without having to choose one over the other. However, the very success of this agile coalition-building has itself created a problem for the independence movement.

The overall political strategy adopted by leading Scottish nationalists since the 1980s had been progressively to downplay how radical a break independence would be from the economic and social status quo under the Union. To win over a cautious Scottish public opinion, the policy stakes were gently lowered so that independence became a gradual process whereby an ever stronger Scottish Parliament could assume more powers while sharing sovereignty with London and Brussels.

---

[39] Nicola Sturgeon, 'Bringing the Powers Home to Build a Better Nation', speech at Strathclyde University, 3 December 2012. For the lively discussion prompted by the speech, see Alex Massie, 'Why Choose Independence if It Means the Same Old, Same Old?', *Think Scotland*, 4 December 2012, at www.thinkscotland.org/todays-thinking/articles.html?read_full=11810 (accessed 2 October 2019); Ian Jack, 'Nicola Sturgeon Used to Be a "Historical Fiction Geek". But Not Any More', *Guardian*, 25 April 2015; Alex Bell, 'Existential versus Utilitarian Nationalism', *Bella Caledonia*, 6 May 2015, at https://bellacaledonia.org.uk/2015/05/06/existential-versus-utilitarian-nationalism (accessed 2 October 2019); Peter Jones, 'Existential and Utilitarian Nationalism in Scotland', in Klaus Peter Müller (ed.), *Scotland 2014 and Beyond – Coming of Age and Loss of Innocence?* (Frankfurt am Main, Peter Lang, 2015), pp. 137–64.

[40] Emmanuel Dalle Mulle, 'New Trends in Justifications for National Self-Determination: Evidence from Scotland and Flanders', *Ethnopolitics*, 15 (2016), pp. 211–29; Emmanuel Dalle Mulle and Ivano Serrano, 'Between a Principled and a Consequentialist Logic: Theory and Practice of Secession in Catalonia and Scotland', *Nations and Nationalism*, 25 (2019), pp. 630–51.

The whole tenor of this nationalist argument was averse to a once-and-for-all transformational moment in which Scotland would suddenly return as a sovereign state. Yet when historical circumstances unexpectedly presented the SNP with the opportunity to run an independence referendum, nationalist leaders found that the rhetoric and the popular mobilisation of such a plebiscite overran the cautious positions they had staked out (perhaps even in terms of their own personal convictions about whether independence was more plausibly regarded as a process or an event). The 2014 referendum created a nationalist movement that was deeply committed to the symbolism of a popular vote for independence and saw the transition to Scottish statehood as a decisive rupture from the British model of politics and economics. How can this more muscular nationalist support base be reconciled with the cautious and gradualist outlook of the SNP leadership? An open debate among Scottish nationalists about independence – its possible forms, its limits, its potential – is therefore an important task if the case for a Scottish state is to be refreshed to face the new political landscape that has been revealed in the wake of the financial crash. Movements that cannot articulate the goals of their leaders with those of their activists and supporters usually find that victory brings disillusionment rather than gratitude.

Select Bibliography

Material has been classified into primary or secondary according to usage in the text. Shorter pieces of journalism, letters to newspapers and brief book reviews are not included. Works by the same author are listed in chronological order.

Primary Sources

Archives

National Library of Scotland
Andrew Dewar Gibb Papers, Acc. 9188
Tom Gibson Papers, Acc. 6057
Gavin Kennedy Papers, Acc. 11565
Robert McIntyre Papers, Acc. 10090, Acc. 12917
Scottish Labour Party Edinburgh Branch Papers, Acc. 7472
Scottish National Party Papers, Acc. 7295, Acc. 10754
Gordon Wilson Papers, Acc. 13099
Douglas Young Papers, Acc. 6419

Official Records

House of Commons Debates, Fifth Series and Sixth Series
MacCormick v. *HM Advocate*, 1953 Session Cases, 396, pp. 396–418

Periodicals and Pamphlet Series

'79 Group News
Bulletin of Scottish Politics
Calgacus
Cencrastus
Chapman
Common Sense
Crann-Tàra
Forward Scotland: Journal of the Scottish Labour Party
Herald
Nevis Quarterly

New Edinburgh Review/Edinburgh Review
New Left Review
Political Quarterly
Question
Radical Scotland
Scots Independent
Scotsman
Scottish Government Yearbook
Scottish International
Scottish Worker
SNP '79 Group Papers Nos. 1–7

Books, Pamphlets, Articles, Lectures and Speeches

Anderson, Perry, 'Origins of the Present Crisis', *New Left Review*, no. 23, 1964, pp. 26–53
'Critique of Wilsonism', *New Left Review*, no. 27, 1964, pp. 3–27
English Questions (London, Verso, 1992)
Anon., 'The Irish Menace', *Scots Independent*, no. 2, December 1926
'Scotland's Answer to the Crisis: Manifesto by the National Party', *Scots Independent*, no. 255, November 1947
'Policy Resolutions by National Party Conference', *Scots Independent*, no. 280, December 1949
'Scotland – Free or Fettered?', *Scots Independent*, no. 305, January 1952
'Court Decision Warning to All Those Who Would Be Free', *Scots Independent*, no. 322, June 1953
'The National Party in Conference', *Scots Independent*, no. 321, May 1953
'Scotland's Dilemma Posed Again by Judicial Opinion', *Scots Independent*, no. 325, September 1953
'Survey: The '79 Group: Where Are They Now?', *Radical Scotland*, no. 5, June/July 1983, pp. 7–9
Archer, Clive and Stephen Maxwell (eds.), *The Nordic Model: Studies in Public Policy Innovation* (Farnborough, Gower, 1980)
Ascherson, Neal, 'The Day the SNP Became a "Normal" Political Party', *Scotsman*, 2 June 1975
'Sillars Decides to Go It Alone', *Scotsman*, 10 June 1975
'Assembly "Stage to Freedom"', *Scotsman*, 22 October 1976
'Nationalists Want Economic Prefects', *Scotsman*, 5 March 1976
'The Salad Days Are Over for the SNP', *Scotsman*, 27 May 1976
'Sillars Puts New Party on Course', *Scotsman*, 19 January 1976
'The World of Woad!', *Forward Scotland: Journal of the Scottish Labour Party*, no. 1, July 1976
'Divine Right of Parliaments', *Scotsman*, 18 February 1977
'Future Imperfect', *New Edinburgh Review*, no. 44, winter 1978, pp. 25–8
'Party in Search of a Strategy', *Scotsman*, 7 June 1978
'SNP Road to Success', *Scotsman*, 21 November 1978
'Back from the Depths on Black Friday', *Scotsman*, 3 March 1979

'MacDiarmid and Politics', in Paul Scott and A. C. Davis (eds.), *The Age of MacDiarmid* (Edinburgh, Mainstream, 1980), pp. 224–37

'Ancient Britons and the Republican Dream', John Mackintosh Memorial Lecture, Edinburgh University, 16 November 1985, *Radical Scotland*, no. 18, December/January 1986; reprinted in Neal Ascherson, *Games with Shadows* (London, Radius, 1988), pp. 146–58

'Devolution Diary', *Cencrastus*, no. 22, winter 1986, pp. 3–12, 49–54

'Local Government and the Myth of Sovereignty', Fifth Sovereignty lecture, 25 February 1994, Royal Museum of Scotland (London, Charter 88 Trust, 1994)

'The "Glorious" Anglo-Scottish Union Belongs to a Past Era', *Financial Times*, 15 July 2014

'Why I'm Voting Yes', *Prospect*, 17 July 2014

Barnett, Anthony, *This Time: Our Constitutional Revolution* (London, Vintage, 1997)

Barrow, Geoffrey, *Robert the Bruce and the Community of the Realm of Scotland* (London, Eyre and Spottiswoode, 1965)

Bell, Alex, 'Existential versus Utilitarian Nationalism', *Bella Caledonia*, 6 May 2015, at https://bellacaledonia.org.uk/2015/05/06/existential-versus-utilitarian-nationalism

Beveridge, Craig and Ronald Turnbull, 'The Myth of Scottish Inarticulacy', *Bulletin of Scottish Politics*, no. 2, spring 1981, pp. 134–8

'Inferiorism', *Cencrastus*, no. 8, spring 1982, pp. 4–5

The Eclipse of Scottish Culture (Edinburgh, Polygon, 1989)

Scotland after Enlightenment: Image and Tradition in Modern Scottish Culture (Edinburgh, Polygon, 1997)

Boyd, Cat and Jenny Morrison, *Scottish Independence: A Feminist Response* (Edinburgh, Word Power Books, 2014)

Brown, Gordon, 'Introduction: The Socialist Challenge', in Gordon Brown (ed.), *The Red Paper on Scotland* (Edinburgh, EUSPB, 1975), pp. 7–21

(ed.), *The Red Paper on Scotland* (Edinburgh, EUSPB, 1975)

'Labour – Where the Strength Lies', *Question*, no. 4, January 1976

Brown, Oliver, *Scotland: The Satellite!* (Glasgow, Scottish Secretariat, 1958)

The Anglo-Scottish Union of 1707: Then and Now (Stirling, Scots Independent, n.d. [*c.* 1959])

Buchanan, George, *The Art and Science of Government among the Scots*, edited by Duncan H. MacNeill (Glasgow, MacLellan, 1964)

Burnett, Ray, 'Scotland and Antonio Gramsci', *Scottish International*, vol. 5, no. 9, November 1972, pp. 12–15

'Socialists and the SNP', in Gordon Brown (ed.), *The Red Paper on Scotland* (Edinburgh, EUSPB, 1975), pp. 108–24

'When the Finger Points at the Moon', in James D. Young (ed.), *Scotland at the Crossroads: A Socialist Answer* (Glasgow, Clydeside Press, 1990), pp. 90–110

'Gramsci and Scotland Revisited', *Scottish Left Review*, no. 99 (2017), pp. 25–6

Burnett, Ray and Eamon McCann, 'Derry: Fighting under the Flag of the Citizens' Army: An Interview with Eamon McCann and Ray Burnett on the Barricades', *Socialist Worker*, 21 August 1969

Campaign for a Scottish Assembly, *A Claim of Right for Scotland*, July 1988, reprinted in Owen Dudley Edwards (ed.), *A Claim of Right for Scotland* (Edinburgh, Polygon, 1989), pp. 9–53

Chiene, Peter, 'Problems for the SLP', *Question*, no. 14, 22 October 1976

'Slimming Session at Stirling', *Question*, no. 15, 5 November 1976

Clark, Angus, 'Scotland a Nation', *Scots Independent*, no. 1, November 1926

Clarty, Tony, 'Scottish Legal Culture and the Withering Away of the State: A Study in MacCormick's Nationalism', *Cencrastus*, no. 14, autumn 1983, pp. 5–9

'Independence and the Scottish Political Imagination', *Cencrastus*, no. 11, New Year 1983, pp. 26–8

Clarty, Tony and Alexander McCall Smith (eds.), *Power and Manoeuvrability: The International Implications of an Independent Scotland* (Edinburgh, Q Press, 1978)

Collie, Liz, 'A Woman's Claim of Right for Scotland', *Radical Scotland*, no. 39, June/July 1989, pp. 12–13

Cooper, T. M. [Lord Cooper of Culross], 'The Declaration of Arbroath Revisited' [1949], in his *Selected Papers 1922–54* (Edinburgh and London, Oliver and Boyd, 1957), pp. 324–32

Cunningham, Roseanna, 'The SNP '79 Group', *Crann-Tàra*, no. 8, autumn 1979

Currie, Andrew, 'The SNP and Participation', *Question*, no. 7, April 1976

'Independence', in *SNP '79 Group Papers No. 1*, papers discussed at founding meeting, 31 May 1979, Belford Hotel, Edinburgh (no publisher/date), pp. 8–9

Davidson, Neil, 'Yes: A Non-Nationalist Argument for Independence', *Radical Philosophy*, no. 185, May/June 2014, pp. 2–7

Davie, George, 'Hume and the Origins of the Common Sense School', *Revue Internationale de Philosophie*, 6 (1952), pp. 213–21

'Common Sense and Sense-Data', *Philosophical Quarterly*, 4 (1954), pp. 229–46

The Democratic Intellect (Edinburgh, Edinburgh University Press, 2013 [1961])

'Anglophobe and Anglophil', *Scottish Journal of Political Economy*, 14 (1967), pp. 291–302

'Discussion', in J. N. Wolfe (ed.), *Government and Nationalism in Scotland: An Enquiry by Members of the University of Edinburgh* (Edinburgh, Edinburgh University Press, 1969), pp. 204–5; reprinted as 'Nationalism and the Philosophy of the Unthinkable', *Edinburgh Review*, no. 83, 1990, pp. 38–9

'The Social Significance of the Scottish Philosophy of Common Sense' [1972], in George Davie, *The Scottish Enlightenment and Other Essays* (Edinburgh, Polygon, 1991), pp. 52–85

The Crisis of the Democratic Intellect (Edinburgh, Polygon, 1986)

'The Threat to Scottish Education', *Edinburgh Review*, no. 83, 1990, pp. 35–7

'The Importance of the Ordinary MA', *Edinburgh Review*, no. 90, 1993, pp. 61–9

The Scotch Metaphysics: A Century of Enlightenment in Scotland (London, Routledge, 2001)

Davies, Ron, *Devolution: A Process Not an Event* (Cardiff, Institute of Welsh Affairs, 1999)

Dewar Gibb, Andrew, *Scotland in Eclipse* (London, H. Toulmin, 1930)
  The Shadow on Parliament House: Has Scots Law a Future? (Edinburgh, Porpoise Press, 1932)
Dudley Edwards, Owen, 'Socialism or Nationalism?', in Gavin Kennedy (ed.), *The Radical Approach: Papers on an Independent Scotland* (Edinburgh, Palingenesis Press, 1976), pp. 98–109
  (ed.), *A Claim of Right for Scotland* (Edinburgh, Polygon, 1989)
Duncan, A. A., *The Nation of Scots and the Declaration of Arbroath (1320)* (London, Historical Association, 1970)
Dunion, Kevin, 'The Philosopher's Stone', *Radical Scotland*, no. 21, June/July 1986, pp. 31–2
Elliot, Walter, 'The Scottish Heritage in Politics', in the Duke of Atholl (ed.), *A Scotsman's Heritage* (London, A. Maclehose, 1932), pp. 53–65
Erskine of Marr, Hon. Ruaraidh, *Changing Scotland* (Montrose, Review Press, 1931)
Evans, Gwynfor, Roy Lewis, J. E. Jones, Arthur Donaldson, David Rollo, Robert McIntyre, John Banks, Douglas Stuckey and Don Bannister, *Our Three Nations: Wales, Scotland, England* (Cardiff, Plaid Cymru/SNP/Common Wealth Party, 1956)
Fitzgerald, Garret, 'Anglo-Irish Relations after 1921', *Scots Independent*, no. 221, August 1989
  'Better Relationships in Europe Than at Home', *Scots Independent*, no. 223, October 1989
  'Evolving Relationships After 1973', *Scots Independent*, no. 222, September 1989
  'The British and Irish in the Context of Europe', John Mackintosh Memorial Lecture, October 1990, Edinburgh University, in Bernard Crick (ed.), *National Identities* (Oxford, Blackwell/Political Quarterly, 1990), pp. 7–24
Foley, James and Pete Ramand, *Yes: The Radical Case for Independence* (London, Pluto, 2014)
Gall, Gregor (ed.), *Scotland's Road to Socialism: Time to Choose* (Glasgow, Scottish Left Press, 2013)
Gallagher, Tom (ed.), *Nationalism in the Nineties* (Edinburgh, Polygon, 1991)
Galloway, John, 'Employment in Scotland', *Scots Independent*, no. 260, April 1948
Gellner, Ernest, 'Nationalism', in Ernest Gellner, *Thought and Change* (London, Weidenfeld & Nicolson, 1964), pp. 147–78
  'Nationalism, or the New Confessions of a Justified Edinburgh Sinner', *Political Quarterly*, 49 (1978), pp. 103–11
  Nations and Nationalism (Ithaca, Cornell University Press, 1983)
Gibson, Tom, 'The Land: The Problem Stated', *Scots Independent*, no. 2, December 1926
  'The Reasons for a National Party', *Scots Independent*, no. 13, November 1927
Grassic Gibbon, Lewis and Hugh MacDiarmid, *Scottish Scene or the Intelligent Man's Guide to Albyn* (London, Jarrolds, 1934)
Gray, Alasdair, *Independence: An Argument for Home Rule* (Edinburgh, Canongate, 2014)

Grieve, C. M., 'Wider Aspects of Scottish Nationalism', *Scots Independent*, no. 13, November 1927

'Neo-Gaelic Economics', *Scots Independent*, no. 14, December 1927

'Neo-Gaelic Economics II', *Scots Independent*, no. 16, February 1928

Gunn, Richard, 'George Davie: Common Sense, Hegelianism and Critique', *Cencrastus*, no. 27, autumn 1987, pp. 48–51

'Marxism and Common Sense', *Common Sense*, no. 11, winter 1991, pp. 79–100

'Scottish Common Sense Philosophy', *Edinburgh Review*, no. 87, winter 1991, pp. 117–40

'Review of Davie, *The Scottish Enlightenment and Other Essays*', *Common Sense*, no. 12, summer 1992, pp. 101–5

'Common Sense: A Presentation', paper for a talk at the Ragged University, Edinburgh, June 2013, pp. 4–5, at www.thiswasnottheplan.com/wp- con tent/uploads/2016/05/9_common_sense_a_presentation.pdf

'Common Sense, Scottish Thought and Current Politics', *Bella Caledonia*, 26 July 2014, at https://bellacaledonia.org.uk/2014/07/26/common-sense-scottish-thought-and-current-politics

Hargrave, Andrew, 'Scotland 1980: A Critique', *Question*, no. 32, 8 July 1977

Hauser, Richard and Hephzibah Menuhin, *The Fraternal Society* (London, Bodley Head, 1962)

Hayek, F. A., *The Road to Serfdom* (London, Routledge, 1944)

Hechter, Michael, *Internal Colonialism: The Celtic Fringe in British National Development* (New Brunswick, Transaction Publishers, 1999 [1975])

'Internal Colonialism Revisited', *Cencrastus*, no. 10, autumn 1982, pp. 8–11

Hepburn, Ian, 'I'll Say That Again', *Radical Scotland*, no. 1, February/March 1983, pp. 21–2

Hobsbawm, Eric, 'Some Reflections on *The Break-Up of Britain*', *New Left Review*, no. 105, 1977, pp. 8–23

Hroch, Miroslav, *Die Vorkämpfer der nationalen Bewegung bei den kleinen Völkern Europas* (Prague, Universita Karlova, 1968); revised and translated as *Social Preconditions of National Revival in Europe* (Cambridge, Cambridge University Press, 1985)

James, Henry, 'Ivan Turgenev', in his *Literary Criticism: French Writers, Other European Writers* (New York, Library of America, 1984), pp. 968–1034

Kennedy, Gavin, 'Scotland's Economy', in Gavin Kennedy (ed.), *The Radical Approach: Papers on an Independent Scotland* (Edinburgh, Palingenesis Press, 1976), pp. 47–59

(ed.), *The Radical Approach: Papers on an Independent Scotland* (Edinburgh, Palingenesis Press, 1976)

Kerevan, George, 'Arguments within Scottish Marxism', *Bulletin of Scottish Politics*, no. 2, spring 1981, pp. 111–33

'Labourism Revisited', *Chapman*, 35/36, July 1983, pp. 25–31

'The Impending Crisis of the Scottish Left and How to Combat It', *Radical Scotland*, no. 24, December 1986/January 1987, pp. 7–9

'Back to the Drawing Board for Nationalists', *Scotsman*, 10 May 1999

'Remember, There Is No Such Thing as Inevitability in Politics', *Scotsman*, 20 September 1999

'Tax System That Can Unite Scotland', *Scotsman*, 16 August 1999

'The Utopian Guff of Tommy Sheridan', *Scotsman*, 17 November 2000

'The Way Forward for SNP Success', *Scotsman*, 17 January 2000

'This Way Forward for the SNP, Mr Swinney', *Scotsman*, 22 September 2000

'SNP on Thin Ice Until It Finds a Real Vision', *Scotsman*, 19 April 2004

'Scotland in the Wider World: Does Size and Sovereignty Matter?', in Gerry Hassan and James Mitchell (eds.), *After Independence* (Edinburgh, Luath, 2013), pp. 151–61

'The Case for Yes', in George Kerevan and Alan Cochrane, *Scottish Independence: Yes or No* (Stroud, The History Press, 2014), pp. 7–95

Lamont, Archie, *Scotland and the War* (Glasgow, Scottish Secretariat, 1943)

Small Nations (Glasgow, William MacLellan, 1944)

Lindsay, Isobel, 'Nationalism, Community and Democracy', in Gavin Kennedy (ed.), *The Radical Approach: Papers on an Independent Scotland* (Edinburgh, Palingenesis Press, 1976), pp. 21–6

'Divergent Trends', *Radical Scotland*, no. 29, October/November 1987, pp. 14–15

'The SNP and the Lure of Europe', in Tom Gallagher (ed.), *Nationalism in the Nineties* (Edinburgh, Polygon, 1991), pp. 84–101

Livingstone, Alison, 'SLP Reconvened Conference Report', *Scottish Worker*, vol. 4, no. 2, February 1977

McAlpine, Robin, 'The Butterfly Rebellion', *Bella Caledonia*, 14 September 2014, at https://bellacaledonia.org.uk/2014/09/14/the-butterfly-rebellion

MacAskill, Kenny, *Building a Nation: Post-Devolution Nationalism in Scotland* (Edinburgh, Luath Press, 2004)

MacCormick, John, *The Flag in the Wind* (London, Gollancz, 1955)

MacCormick, Neil, 'Independence and Constitutional Change' in Neil MacCormick (ed.), *The Scottish Debate* (Oxford, Oxford University Press, 1970), pp. 52–64

'Westminster Must Beware of Pushing the SNP into an All-Out Battle', *The Times*, 17 May 1977

'Does the United Kingdom have a Constitution? Reflections on *MacCormick v Lord Advocate*', *Northern Ireland Legal Quarterly*, 29 (1978), pp. 1–20

'Constitution', in Colin MacLean (ed.), *The Crown and the Thistle: The Nature of Nationhood* (Edinburgh, Scottish Academic Press, 1979), pp. 149–55

'Nation and Nationalism', in Colin MacLean (ed.), *The Crown and the Thistle: The Nature of Nationhood* (Edinburgh, Scottish Academic Press, 1979), pp. 99–111

Legal Right and Social Democracy (Oxford, Oxford University Press, 1982)

'The Idea of Liberty: Some Reflections on Lorimer's Institutes', in Vincent Hope (ed.), *Philosophers of the Scottish Enlightenment* (Edinburgh, Edinburgh University Press, 1984), pp. 233–48

'Unrepentant Gradualism', in Owen Dudley Edwards (ed.), *A Claim of Right for Scotland* (Edinburgh, Polygon, 1989), pp. 99–109

'An Idea for a Scottish Constitution', in Wilson Finnie, Chris Himsworth and Neil Walker (eds.), *Edinburgh Essays in Public Law* (Edinburgh, Edinburgh University Press, 1991), pp. 159–84

'Beyond the Sovereign State', *Modern Law Review*, 56 (1993), pp. 1–18

'Liberalism, Nationalism and the Post-Sovereign State', *Political Studies*, 44 (1996), pp. 553–67

'Institutional Normative Order: A Conception of Law', *Cornell Law Review*, 82 (1997), pp. 1051–70

Questioning Sovereignty: Law, State and Nation in the European Commonwealth (Oxford, Oxford University Press, 1999)

'Doubts about the "Supreme Court" and Reflections on *MacCormick v Lord Advocate*', *Juridical Review*, 2004, pt 3, pp. 236–50

'New Unions for Old', in William Miller (ed.), *Anglo-Scottish Relations from 1900 to Devolution and Beyond* (Oxford, Oxford University Press/British Academy, 2005), pp. 249–55

MacCormick, Neil (ed.), *The Scottish Debate: Essays on Scottish Nationalism* (Oxford, Oxford University Press, 1970)

MacDiarmid, Hugh, *Albyn* [1927], in Hugh MacDiarmid, *Albyn: Shorter Books and Monographs*, edited by Alan Riach (Manchester, Carcanet, 1996), pp. 1–39

At the Sign of the Thistle (London, Stanley Nott, 1934)

Cunninghame Graham: A Centenary Study (Glasgow, Caledonian Press, 1952)

Collected Poems (Edinburgh, Oliver and Boyd, 1962)

The Company I've Kept (London, Hutchinson, 1966)

A Political Speech (Edinburgh, Reprographia, 1972)

McGrath, John, *The Cheviot, the Stag and the Black, Black Oil* (London, Bloomsbury, 2015 [1974])

'Scotland: Up against It', in Gordon Brown (ed.), *The Red Paper on Scotland* (Edinburgh, EUSPB, 1975), pp. 134–40

McIlvanney, William, 'Stands Scotland Where It Did?', Donaldson lecture, 1987, in his *Surviving the Shipwreck* (Edinburgh, Mainstream, 1991), pp. 241–53; also in *Radical Scotland*, no. 30, December 1987/January 1988, pp. 19–22

Dreaming Scotland (Edinburgh, Saltire Society, 2014)

MacIntyre, Alasdair, *After Virtue* (Notre Dame, University of Notre Dame Press, 1981)

'The Idea of an Educated Public', in Paul Hirst (ed.), *Education and Values* (London, Institute of Education, 1987), pp. 15–36

Whose Justice? Which Rationality? (Notre Dame, University of Notre Dame Press, 1988)

Three Rival Versions of Moral Enquiry (Notre Dame, University of Notre Dame Press, 1990)

McIntyre, Robert, *Some Principles for Scottish Reconstruction* (Glasgow, SNP, 1944)

'European Union', *Scots Independent*, no. 260, April 1948

'National Party Annual Conference: Chairman's Opening Remarks', *Scots Independent*, no. 262, June 1948

'Nationalists Annual Conference: Chairman's Opening Remarks', *Scots Independent*, no. 275, July 1949

'England Turns Back: The National Idea', *Scots Independent*, no. 287, July 1950

'Freedom, Power and Democracy', *Scots Independent*, no. 286, June 1950

'The Challenge of Today', *Scots Independent*, no. 299, July 1951

MacKay, Donald (ed.), *Scotland 1980: The Economics of Self-Government* (Edinburgh, Q Press, 1977)

MacKenzie, Agnes Mure, *Scotland in Modern Times 1720–1939* (London, W & R Chambers, 1941)

Scottish Principles of Statecraft and Government (Glasgow, Scottish Convention, 1942)

On the Declaration of Arbroath (Edinburgh, Saltire Society, 1951)

MacLeod, Dennis and Michael Russell, *Grasping the Thistle* (Glendaruel, Argyll Publishing, 2006)

MacNeill, Duncan H., *The Scottish Constitution* (Glasgow, SNP, 1943)

The Scottish Realm: An Approach to the Political and Constitutional History of Scotland (Glasgow, A. and J. Donaldson, 1947)

Marwick, William H., *Scottish Devolution* (London, Fabian Society, 1950)

Massie, Alex, 'Why Choose Independence if It Means the Same Old, Same Old?', *Think Scotland*, 4 December 2012, at www.thinkscotland.org/todays-thinking/articles.html?read_full=11810

Maxwell, Stephen, 'Treason of the Clerks', *Scottish International*, vol. 5, no. 6, August 1972, pp. 18–20

'Treason of the Clerks II', *Scottish International*, vol. 5, no. 7, September 1972, pp. 14–17

'Beyond Social Democracy', in Gavin Kennedy (ed.), *The Radical Approach: Papers on an Independent Scotland* (Edinburgh, Palingenesis Press, 1976), pp. 7–20

'Can Scotland's Political Myths Be Broken?', *Question*, no. 16, 19 November 1976

'Scotland's Foreign Policy', *Question*, no. 12, September 1976

'The English in Scotland', *New Edinburgh Review*, no. 37, spring 1977, pp. 44–5

'Politics and Culture', *Question*, no. 25, 1 April 1977

'Review: *The Break-Up of Britain*', *Question*, no. 31, 24 June 1977

'The Sacred Bullock', *Question*, no. 21, 4 February 1977

'The Implications of Prospective Independence: The Problem of State Power', *Nevis Quarterly*, no. 2, January 1979, pp. 11–20

'Labourism or Socialism', in *SNP '79 Group Papers No. 1*, papers discussed at founding meeting, 31 May 1979, Belford Hotel, Edinburgh (no publisher/date), pp. 10–11

'Radical Strategy for an SNP Revival', *Scotsman*, 15 June 1979

'The Nationalism of Hugh MacDiarmid', in Paul Scott and A. C. Davis (eds.), *The Age of MacDiarmid* (Edinburgh, Mainstream, 1980), pp. 202–23

'Scotland and the British Crisis', in *SNP '79 Group Papers No. 3*, report and commentary on conference on 'Scotland and the British Crisis', 23 February 1980 (no publisher/date), pp. 1–11

'The Case for Left-Wing Nationalism', *SNP '79 Group Paper No. 6* (Hamilton, Aberdeen People's Press, 1981)

'Lothian Region: Showdown or Copout?', *'79 Group News*, September 1981

'The Secular Pulpit: Presbyterian Democracy in the Twentieth Century', *Scottish Government Yearbook*, 1982, pp. 181–98

'Scotland's Cruel Paradox', *Radical Scotland*, no. 1, February/March 1983, pp. 12–14

'Scottish Universities', *Radical Scotland*, no. 7, February/March 1984, pp. 12–13

'The '79 Group: A Critical Retrospect', *Cencrastus*, no. 21, 1985, pp. 11–16

'*The Crisis of the Democratic Intellect*', *Radical Scotland*, no. 23, October/November 1986, pp. 16–17

'Norway's Economic Lessons for Scotland', *Radical Scotland*, no. 25, February/March 1987, pp. 14–17

'Scotland in a Wider Europe', *Radical Scotland*, no. 40, August/September 1989, pp. 24–6

'Scotland International', *Cencrastus*, no. 35, winter 1989, pp. 15–18

'Social Policy and the Constitutional Debate', *Radical Scotland*, no. 39, June/July 1989, pp. 16–17

'The Scottish Middle Class and the National Debate', in Tom Gallagher (ed.), *Nationalism in the Nineties* (Edinburgh, Polygon, 1991), pp. 126–51

'Social Justice and the SNP', in Gerry Hassan (ed.), *The Modern SNP: From Protest to Power* (Edinburgh, Edinburgh University Press, 2009), pp. 120–34

'Tackling Scottish Poverty – Principles and Absences: A Critique of the Scottish Government's Approach to Combating Scotland's Problem of Poverty and Inequality', *Scottish Affairs*, no. 67 (2009), pp. 57–69

Arguing for Independence: Evidence, Risk and the Wicked Issues (Edinburgh, Luath Press, 2012)

The Case for Left-Wing Nationalism, edited by Jamie Maxwell (Edinburgh, Luath Press, 2013)

Maxwell, Stephen (ed.), *Scotland, Multinationals and the Third World* (Edinburgh, Mainstream, 1982)

Miliband, Ralph, *Parliamentary Socialism* (London, Allen & Unwin, 1961)

Muirhead, Roland, Robert McIntyre and Mary Dott, 'The Scottish Nation's Claim of Right to UNO', *Scots Independent*, no. 254, October 1947

Nairn, Tom, 'The English Working Class', *New Left Review*, no. 24, 1964, pp. 43–57

'The Nature of the Labour Party I', *New Left Review*, no. 27, 1964, pp. 38–65

'The Nature of the Labour Party II', *New Left Review*, no. 28, 1964, pp. 33–62

'Labour Imperialism', *New Left Review*, no. 32, 1965, pp. 3–15

'The Three Dreams of Scottish Nationalism', *New Left Review*, no. 49, 1968, pp. 3–18

'The Three Dreams of Scottish Nationalism', in Karl Miller (ed.), *Memoirs of a Modern Scotland* (London, Faber and Faber, 1970), pp. 34–54

'Culture and Nationalism: An Open Letter from Tom Nairn', *Scottish International*, vol. 6, no. 4, April 1973, pp. 8–9

The Left against Europe? (London, Pelican, 1973)

'Scotland and Europe', *New Left Review*, no. 83, 1974, pp. 57–82

'The Modern Janus', *New Left Review*, no. 94, 1975, pp. 3–29

'Old Nationalism and New Nationalism', in Gordon Brown (ed.), *The Red Paper on Scotland* (Edinburgh, EUSPB, 1975), pp. 22–57

'The National Question', *Scottish Worker*, vol. 3, no. 10, December 1976

'The Radical Approach', *Question*, no. 10, July 1976

'Revolutionaries versus Parliamentarists', *Question*, no. 16, 19 November 1976

'Scotland the Misfit', *Question*, no. 13, 8 October 1976

The Break-Up of Britain (London, New Left Books, 1977)

'The SLP: Report on the First Year of a New Party', *Planet*, no. 37/38, May 1977, pp. 14–17

'Twilight of the British State', *New Left Review*, no. 101/102, 1977, pp. 3–61

'After the Referendum', *New Edinburgh Review*, no. 46, summer 1979, pp. 3–10

'Scotland after the Elections', in *SNP '79 Group Papers No. 1*, papers discussed at founding meeting, 31 May 1979, Belford Hotel, Edinburgh (no publisher/ date), pp. 5–7

'Dr Jekyll's Case: Model or Warning?', *Bulletin of Scottish Politics*, no. 1, autumn 1980, pp. 136–42

The Enchanted Glass (London, Radius, 1988)

'The Timeless Girn', in Owen Dudley Edwards (ed.), *A Claim of Right for Scotland* (Edinburgh, Polygon, 1989), pp. 163–78

'Scottish Identity: A Cause Unwon', *Chapman*, 67, winter 1991/92, pp. 2–12

'Gender Goes Top of the Agenda' [1994], in Fiona MacKay and Esther Breitenbach (eds.), *Women and Contemporary Scottish Politics: An Anthology* (Edinburgh, Polygon, 2001), pp. 195–6

Faces of Nationalism (London, Verso, 1997)

After Britain (London, Granta, 2000)

'Twenty-First Century Hindsight: *Break-Up* Twenty-Five Years on', in Tom Nairn, *The Break-Up of Britain* (3rd ed., Altona, Common Ground, 2003), pp. xi–xxx

Gordon Brown: Bard of Britishness (Cardiff, Institute of Welsh Affairs, 2006)

'Preface' to Stephen Maxwell, *The Case for Left-Wing Nationalism*, edited by Jamie Maxwell (Edinburgh, Luath Press, 2013), pp. 9–12

'Globalisation and Nationalism: The New Deal', Edinburgh lecture, 4 March 2008, in Tom Nairn, *Old Nations, Auld Enemies, New Times: Selected Essays*, edited by Jamie Maxwell and Pete Ramand (Edinburgh, Luath Press, 2014), pp. 396–405

'Old Nation, New Age', April 2014, in Tom Nairn, *Old Nations, Auld Enemies, New Times: Selected Essays*, edited by Jamie Maxwell and Pete Ramand (Edinburgh, Luath Press, 2014), pp. 416–19

Page, Edward, 'Michael Hechter's Internal Colonial Thesis: Some Theoretical and Methodological Problems', *European Journal of Political Research*, 6 (1978), pp. 295–317

Paterson, Lindsay, 'What Kind of Scotland?', *Crann-Tàra*, no. 1, winter 1977

Paton, H. J., *The Claim of Scotland* (London, George Allen & Unwin, 1968)

Reid, George, 'A State of Flux', *Question*, no. 5, February 1976

'Oh, to Be in Britain?', Donaldson lecture, 1995 (Edinburgh, SNP, September 1995)

Ross, Jim, 'Towards a New Scotland: A Choice of Weapons', *Cencrastus*, no. 35, winter 1989, pp. 25–8

Salmond, Alex, 'The Economics of Independence', *West Lothian Standard*, spring 1977

'Scotland in Europe: Living with the Single European Act', *Radical Scotland*, no. 34, August/September 1988, pp. 10–11

'Unleash the Power to Create Our Own Tiger Economy', *Herald*, 20 March 1996

'Irish Show Scots Road to Success', *Irish Times*, 1 May 1997

'Learning to Love the Euro', *Herald*, 7 November 1997

The Economics of Independence (Glasgow, Strathclyde University Economics Department, 2003)

'Free to Prosper: Creating the Celtic Lion Economy', speech, Harvard University, 31 March 2008, at www.gov.scot/News/Speeches/Speeches/First-Minister/harvard-university

'Scotland's Place in the World', Hugo Young lecture, 24 January 2012, at www.theguardian.com/politics/2012/jan/25/alex-salmond-hugo-young-lecture

'The Six Unions', speech, Nigg Fabrication Yard, 12 July 2013, at http://news.scotland.gov.uk/Speeches-Briefings/The-six-unions-introduction-51e.aspx

et al., 'The Scottish Industrial Resistance', *'79 Group Paper No. 7* (Hamilton, Aberdeen People's Press, 1982)

Scottish Centre for Economic and Social Research, *Monetary Policy Options for an Independent Scotland* (Edinburgh, Scottish Centre for Economic and Social Research, n.d. [1989])

The Power of Small Nations in the New Europe (Edinburgh, Scottish Centre for Economic and Social Research, 1994)

Scottish Constitutional Convention, *Towards Scotland's Parliament* (Edinburgh, Scottish Constitutional Convention, 1990)

Scottish Government, *Scotland's Future: Your Guide to an Independent Scotland* (Edinburgh, Scottish Government, November 2013)

The Scottish Independence Bill: A Consultation on an Interim Constitution for Scotland (Edinburgh, Scottish Government, 2014)

Sillars, Jim, 'Let's Sit at the Top Table in Europe', *The Highway*, July 1975

'Why I'm Not in the SNP', *Crann-Tàra*, no. 1, winter 1977

Scotland: Moving on and up in Europe (no publisher/place of publication, June 1985)

Scotland: The Case for Optimism (Edinburgh, Polygon, 1986)

No Turning Back: The Case for Scottish Independence within the European Community and How We Face the Challenge of 1992 (no publisher/place of publication, August 1988)

Independence in Europe (Glasgow, SNP, June 1989)

'Freedom and Order', *Cencrastus*, no. 34, summer 1989, pp. 14–17

In Place of Fear II: A Socialist Programme for an Independent Scotland (Glasgow, Vagabond Voices, 2014)

'Why Scottish Nationalists Should Back Brexit', *CommonSpace*, 9 May 2016, at www.commonspace.scot/articles/3976/jim-sillars-why-scottish-nationalists-should-back-brexit

Simpson, David, *The Economics of Self-Government* (Edinburgh, SNP Research Office, n.d. [*c.* 1982])

Smith, T. B., *British Justice: The Scottish Contribution* (London, Stevens & Sons, 1961)

Smout, T. C., 'Centre and Periphery in History; With Some Thoughts on Scotland as a Case Study', *Journal of Common Market Studies*, 18 (1980), pp. 256–71

'Scotland and England: Is Dependency a Symptom or a Cause of Underdevelopment?', *Review*, 3 (1980), pp. 601–30

Snow, C. P., 'Miasma, Darkness and Torpidity', *New Statesman*, 11 August 1961

SNP, *Statement of Aim and Policy of the Scottish National Party* (Stirling, Scots Independent, January 1947)

The SNP and You: Aims and Policy of the Scottish National Party (Edinburgh, SNP, 1964)

The New Scotland – Your Scotland (Edinburgh, SNP, 1970)

For the Good of Scotland: Towards a Better Scotland (Edinburgh, SNP, November 1995)

Spence, Lewis, *The National Party of Scotland* (Glasgow, National Party of Scotland, 1928) [reprinted from *Edinburgh Review*, 1928]

Stewart Black, Charles, *The Case for Scotland* (Edinburgh, National Party of Scotland, 1930)

Scottish Nationalism: Its Inspiration and Aims (Glasgow, National Party of Scotland, 1933)

Sturgeon, Nicola, 'Bringing the Powers Home to Build a Better Nation', speech, Strathclyde University, 3 December 2012

'The Constitutional Future of an Independent Scotland', speech, Edinburgh Centre for Constitutional Law, 16 June 2014, at https://news.gov.scot/speeches-and-briefings/the-constitutional-future-of-an-independent-scotland

Tait, Bob, 'The Left, the SNP and Oil', in Gordon Brown (ed.), *The Red Paper on Scotland* (Edinburgh, EUSPB, 1975), pp. 125–33

'Scottish Education in Dubious Battle', *Cencrastus*, no. 25, spring 1987, pp. 4–5

Tamir, Yael, *Liberal Nationalism* (Princeton, NJ, Princeton University Press, 1993)

Taylor, Charles, *Sources of the Self* (Cambridge, MA, Harvard University Press, 1989)

Reconciling the Solitudes: Essays on Canadian Federalism and Nationalism (Quebec City, McGill-Queens University Press, 1993)

Thompson, E. P., 'The Peculiarities of the English', *Socialist Register*, 2 (1965), pp. 311–62

Thomson, George, *Caledonia or the Fate of the Scots* (London, Kegan Paul, 1927)

Turnbull, Ronald, 'Reviving Critique', *Irish Review*, no. 28, winter 2001, pp. 98–107

'Nairn's Nationalisms', in Eleanor Bell and Gavin Miller (eds.), *Scotland in Theory* (Edinburgh, Rodopi, 2004), pp. 35–48

Turnbull, Ronald and Craig Beveridge, 'Philosophy and Autonomy', *Cencrastus*, no. 3, summer 1980, pp. 2–4

'Scottish Nationalist, British Marxist: The Strange Case of Tom Nairn', *Cencrastus*, no. 13, summer 1983, pp. 2–5

'The Historiography of External Control', *Cencrastus*, no. 23, June/August 1986, pp. 41–4

'Towards Postmodernism: An Introduction to MacIntyre', *Cencrastus*, no. 26, autumn 1988, pp. 1–3

Wallerstein, Immanuel, *The Modern World-System I* (New York, Academic Press, 1974)

'One Man's Meat: The Scottish Great Leap Forward', *Review*, 3 (1980), pp. 631–40

Wanniski, Jude, 'Taxes, Revenues, and the "Laffer Curve"', *Public Interest*, winter 1978, pp. 3–16

Welsh, Irvine, 'Scottish Independence and British Unity', *Bella Caledonia*, 10 January 2013, at https://bellacaledonia.org.uk/2013/01/10/irvine-welsh-on-scottish-independence-and-british-unity

Williamson, Neil, 'Ten Years After – The Revolutionary Left in Scotland', *Scottish Government Yearbook*, 1979, pp. 61–77

Wolfe, Billy, *Scotland Lives* (Edinburgh, Reprographia, 1973)

Women's Claim of Right Group (ed.), *A Woman's Claim of Right* (Edinburgh, Polygon, 1991)

Wright, Kenyon, *The People Say Yes* (Glendaruel, Argyll, 1997)

Young, Douglas, *Quislings in Scotland* (Glasgow, Scottish Secretariat, 1942)

The Free-Minded Scot (Glasgow, Scottish Secretariat, 1942)

Fascism for the Highlands? Gauleiter for Wales? (Glasgow, SNP, 1943)

An Appeal to Scots Honour: A Vindication of the Right of the Scottish People to Freedom from Industrial Conscription and Bureaucratic Despotism under the Treaty of Union with England (Glasgow, Scottish Secretariat, 1944)

British Invasion of Scottish Rights: Douglas Young's Speech in Paisley Sheriff Court on 12th June (Glasgow, Scottish Secretariat, 1944)

The International Importance of Scottish Nationalism (Glasgow, Scottish Secretariat, 1947)

Chasing an Ancient Greek (London, Hollis & Carter, 1950)

Young, J. D., *The Rousing of the Scottish Working Class* (London, Croom Helm, 1979)

Secondary Sources

Anderson, Robert, *Education and Opportunity in Victorian Scotland* (Oxford, Oxford University Press, 1983)

'Education and Society in Modern Scotland: A Comparative Perspective', *History of Education Quarterly*, 25 (1985), pp. 459–81

'Democracy and Intellect', *Cencrastus*, no. 25, Spring 1987, pp. 3–4

'The Scottish University Tradition: Past and Future', in Jennifer Carter and Donald Withrington (eds.), *Scottish Universities: Distinctiveness and Diversity* (Edinburgh, John Donald, 1992), pp. 67–78

Ascherson, Neal, *Stone Voices* (London, Granta, 2002)

Tom Nairn: 'Painting Nationalism Red?' (Dundee, Democratic Left Scotland, 2018)

Aughey, Arthur, *The Politics of Englishness* (Manchester, Manchester University Press, 2007)

Barnes, Eddie, 'What the New Form of Independence Is All about', *Scotsman*, 14 May 2011

Barr, Jean, 'Re-framing the Democratic Intellect', *Scottish Affairs*, no. 55 (2006), pp. 23–46

Bayne, Ian O., 'The Impact of 1979 on the SNP', in Tom Gallagher (ed.), *Nationalism in the Nineties* (Edinburgh, Polygon, 1991), pp. 46–65

Bell, Eleanor, *Questioning Scotland: Literature, Nationalism, Postmodernism* (Basingstoke, Palgrave, 2004)

Bell, Eleanor and Gavin Miller (eds.), *Scotland in Theory* (Edinburgh, Rodopi, 2004)

Blackburn, Dean, 'Still the Stranger at the Feast? Ideology and the Study of Twentieth Century British Politics', *Journal of Political Ideologies*, 22 (2017), pp. 116–30

Blackledge, Paul, 'Freedom, Desire and Revolution: Alasdair MacIntyre's Early Marxist Ethics', *History of Political Thought*, 26 (2004), pp. 696–720

Blane, Neil and David Hutchison with Gerry Hassan (eds.), *Scotland's Referendum and the Media* (Edinburgh, Edinburgh University Press, 2016)

Bourke, Richard, 'Reflections on the Political Thought of the Irish Revolution', *Transactions of the Royal Historical Society*, 27 (2017), pp. 175–91

Brand, Jack, *The National Movement in Scotland* (London, Routledge, 1978)

Brotherstone, Terry and David Ditchburn, '1320 and a' that: The Declaration of Arbroath and the Remaking of Scottish History', in Terry Brotherstone and David Ditchburn (eds.), *Freedom and Authority: Scotland c.1050–c. 1650* (East Linton, Tuckwell Press, 2000), pp. 10–31

Brown, Alice, 'Deepening Democracy: Women and the Scottish Parliament' [1998], in Fiona MacKay and Esther Breitenbach (eds.), *Women and Contemporary Scottish Politics: An Anthology* (Edinburgh, Polygon, 2001), pp. 213–29

Brown Swan, Coree and Bettina Petersohn, 'The Currency Issue', in Michael Keating (ed.), *Debating Scotland: Issues of Independence and Union in the 2014 Referendum* (Oxford, Oxford University Press, 2017), pp. 65–83

Bulmer, W. Elliot, 'An Analysis of the Scottish National Party's Draft Constitution for Scotland', *Parliamentary Affairs*, 64 (2011), pp. 674–93

Constituting Scotland: The Scottish National Movement and the Westminster Model (Edinburgh, Edinburgh University Press, 2016)

Burness, Catriona, 'Drunk Women Don't Look at Thistles: Women and the SNP 1934–94', *Scotlands*, 2 (1994), pp. 131–54

Cameron, Ewen, *Impaled upon a Thistle: Scotland since 1880* (Edinburgh, Edinburgh University Press, 2010)

Chun, Lin, *The British New Left* (Edinburgh, Edinburgh University Press, 1993)

Cohen, Anthony, 'Personal Nationalism: A Scottish View of Some Rites, Rights, and Wrongs', *American Ethnologist*, 23 (1996), pp. 802–15

Cocks, Joan, 'In Defence of Ethnicity, Locality, Nationality: The Curious Case of Tom Nairn', in Joan Cocks, *Passion and Paradox: Intellectuals Confront the National Question* (Princeton, NJ, Princeton University Press, 2002), pp. 111–32

Cowan, E. J., 'Identity, Freedom, and the Declaration of Arbroath', in Dauvit Broun, Richard Finlay and Michael Lynch (eds.), *Image and Identity: The Making and Re-making of Scotland through the Ages* (Edinburgh, John Donald, 1998), pp. 38–68

Craig, Cairns, *Out of History* (Edinburgh, Polygon, 1996)
The Modern Scottish Novel (Edinburgh, Edinburgh University Press, 1999)
Intending Scotland (Edinburgh, Edinburgh University Press, 2009)
The Wealth of the Nation: Scotland, Culture and Independence (Edinburgh, Edinburgh University Press, 2018)

Craig, Carol, *The Scots' Crisis of Confidence* (Glendaruel, Argyll Publishing, 2011 [2003])

Crawford, Robert, *Devolving English Literature* (Edinburgh, Edinburgh University Press, 2000)
Scotland's Books (London, Penguin, 2009)
Bannockburns: Scottish Independence and Literary Imagination, 1314–2014 (Edinburgh, Edinburgh University Press, 2014)

Cumbers, Andrew, 'The Scottish Independence Referendum and the Dysfunctional Economic Geography of the UK', *Political Geography*, 41 (2014), pp. 33–6

Dalle Mulle, Emmanuel, 'New Trends in Justifications for National Self-Determination: Evidence from Scotland and Flanders', *Ethnopolitics*, 15 (2016), pp. 211–29

Dalle Mulle, Emmanuel and Ivano Serrano, 'Between a Principled and a Consequentialist Logic: Theory and Practice of Secession in Catalonia and Scotland', *Nations and Nationalism*, 25 (2019), pp. 630–51

Dardanelli, Paolo, *Between Two Unions: Europeanisation and Scottish Devolution* (Manchester, Manchester University Press, 2006)

Davidson, Neil, 'Alasdair MacIntyre as a Marxist', in Neil Davidson, *Holding Fast to an Image of the Past* (Chicago, Haymarket, 2014), pp. 129–81
'Antonio Gramsci's Reception in Scotland', in Neil Davidson, *Holding Fast to an Image of the Past* (Chicago, Haymarket Books, 2014), pp. 253–86
'Tom Nairn and the Inevitability of Nationalism', in Neil Davidson, *Holding Fast to an Image of the Past* (Chicago, Haymarket Books, 2014), pp. 1–44
'A Scottish Watershed', *New Left Review*, no. 89, 2014, pp. 5–26

Davis, Madeleine, 'The Marxism of the British New Left', *Journal of Political Ideologies*, 11 (2006), pp. 335–58
'Arguing Affluence: New Left Contributions to the Socialist Debate 1957–63', *Twentieth Century British History*, 23 (2012), pp. 496–528
'Reappraising British Socialist Humanism', *Journal of Political Ideologies*, 18 (2013), pp. 1–25
'"Among the Ordinary People": New Left Involvement in Working Class Mobilisation 1956–68', *History Workshop Journal*, 86 (2018), pp. 133–59

Devine, Tom, 'The Break-Up of Britain? Scotland and the End of Empire', *Transactions of the Royal Historical Society*, 16 (2006), pp. 163–80
To the Ends of the Earth: Scotland's Global Diaspora (London, Penguin, 2011)
Independence or Union: Scotland's Past and Scotland's Future (London, Penguin, 2016)

Donaldson, William, 'Agnes Mure MacKenzie (1891–1955)', *Oxford Dictionary of National Biography* (Oxford, Oxford University Press, online ed., 28 September 2006), at https://doi.org/10.1093/ref:odnb/57342

Douglas, Dick, *At the Helm: The Life and Times of Dr Robert D McIntyre* (Portessie, Buckie, NPFI Publications, 1996)

Drucker, Henry, *Breakaway: The Scottish Labour Party* (Edinburgh, EUSPB, 1978)

'Crying Wolfe: Recent Divisions in the SNP', *Political Quarterly*, 50 (1979), pp. 503–8

Dworkin, Dennis, *Cultural Marxism in Post-War Britain* (Durham, NC, Duke University Press, 1997)

Edgerton, David, *The Rise and Fall of the British Nation: A Twentieth Century History* (London, Allen Lane, 2018)

Erdos, David, 'Charter 88 and the Constitutional Reform Movement: A Retrospective', *Parliamentary Affairs*, 62 (2009), pp. 537–51

Erskine, Caroline, 'George Buchanan, English Whigs and Royalists and the Canon of Political Theory', in Caroline Erskine and Roger Mason (eds.), *George Buchanan: Political Thought in Early Modern Britain and Europe* (Aldershot, Ashgate, 2012), pp. 229–45

Farmer, Lindsay, 'Under the Shadow over Parliament House: The Strange Case of Legal Nationalism', in Lindsay Farmer and Scott Veitch (eds.), *The State of Scots Law: Law and Government after the Devolution Settlement* (London, Bloomsbury, 2001), pp. 151–64

Fieldhouse, Edward and Christopher Prosser, 'The Limits of Partisan Loyalty: How the Independence Referendum Cost Labour', *Electoral Studies*, 52 (2018), pp. 11–25

Finlay, Richard, '"For or against?" Scottish Nationalists and the British Empire 1919–39', *Scottish Historical Review*, 71 (1992), pp. 184–206

'Controlling the Past: Scottish Historiography and Scottish Identity in the 19th and 20th Centuries', *Scottish Affairs*, no. 9 (1994), pp. 127–42

Independent and Free: Scottish Politics and the Origins of the Scottish National Party 1918–45 (Edinburgh, John Donald, 1994)

'National Identity in Crisis: Politicians, Intellectuals and the "End of Scotland"', *History*, 79 (1994), pp. 242–59

'Thatcherism, Unionism and Nationalism: A Comparative Study of Scotland and Wales', in Ben Jackson and Robert Saunders (eds.), *Making Thatcher's Britain* (Cambridge, Cambridge University Press, 2012), pp. 165–79

'Thomas Hill Gibson (1893–1975)', *Oxford Dictionary of National Biography* (Oxford, Oxford University Press, online ed., 4 October 2012), at https://doi.org/10.1093/ref:odnb/71329

'Robert McIntyre (1913–98)', *Oxford Dictionary of National Biography* (Oxford, Oxford University Press, online ed., 28 May 2015), at https://doi.org/10.1093/ref:odnb/59442

'Robert McIntyre', in Gerry Hassan and James Mitchell (eds.), *Scottish National Party Leaders* (London, Biteback, 2016), pp. 177–99

Forgacs, David, 'Gramsci and Marxism in Britain', *New Left Review*, no. 176, 1989, pp. 70–88

Freeden, Michael, 'Stranger at the Feast: Ideology and Public Policy in Twentieth-Century Britain', *Twentieth Century British History*, 1 (1990), pp. 9–34

Ideologies and Political Theory (Oxford, Oxford University Press, 1996)

'The Coming of the Welfare State', in Terence Ball and Richard Bellamy (eds.), *Cambridge History of Twentieth Century Political Thought* (Cambridge, Cambridge University Press, 2003), pp. 5–44

Freeman, Tom, 'Isobel Lindsay's Radical Road to Devolution', *Holyrood*, 1 March 2019, at www.holyrood.com/articles/inside-politics/isobel-lind says-radical-road-devolution

Fry, Michael, *Patronage and Principle: A Political History of Modern Scotland* (Aberdeen, Aberdeen University Press, 1987)

Gardiner, Michael, *The Cultural Roots of British Devolution* (Edinburgh, Edinburgh University Press, 2004)

Geekie, Jack and Roger Levy, 'Devolution and the Tartanisation of the Labour Party', *Parliamentary Affairs*, 42 (1989), pp. 399–411

Geoghegan, Peter, *The People's Referendum* (Edinburgh, Luath Press, 2015)

Gibbs, Ewan, 'The Moral Economy of the Scottish Coalfields: Managing Deindustrialisation, *c.* 1947–83', *Enterprise and Society*, 19 (2018), pp. 124–52

Gibbs, Ewan and Rory Scothorne, '"Origins of the Present Crisis?": The Emergence of "Left-Wing" Scottish Nationalism, 1956–79', in Evan Smith and Matthew Worley (eds.), *Waiting for the Revolution: The British Far Left from 1956* (Manchester, Manchester University Press, 2017), pp. 163–81

Glyn, Andrew (ed.), *Social Democracy in Neo-Liberal Times: The Left and Economic Policy since 1980* (Oxford, Oxford University Press, 2001)

Gow, David, 'Obituary: Bob Tait, Writer and Intellectual', *Scotsman*, 2 January 2018

Gunn, Linda and Richard Cleary, 'Wasps in a Jam Jar: Scottish Literary Magazines and Political Culture 1979–99', in Aimee McNair and Jacqueline Ryder (eds.), *Further from the Frontiers* (Aberdeen, Centre for Irish and Scottish Studies, 2009), pp. 41–52

Gutiérrez, Ramón A., 'Internal Colonialism: An American Theory of Race', *Du Bois Review*, 1 (2004), pp. 281–95

Hames, Scott, *The Literary Politics of Scottish Devolution* (Edinburgh, Edinburgh University Press, 2019)

Hamilton, Scott, *The Crisis of Theory: E. P. Thompson, the New Left and Postwar British Politics* (Manchester, Manchester University Press, 2011)

Hanham, H. J., *Scottish Nationalism* (London, Faber, 1969)

Harris, Jose, 'Political Thought and the Welfare State 1870–1940: An Intellectual Framework for British Social Policy', *Past and Present*, 135 (1992), pp. 116–41

Harvie, Christopher, 'Nationalism, Journalism and Cultural Politics', in Tom Gallagher (ed.), *Nationalism in the Nineties* (Edinburgh, Polygon, 1991), pp. 29–45

Fool's Gold: The Story of North Sea Oil (London, Penguin, 1995)

Scotland and Nationalism: Scottish Society and Politics 1707 to the Present (London, Routledge, 2004)

'William Wolfe', in Gerry Hassan and James Mitchell (eds.), *Scottish National Party Leaders* (London, Biteback, 2016), pp. 247–64

Hassan, Gerry, 'The Forward March of Scottish Nationalism', *Renewal*, 19 (2011), pp. 50–63

Caledonia Dreaming: The Quest for a Different Scotland (Edinburgh, Luath Press, 2014)

Independence of the Scottish Mind: Elite Narratives, Public Spaces and the Making of a Modern Nation (Basingstoke, Palgrave, 2014)

'Jim Sillars', in Gerry Hassan and James Mitchell (eds.), *Scottish National Party Leaders* (London, Biteback, 2016), pp. 409–34

Hassan, Gerry and Eric Shaw, *The Strange Death of Labour Scotland* (Edinburgh, Edinburgh University Press, 2013)

Hassan, Gerry (ed.), *The Modern SNP* (Edinburgh, Edinburgh University Press, 2009)

Hassan, Gerry and James Mitchell (eds.), *After Independence* (Edinburgh, Luath Press, 2013)

(eds.), *Scottish National Party Leaders* (London, Biteback, 2016)

Hearn, Jonathan, *Claiming Scotland: National Identity and Liberal Culture* (Edinburgh, Polygon, 2000)

Rethinking Nationalism (Basingstoke, Palgrave, 2006)

'Nationalism and Normality: A Comment on the Scottish Independence Referendum', *Dialectical Anthropology*, 38 (2014), pp. 505–12

Hepburn, Eve, *Using Europe: Territorial Party Strategies in a Multi-Level System* (Manchester, Manchester University Press, 2010)

Herdman, John, *Another Country: An Era in Scottish Politics and Letters* (Edinburgh, Thirsty Books, 2013)

Hill, Christopher, 'Nations of Peace: Nuclear Disarmament and the Making of National Identity in Scotland and Wales', *Twentieth Century British History*, 27 (2016), pp. 26–50

Horn, Gerd-Rainer, *The Spirit of '68: Rebellion in Western Europe and North America, 1956–76* (Oxford, Oxford University Press, 2007)

Howe, Stephen, 'Some Intellectual Origins of Charter 88', *Parliamentary Affairs*, 62 (2009), pp. 552–67

Hutcheon, Paul, 'Salmond Causes Rival to Change "Dangerous" Book', *Sunday Herald*, 1 October 2006

Hutchinson, Francis and Brian Burkitt, *The Political Economy of Social Credit and Guild Socialism* (London, Routledge, 1997)

Ichijo, Atsuko, *Scottish Nationalism and the Idea of Europe* (London, Routledge, 2004)

Immerwahr, Daniel, 'Polanyi in the United States: Peter Drucker, Karl Polanyi and the Mid-Century Critique of Economic Society', *Journal of the History of Ideas*, 70 (2009), pp. 445–66

Invernizzi Accetti, Carlo, *What Is Christian Democracy?* (Cambridge, Cambridge University Press, 2019)

Jack, Ian, 'Nicola Sturgeon Used to Be a "Historical Fiction Geek". But Not Any More', *Guardian*, 25 April 2015

Jackson, Ben, *Equality and the British Left* (Manchester, Manchester University Press, 2007)

'Property-Owning Democracy: A Short History', in Martin O'Neill and Thad Williamson (eds.), *Property-Owning Democracy: Rawls and Beyond* (Oxford, Wiley-Blackwell, 2012), pp. 33–52

'Social Democracy', in Michael Freeden, Lyman Tower Sargeant and Marc Stears (eds.), *Oxford Handbook of Political Ideologies* (Oxford, Oxford University Press, 2013), pp. 348–63

'A Union of Hearts? Republican Social Democracy and Scottish Nationalism', in Hans Schattle and Jeremy Nuttall (eds.), *Making Social Democrats: Citizens, Mindsets, Realities: Essays for David Marquand* (Manchester, Manchester University Press, 2018), pp. 161–73

Jones, Peter, 'SNP Leader Signals Economic Policy Shift', *Scotsman*, 7 August 1993

'Salmond Set for Test of New Policies', *Scotsman*, 18 August 1993

'Dedicated Leader of the Band', *Scotsman*, 19 August 1993

'Existential and Utilitarian Nationalism in Scotland', in Klaus Peter Müller (ed.), *Scotland 2014 and Beyond – Coming of Age and Loss of Innocence?* (Frankfurt am Main, Peter Lang, 2015), pp. 137–64

Jones, Tudor, *The Revival of British Liberalism* (Basingstoke, Palgrave, 2011)

Kearney, Richard, 'Towards a Post-Nationalist Archipelago', *Edinburgh Review*, no. 103, 2000, pp. 21–35

Kearton, Antonia, 'Imagining the "Mongrel Nation": Political Uses of History in the Recent Scottish Nationalist Movement', *National Identities*, 7 (2005), pp. 23–50

Keating, Michael, *Plurinational Democracy: Stateless Nations in a Post-Sovereignty Era* (Oxford, Oxford University Press, 2001)

The Independence of Scotland (Oxford, Oxford University Press, 2009)

(ed.), *Debating Scotland: Issues of Independence and Union in the 2014 Referendum* (Oxford, Oxford University Press, 2017)

Keating, Michael and Richard Bleiman, *Labour and Scottish Nationalism* (London, Macmillan, 1979)

Kemp, Arnold, *Hollow Drum: Scotland since the War* (Glasgow, Neil Wilson Publishing, 1993)

Kenny, Meryl, 'Engendering the Independence Debate', *Scottish Affairs*, 23 (2014), pp. 323–31

Kenny, Michael, *The First New Left* (London, Lawrence & Wishart, 1995)

The Politics of English Nationhood (Oxford, Oxford University Press, 2014)

Kidd, Colin, *Subverting Scotland's Past* (Cambridge, Cambridge University Press, 1993)

'Sovereignty and the Scottish Constitution before 1707', *Juridical Review*, 2004, pt 3, pp. 225–36

'Lord Dacre and the Politics of the Scottish Enlightenment', *Scottish Historical Review*, 84 (2005), pp. 202–20

Union and Unionisms: Political Thought in Scotland, 1500–2000 (Cambridge, Cambridge University Press, 2008)

Lee, Geoffrey, 'North Sea Oil and Scottish Nationalism', *Political Quarterly*, 47 (1976), pp. 307–17

Leith, Murray Stewart and Daniel Soule, *Political Discourse and National Identity in Scotland* (Edinburgh, Edinburgh University Press, 2011)

Levy, Roger, *Scottish Nationalism at the Crossroads* (Edinburgh, Scottish Academic Press, 1990)

Little, Gavin, 'A Flag in the Wind: *MacCormick v Lord Advocate*', in John Grant and Elaine Sutherland (eds.), *Scots Law Tales* (Dundee, Dundee University Press, 2010), pp. 23–44

Lyall, Scott, *Hugh MacDiarmid's Poetry and Politics of Place: Imagining a Scottish Republic* (Edinburgh, Edinburgh University Press, 2006)

'Hugh MacDiarmid and the Scottish Renaissance', in Gerard Carruthers and Liam McIlvanney (eds.), *The Cambridge Companion to Scottish Literature* (Cambridge, Cambridge University Press, 2012), pp. 173–87

Lynch, Peter, *Minority Nationalism and European Integration* (Cardiff, University of Wales Press, 1996)

'From Social Democracy Back to No Ideology – The Scottish National Party and Ideological Change in a Multi-Level Electoral Setting', *Regional and Federal Studies*, 19 (2009), pp. 619–37

SNP: The History of the Scottish National Party (Cardiff, Welsh Academic Press, 2013)

McCreadie, Robert, 'Scottish Identity and the Constitution', in Bernard Crick (ed.), *National Identities* (Oxford, Blackwell/Political Quarterly, 1990), pp. 38–56

McCrone, David, 'Post-Nationalism and the Decline of the Nation State', *Radical Scotland*, no. 49, February/March 1991, pp. 6–8

Understanding Scotland: The Sociology of a Nation (2nd ed., London, Routledge, 2001)

'Cultural Capital in an Understated Nation: The Case of Scotland', *British Journal of Sociology*, 56 (2005), pp. 65–80

McCulloch, Margarey Palmer, *Scottish Modernism and Its Contexts 1918–59: Literature, National Identity and Cultural Exchange* (Edinburgh, Edinburgh University Press, 2009)

MacDonald, Catriona M. M., 'Alba Mater: Scottish University Students, 1889–1945', in Robert Anderson, Mark Freeman and Lindsay Paterson (eds.), *The Edinburgh History of Education in Scotland* (Edinburgh, Edinburgh University Press, 2015), pp. 286–303

McEwen, Nicola, *Nationalism and the State: Welfare and Identity in Scotland and Quebec* (Brussels, Peter Lang, 2006)

McHarg, Aileen, Tom Mullen, Alan Page and Neil Walker (eds.), *The Scottish Independence Referendum: Constitutional and Political Implications* (Oxford, Oxford University Press, 2016)

MacKay, Fiona and Meryl Kenny, 'Women's Political Representation and the SNP: Gendered Paradoxes and Puzzles', in Gerry Hassan (ed.), *The Modern SNP* (Edinburgh, Edinburgh University Press, 2009), pp. 42–54

McLean, Bob, *Getting It Together: The History of the Campaign for a Scottish Assembly/Parliament 1980–99* (Edinburgh, Luath Press, 2005)

McLean, Iain, 'The Rise and Fall of the Scottish National Party', *Political Studies*, 18 (1970), pp. 357–72

McLean, Iain, Jim Gallagher and Guy Lodge, *Scotland's Choices: The Referendum and What Happens Afterwards* (Edinburgh, Edinburgh University Press, 2013)

MacPherson, C. B., *Democracy in Alberta: Social Credit and the Party System* (Toronto, University of Toronto Press, 2013 [1953])

MacQueen, Hector, 'Legal Nationalism: Lord Cooper, Legal History and Comparative Law', *Edinburgh Law Review*, 9 (2005), pp. 395–406

    'Two Toms and an Ideology for Scots Law: T. B. Smith and Lord Cooper of Culross', in Elspeth Reid and David Carey Miller (eds.), *A Mixed Legal System in Transition: T. B. Smith and the Progress of Scots Law* (Edinburgh, Edinburgh University Press, 2005), pp. 44–72

    'Public Law, Private Law, and National Identity', in Cormac Mac Amhlaigh, Claudio Michelon and Neil Walker (eds.), *After Public Law* (Oxford, Oxford University Press, 2013), pp. 168–98

Macwhirter, Iain, *Disunited Kingdom: How Westminster Won a Referendum But Lost Scotland* (Glasgow, Cargo, 2014)

Mansbach, Richard, 'The SNP: A Revised Political Profile', *Comparative Politics*, 5 (1973), pp. 185–210

Marr, Andrew, *The Battle for Scotland* (London, Penguin, 1995)

Mason, Roger, 'Introduction' to George Buchanan, *A Dialogue on the Law of Kingship Among the Scots* [1579], translated and edited by Martin Smith and Roger Mason (Edinburgh, Saltire Society, 2006), pp. 1–32

    'Beyond the Declaration of Arbroath: Kingship, Counsel and Consent in Late Medieval and Early Modern Scotland', in Steve Boardman and Julian Goodare (eds.), *Kings, Lords and Men in Scotland and Britain, 1300–1625* (Edinburgh, Edinburgh University Press, 2014), pp. 265–82

Matthews, Wade, *The New Left, National Identity and the Break-Up of Britain* (Chicago, Haymarket, 2014)

Miller, David, *On Nationality* (Oxford, Oxford University Press, 1995)

Miller, William, *The End of British Politics?* (Oxford, Oxford University Press, 1981)

    'Modified Rapture All Round: The First Elections to the Scottish Parliament', *Government and Opposition*, 34 (1999), pp. 299–322

Mitchell, James, *Strategies for Self-Government* (Edinburgh, Polygon, 1996)

    'Varieties of Independence', in Gerry Hassan and James Mitchell (eds.), *After Independence* (Edinburgh, Luath Press, 2013), pp. 45–54

    The Scottish Question (Oxford, Oxford University Press, 2014)

    'Alex Salmond (Act II)', in James Mitchell and Gerry Hassan (eds.), *Scottish National Party Leaders* (London, Biteback, 2016), pp. 325–48

    Hamilton 1967: The By-Election That Transformed Scotland (Edinburgh, Luath, 2017)

    'The Meaning of Independence', in Gerry Hassan and Simon Barrow (eds.), *A Nation Changed? The SNP and Scotland Ten Years on* (Edinburgh, Luath Press, 2017), pp. 299–304

Mitchell, James and Rob Johns, *Takeover: Explaining the Extraordinary Rise of the SNP* (London, Biteback, 2016)

Morton, Graeme, *Unionist-Nationalism: Governing Urban Scotland 1830–60* (East Linton, Tuckwell Press, 1999)

Moyn, Samuel, *Christian Human Rights* (Philadelphia, University of Pennsylvania Press, 2015)

Mudge, Stephanie, *Leftism Reinvented: Western Parties from Socialism to Neo-Liberalism* (Cambridge, MA, Harvard University Press, 2018)

Mulhall, Stephen and Adam Swift, *Liberals and Communitarians* (Oxford, Wiley-Blackwell, 1996)

Mycock, Andrew, 'SNP, Identity and Citizenship: Reimagining State and Nation', *National Identities*, 14 (2012), pp. 53–69

Nehring, Holger, '"Out of Apathy": Genealogies of the British "New Left" in a Transnational Context, 1956–62', in Martin Klimke, Jakko Pekelder and Joachim Scharloth (eds.), *Between Prague Spring and French May: Opposition and Revolt in Europe, 1960–80* (New York, Berghahn Books, 2013), pp. 15–31

Nicoll, Laurence, 'Philosophy, Tradition, Nation', in Eleanor Bell and Gavin Miller (eds.), *Scotland in Theory* (Edinburgh, Rodopi, 2004), pp. 211–28

Østergaard Neilsen, Jimmi and Stuart Ward, '"Cramped and Restricted at Home?" Scottish Separatism at Empire's End', *Transactions of the Royal Historical Society*, 25 (2015), pp. 159–85

'Three Referenda and a By-Election: The Shadow of Empire in Devolutionary Politics', in John MacKenzie and Bryan Glass (eds.), *Scotland, Empire and Decolonisation in the Twentieth Century* (Manchester, Manchester University Press, 2015), pp. 200–22

Paterson, Lindsay, 'Ane End of Ane Auld Sang: Sovereignty and the Re-Negotiation of the Union', *The Scottish Government Yearbook*, 1991, pp. 104–22

The Autonomy of Modern Scotland (Edinburgh, Edinburgh University Press, 1994)

Scottish Education in the Twentieth Century (Edinburgh, Edinburgh University Press, 2003)

'Democracy or Intellect: The Scottish Educational Dilemma of the Twentieth Century', in Robert Anderson, Mark Freeman and Lindsay Paterson (eds.), *The Edinburgh History of Education in Scotland* (Edinburgh, Edinburgh University Press, 2015), pp. 226–45

'George Davie and the Democratic Intellect', in Gordon Graham (ed.), *Scottish Philosophy in the Nineteenth and Twentieth Centuries* (Oxford, Oxford University Press, 2015), pp. 236–69

'Utopian Pragmatism: Scotland's Choice', *Scottish Affairs*, 24 (2015), pp. 22–46

Pattie, Charles and Ron Johnston, 'Sticking to the Union? Nationalism, Inequality and Political Disaffection and the Geography of Scotland's 2014 Independence Referendum', *Regional and Federal Studies*, 27 (2017), pp. 83–96

Pentland, Gordon, 'Douglas Young', in Gerry Hassan and James Mitchell (eds.), *Scottish National Party Leaders* (London, Biteback, 2016), pp. 145–64

Petrie, Malcolm, 'John MacCormick', in Gerry Hassan and James Mitchell (eds.), *Scottish National Party Leaders* (London, Biteback, 2016), pp. 43–63

'Anti-socialism, Liberalism and Individualism: Rethinking the Realignment of Scottish Politics, 1945–70', *Transactions of the Royal Historical Society*, 28 (2018), pp. 197–217

Phillips, Jim, *The Industrial Politics of Devolution* (Manchester, Manchester University Press, 2008)

'Deindustrialisation and the Moral Economy of the Scottish Coalfields, 1947–91', *International Labor and Working Class History*, 84 (2013), pp. 99–115

'The Closure of Michael Colliery in 1967 and the Politics of Deindustrialisation in Scotland', *Twentieth Century British History*, 26 (2015), pp. 551–72

Phillips, Jim, Valerie Wright and Jim Tomlinson, 'Deindustrialisation, the Linwood Car Plant and Scotland's Political Divergence from England in the 1960s and 1970s', *Twentieth Century British History*, 30 (2019), pp. 399–423

Pittock, Murray, *The Road to Independence? Scotland in the Balance* (London, Reaktion, 2013)

Price, Richard, 'Some Questions about Literary Infrastructure in the 1960s', in Eleanor Bell and Linda Gunn (eds.), *The Scottish Sixties: Reading, Rebellion, Revolution?* (Amsterdam, Rodopi, 2013), pp. 93–114

Purdie, Bob, *Hugh MacDiarmid: Black, Green, Red and Tartan* (Cardiff, Welsh Academic Press, 2012)

Redhead, Mark, *Charles Taylor: Thinking and Living Deep Diversity* (Lanham, Rowman & Littlefield, 2002)

Ritchie, Murray, 'Alex Salmond (Act I)', in James Mitchell and Gerry Hassan (eds.), *Scottish National Party Leaders* (London, Biteback, 2016), pp. 281–99

Robertson, John, 'An Elusive Sovereignty: The Course of the Union Debate in Scotland 1698–1707', in John Robertson (ed.), *A Union for Empire* (Cambridge, Cambridge University Press, 1995), pp. 198–227

Robinson, Emily, Camilla Schofield, Florence Sutcliffe-Braithwaite and Natalie Thomlinson, 'Telling Stories about Post-War Britain: Popular Individualism and the "Crisis" of the 1970s', *Twentieth Century British History*, 28 (2017), pp. 268–304

Rosenfeld, Sophia, *Common Sense: A Political History* (Cambridge, MA, Harvard University Press, 2011)

Saunders, Robert, '"An Auction of Fear?" The Scotland in Europe Referendum, 1975', *Renewal*, 22 (2014), pp. 87–95

Yes to Europe! The 1975 Referendum and Seventies Britain (Cambridge, Cambridge University Press, 2018)

Scothorne, Rory, 'The "Radical Current": Nationalism and the Radical Left in Scotland, 1967–79', *H-Nationalism*, 25 May 2018, at https://networks.h-net.org/node/3911/discussions/1862513/left-and-nationalism-monthly-series-%E2%80%9C-%E2%80%98radical-current%E2%80%99

'From the Outer Edge', *London Review of Books*, vol. 40, no. 23, 6 December 2018, pp. 35–8

Scott, Drew, 'Neil MacCormick: Public Intellectual', in Neil Walker (ed.), *MacCormick's Scotland* (Edinburgh, Edinburgh University Press, 2012), pp. 205–19

Scott, Paul Henderson, *Scotland Resurgent* (Edinburgh, Saltire Society, 2003)

Simpson, Grant, 'The Declaration of Arbroath Revitalised', *Scottish Historical Review*, 56 (1977), pp. 11–33

Sloman, Peter, *The Liberal Party and the Economy, 1929–64* (Oxford, Oxford University Press, 2015)

Smith, Anthony, *Nationalism* (2nd ed., Cambridge, Polity, 2010)

Smith, Ken, 'Salmond Puts the Case for the Economics of Independence', *Herald*, 7 August 1993

Somerville, Paula, *Through the Maelstrom: A History of the Scottish National Party 1945–67* (Stirling, Scots Independent, 2013)

Stafford, James, 'The Revenge of Sovereignty: The SNP, the Financial Crisis and UK Constitutional Reform', *SPERI Paper No. 20* (Sheffield, SPERI, March 2015)

Stedman Jones, Gareth, 'Rethinking Chartism', in his *Languages of Class* (Cambridge, Cambridge University Press, 1984), pp. 90–178

Stevenson, Randall and Gavin Wallace (eds.), *Scottish Theatre since the Seventies* (Edinburgh, Edinburgh University Press, 1996)

Stewart, David, *The Path to Devolution and Change: A Political History of Scotland under Margaret Thatcher* (London, IB Tauris, 2009)

Stewart, Thomas, '"A Disguised Liberal Party Vote?" Third Party Voting and the SNP under Gordon Wilson in Dundee in the 1970s and 1980s', *Contemporary British History*, 33 (2019), pp. 357–82

Taylor, Alice, *The Shape of the State in Medieval Scotland, 1124–1290* (Oxford, Oxford University Press, 2016)

Thompson, William, 'Tom Nairn and the Crisis of the British State', *Contemporary Record*, 6 (1992), pp. 306–25

Tomkins, Adam, 'The Constitutional Law in *MacCormick v Lord Advocate*', *Juridical Review*, 2004, pt 3, pp. 213–24

Tomlinson, Jim, 'Imagining the Economic Nation: The Scottish Case', *Political Quarterly*, 85 (2014), pp. 170–7

The Politics of Decline: Understanding Post-War Britain (London, Routledge, 2014)

'Deindustrialisation Not Decline: A New Meta-Narrative for Post-War British History', *Twentieth Century British History*, 27 (2016), pp. 76–99

Tomlinson, Jim and Ewan Gibbs, 'Planning the New Industrial Nation: Scotland 1931 to 1979', *Contemporary British History*, 30 (2016), pp. 584–606

Torrance, David, 'The Journey from the '79 Group to the Modern SNP', in Gerry Hassan (ed.), *The Modern SNP* (Edinburgh, Edinburgh University Press, 2009), pp. 162–76

Salmond: Against the Odds (Edinburgh, Birlinn, 2011)

Vinen, Richard, *The Long '68: Radical Protest and Its Enemies* (London, Allen Lane, 2018)

Walker, Neil, 'Scottish Nationalism for and against the Union State', in Neil Walker (ed.), *MacCormick's Scotland* (Edinburgh, Edinburgh University Press, 2012), pp. 163–90

(ed.), *MacCormick's Scotland* (Edinburgh, Edinburgh University Press, 2012)

Webb, Keith, *The Growth of Nationalism in Scotland* (Harmondsworth, Penguin, 1978)

Wellings, Ben and Michael Kenny, 'Nairn's England and the Progressive Dilemma: Reappraising Tom Nairn on English Nationalism', *Nations and Nationalism*, 25 (2019), pp. 847–65

Whigham, Stuart, 'Nationalism, Party Political Discourse and Scottish Independence: Comparing Discursive Visions of Scotland's Constitutional Status', *Nations and Nationalism*, 25 (2019), pp. 1212–37

White, Stuart, '"Revolutionary Liberalism?" The Philosophy and Politics of Ownership in the Post-War Liberal Party', *British Politics*, 4 (2009), pp. 164–87

'A Marquandian Moment? The Civic Republican Political Theory of David Marquand', in Hans Schattle and Jeremy Nuttall (eds.), *Making Social Democrats: Citizens, Mindsets, Realities: Essays for David Marquand* (Manchester, Manchester University Press, 2018), pp. 139–59

Williamson, Philip, *Stanley Baldwin* (Cambridge, Cambridge University Press, 1999)

Willock, Ian, 'The Scottish Legal Heritage Revisited', in John Grant (ed.), *Independence and Devolution: The Legal Implications for Scotland* (Edinburgh, W. Green & Sons, 1976), pp. 1–14

Wilson, Gordon, *The SNP: The Turbulent Years 1960–90* (Stirling, Scots Independent, 2009)

Yack, Bernard, *Nationalism and the Moral Psychology of Community* (Chicago, University of Chicago Press, 2012)

Zimmer, Oliver, 'Boundary Mechanisms and Symbolic Resources: Towards a Process-Oriented Approach to National Identity', *Nations and Nationalism*, 9 (2003), pp. 173–93

Nationalism in Europe, 1890–1940 (Basingstoke, Palgrave, 2003)

Unpublished Theses

Campsie, Alexandre, 'A Social and Intellectual History of British Socialism from New Left to New Times' (PhD, Cambridge University, 2017)

Scothorne, Rory, 'Nationalism and the Radical Left in Scotland, 1968–92' (PhD, Edinburgh University, in progress)

Index